CONVERSATIONS WITH CARDUS

CONVERSATIONS WITH CARDUS

ROBIN DANIELS

With a Foreword by
YEHUDI MENUHIN

"In my own way I've tried to be an artist"
*from the conversation
on music criticism*

LONDON
VICTOR GOLLANCZ LTD
1976

ISBN 0 575 02126 8

First published July 1976
Second impression August 1976

Printed in Great Britain by
The Camelot Press Ltd, Southampton

To
Mae Savell Croy

ACKNOWLEDGEMENTS

I AM MOST thankful to: Yehudi Menuhin for his finely felt and graciously written Foreword; Susan Fawcus; Eleanor Hope; Bill Grundy; Alan Rowlands; Peter Halban; John Marsh; David Castell, former Arts Editor of the *Croydon Times*; Maria Bartha; Joseph C. Ingram; David Ayerst, the *Guardian*'s official historian; John Ryan, assistant to the Editor of the *Guardian*; Christopher Pearson; Mary Vallentine of the Australian Council for the Arts; Peter Welsh; L. W. Duck of the Henry Watson Music Library, Manchester; Ellis Ashton, Chairman of the British Music Hall Society; Ina Vincent and Marie Mann, my cheerful and hard-working typists; Momoyo Tsuboi of the Japan Information Centre, Embassy of Japan, London; the staff of the Buckingham Palace Road Library and Central Music Library, Westminster; the staff of the Reading Room of the British Museum and of the Newspaper Library, Colindale; the staff of the French Institute, London; the Editor of the *Guardian* for permission to quote extracts from music notices by Samuel Langford and Neville Cardus; The Society of Authors, acting on behalf of the Bernard Shaw Estate, for permission to quote from *Music in London*; to the following publishers for permission to quote extracts from the books named, all by, or edited by, Neville Cardus: Hamish Hamilton, *Kathleen Ferrier: A Memoir*; Oxford University Press, *Samuel Langford—Music Criticisms*; Collins, *Sir Thomas Beecham: A Memoir*.

Quotations, the sources of which have not been traced, will be acknowledged in any future edition if the copyright holders have by then notified my publishers.

R. D.

CONTENTS

ILLUSTRATIONS

following page 128

BOOKS BY NEVILLE CARDUS

AUTOBIOGRAPHY AND GENERAL ANTHOLOGIES

Autobiography, Collins, 1947
The Essential Neville Cardus (selected by Rupert Hart-Davis),
   Cape, 1949
Second Innings—More Autobiography, Collins, 1950
My Life (compiled by H. G. Earnshaw), Collins, 1965
Full Score, Cassell, 1970

MUSIC

Samuel Langford—Musical Criticisms (editor), O.U.P., 1929
Music For Pleasure, Angus and Robertson (Sydney, London),
   1942
Ten Composers, Cape, 1945
Kathleen Ferrier—A Memoir (editor), Hamish Hamilton, 1954
Talking of Music, Collins, 1957
A Composers Eleven, Cape, 1958
Sir Thomas Beecham—A Memoir, Collins, 1961
Gustav Mahler: His Mind and his Music, Gollancz, 1965
The Delights of Music: A Critic's Choice, Gollancz, 1966

CRICKET

A Cricketer's Book, Grant Richards, 1922
Days in the Sun—A Cricketer's Journal, Grant Richards, 1924
The Summer Game—A Cricketer's Journal, Hart-Davis, 1929
Cricket, Longmans, Green, 1930
Good Days, Hart-Davis, 1934
Australian Summer—The Test Matches of 1936–37, Hart-Davis,
   1937
English Cricket, Collins, 1945
Cricket All The Year, Collins, 1952
Close of Play, Collins, 1956
The Playfair Cardus, Dickens Press, 1963
The Noblest Game (with John Arlott), Harrap, 1969

FOREWORD

SHOULD PREFACES BE prologues or epilogues: should they
precede a book or follow it? If they attempt to sum up the
qualities of an author, are they not abrogating to themselves
a task which the intelligent reader would feel should be left
to his own interpretation? It would seem then that they should
rather appear at the end where all good mathematical equations
are properly situated, serving as a kind of mental nudge to
those whose percipience proved unequal to the challenge and
who may have missed many a fine point or special subtlety in
what went before. I therefore feel I should first apologize out of
courtesy to the reader and then proceed to belabour him with
my own opinions—which in the case of this particular book I
can do in all confidence.

For decades I have felt the greatest empathy with Neville
Cardus: for the man, and now for the sage who can *relate* art
to life, music to sport, the beauty of a squirrel to a Beethoven
symphony. Neville Cardus recognizes the common thread
linking vision to illusion, to dreams and delusions and halluci-
nations, and he acknowledges the inseparable human com-
pound of ecstasy and terror, genius and madness, and therefore
the eternal truth of great art, which can translate every
manifestation of that common thread into beauty and
meaning.

From the first pages of this intensely human book the reader
recognizes the man in the boy, that boy whose first loves in
music were the spontaneous and romantic melodies from the
Vienna of Lehár and the Strausses, that man who, as he
graduated to more weighty composers, never lost the intrinsic
values of his first fine careless rapture, and has always been able
to relate the one to the other, seeing in them all an organic
whole. This growth upwards from roots grounded in a variety
of soils is consolingly natural and so unlike those mechanical
shifts of opinion springing from uncertain beginnings, based

(because they cannot be rooted) on concrete platforms on which the unfortunate protagonist unsteadily stands, a victim of the latest squall of fashion, clinging desperately to the nearest lamp-post, which can offer only *rigid* support and can cast no more than a pale light upon a shadowed and perplexed mind.

The term "critic" hardly suits Neville Cardus, because today—unlike a "critique" which in Dr Johnson's time meant "an appreciation"—we tend to associate the word with a taking-apart and not with a putting-together.

In Neville Cardus the artist has an ally, for he encourages and supports that deepest urge of every art and every artist: to communicate, to share, to give and to receive, to establish a oneness, a unity with one's endeavour and with humanity at large. Every endeavour of man and woman when guided by generosity and love and by an artist's dedication and his desire to communicate to everyone irrespective of categories and divisions, to unite rather than to separate—every such endeavour becomes the carrier of a message containing a portion of truth, a commentary on a particular human situation, condition, time, and place, in the light of timelessness and infinity.

We are inclined to assume that "understanding" itself implies analysis and, finally, a sum of parts, but true understanding must always mean much more, for sympathy and love exceed the analytical, just as, conversely, prejudice and hate defy reason.

Neville Cardus reminds us that there is an understanding of the heart as well as of the mind. There can surely be no two opinions about the blend of passionate commitment, sweet reasonableness, and unquenchable youngness of heart, which together make Neville Cardus unique among those who belong to his dedicated and arduous profession.

I am heartbroken to think that the Foreword I wrote for Sir Neville's new book should have become a tribute to his memory. His zest for life was such that I could not foresee the moment when his warmth and vitality would no longer be audible and present. Fortunately, for those who knew him, his voice still rings in their ears.

Y. M.

NEVILLE CARDUS

I AM FOREVER indebted to Neville Cardus for my love of two of the three Rs—namely, reading and writing; I have never learned to cope with the third R. As a teenager, I was often deeply moved by poetry. I was overcome by the musicality of "Le Lac" of Lamartine, and by "The Great Lover" of Rupert Brooke, so sensitive of observation: "radiant raindrops *couching* in cool flowers . . . sweet water's dimpling laugh from tap or spring". But my lack of appreciation of prose-writing made me, at that stage of my life, a literary waste-land. Blushingly I recall a fourth-form essay in which I was invited to list "The six books I would take to my desert island". They were, in order of preference: the Collected Sherlock Holmes short stories, C. S. Forester's *Flying Colours*, *The Wooden Horse*, *William in Trouble*, *Sergeant Bigglesworth C.I.D.*, and *Robinson Crusoe*. My form-master, "Pills" Parker, awarded me 7 marks out of 10, and commented with chastening irony: "I think some of these would be rather tedious as you grow older—but perhaps you are going to be saved!"

At this formative time of my life—tall, languid, and tousle-haired—I knew deep down inside me that I could become a reader, a book lover, if only I could find the right author to start me off. Then one day I read, for the first time, the *Guardian*. The date is etched on my mind and memory: September 27, 1960. That day I read Cardus for the first time. He was writing about the great C major symphony of Schubert. This was not music criticism; this was literature:

> Mr Horenstein gave us a strong-muscled Schubert, sure of himself in action, especially during the firmly and vitally handled *scherzo*, though even here we could have had a freer swing and curve in the second subject, where the young gods on Olympus toss the golden ball about. The proportions of the symphony were superbly encompassed, and the

onward energy and stride along the giant's causeway of the
finale, with the terrific stamp of four repeated notes, were
defiant and inexorable.

". . . . we could have had a freer swing and curve". Cardus:
he was the writer I had been searching for, for so long. I still
have that *Guardian* cutting, now brittle and brown with age.
Since that September day, I have never missed a copy of the
Guardian. Along with tens of thousands of music lovers, cricket
fans, and admirers of fine English prose, I am sad and impover-
ished that the name *Cardus* has appeared for the last time in his
beloved newspaper. Every morning, when bleary-eyed I had
tugged the *Guardian* from my stiff-flapped post box, I used to
turn eagerly to the arts page, and during the summer also to
the sports pages, in the hope of seeing the by-line *Neville Cardus*.

Two years after that first "meeting" with Cardus, I wrote
to him, sending a copy of a music notice I had written. He
replied promptly, with these words of encouragement: "Your
notice of the Lili Kraus concert is a promising beginning; and
I have no fault to find, as far as it goes. But try to make your
vocabulary more selective. And try to get a surprise into a
sentence. . . ."

Another two years passed, and we corresponded again. By
this time my own writings on music were being published week
by week. I decided I wanted to read some of Cardus's early
notices, and I rang him to ask a question about his pre-
Manchester Guardian days when he was writing for the *Daily
Citizen*. He was delighted that someone should want to read his
music notices of half a century ago, and he invited me to join him
for tea later in that week, curious no doubt to meet so devoted a
reader. At the National Liberal Club a friendship was born.

I clearly remember my first sight of Neville Cardus. Down
the grand staircase he came, elegantly straight-backed, loose
and free and lissom in his movements, belying a man then in
his mid-seventies. As he came closer, I could see that he was
simply and modestly dressed, with magnificent hair silvery-
grey, the face weather-beaten, of fine sensitivity, with lines—
on forehead and cheeks, and around the eyes—that wit, wisdom,
and goodwill, had furrowed.

I held out my hand, as a gesture of greeting, and found to
my consternation that, with my hand still poised in mid-air,

still not shaken, he was leading me to the cloakroom. On my way home, and not until then, I discovered the reason: Neville was disdainful of formalities. This was his way of saying: "We are *already* friends."

We sat down to our tea. Of the tea itself I have no memory. For all I know, we might have been drinking cocoa or Bovril. Neville's conversation was riveting. Out of the corner of my eye, I could see that people seated nearby were moving their chairs closer so they could tune-in to Neville's speech (his speech and his Speech), delivered with scarcely a pause for breath, illustrated now and then with hummed melodies, and conducted, as it were, by arm and hand gestures that were spontaneous, expressive, and flamboyant: a touch of Colin Davis, perhaps; not, definitely not, Sir Adrian Boult.

In every one of our subsequent meetings, Neville always matched, and sometimes even excelled, that "first performance". A meeting with Neville Cardus was never predictable —of pace, direction, or length—but was always endearing, always memorable, and often full of unexpected turns, a sort of conversational Big Dipper.

At *any* moment, in the middle of a conversation, he was likely to imitate the diction of Klemperer, or, arms aloft, the conducting style of Herbert von Karajan, or perch on his piano stool and parody the non-music of Stockhausen, or sing the opening bars of the slow movement of Mozart's clarinet concerto. Had I been an impresario years ago, I would have signed Neville Cardus on a long-term contract, as a music-hall artist. His flow of anecdote and mimicry was unquenchable. Even without the advantage of television's mass audiences, he would have won nation-wide fame, within weeks. But Neville Cardus chose to be a writer, and he gained not only a nation-wide, but a truly international, renown and following.

If I were to have called Neville Cardus "a musicologist", he would *not* have been flattered, and his amusement would have known no bounds. I can picture him now. "Oh dear, no", he would exclaim, shaking his head from side to side, arms raised in mock despair, the whole body quivering with laughter. His reply would be swift and devastating: "You must be suffering from sun-stroke, Robert."* He would then enquire, with the most pointed politeness, if I needed a doctor.

* The name Neville Cardus invariably used for me.

Of course I would never dream of calling Neville "a musico-logist". He was the very opposite of the narrow-minded, narrow-eyed specialist who sits up all night reading music scores. Neville's writings on music are the writings of a full man, who had known hardships as well as luxury; who had eaten in the cafés of Manchester as well as in the most select restaurants of Edinburgh and Vienna; who had been pavement artist and insurance clerk, cricket coach and music-hall chocolate-seller. This variety of background, this range of worldly experience, enabled Neville Cardus to regard music not merely as the rich man's pleasure and the poor man's solace, but as a subject which must be related to the smells and the tastes, the sights and sounds, of life itself.

Neville Cardus owes not one atom or particle of his fame to advantages of family or schooling or influential friends. His *Guardian* columns of the past half-century and his autobio-graphy—which ranks among the best and most absorbing of all those written in the twentieth century—and his many other books, all of which have become classics: these literary achieve-ments are all his own work, the products of self-education and noble individuality of character.

Neville Cardus continued, in his mid-eighties, to write compellingly. What was his secret? He had superbly-trained powers of observation; a wonderfully retentive memory, which he had stocked richly; joy in use of words; wit unlimited; an absolutely boyish enthusiasm, even in so-called old age; and, above all, a love of people.

Here is Neville Cardus describing his predecessor as music critic of the *Manchester Guardian*, Samuel Langford:

I shall never forget an evening in June, very late and silent, when he leaned over his garden gate and talked to me of Shakespeare's lyrics and the fragility of loveliness in life. The air was full of the scent of flowers, and the simple tender wisdom of his speech seemed part of the beauty of the summer night. But of all my memories of 'S.L.' perhaps I shall hold tightest the picture he made once at Old Trafford during a Test Match. He sat in the front row, with the grass in front of him, between two perfect strangers, both honest uncouth men. And as he chatted lightheartedly to them, he ate a huge piece of currant cake and the crumbs fell down his crinkled, untidy waistcoat. Dear old Sammy; is it true that the great juice of him will flow no more? It is hard to believe we shall not again find him amongst us, for there was as much about him, surely, of elemental and undying nature as there was of mortal, lovable man.

This is Cardus writing about Kathleen Ferrier:

> She had the gift that radiates happiness. Her personal qualities even transcended her art; for great though she was as a singer, she was greater still as Kathleen Ferrier. Those of us who had the good luck and blessing to know her will never be able to separate in memory the artist in her from the warm, laughing, kind, serious, fervent, great-hearted and always uninhibitedly alive and human girl and woman that she was day in and day out, in good times or ill.

As critic and writer, Neville Cardus was the natural successor of a noble dynasty: Pater, Ruskin, Shaw, Newman. What is more, Cardus had many of the gifts of all four of them: the aesthetic sensibility of Pater; the metaphysics of John Ruskin, and his aptness of metaphor; Shaw's wit; and Newman's fluency. But not one of this illustrious quartet of writers excelled Cardus in humanity, nor in vividness of anecdote, nor in grace of language, nor in nature-rooted bloom of imagery.

Cardus's love for Kathleen Ferrier is certain to awaken the romantic in us:

> With her life now before us, as we contemplate the course of it, quick to ripen after a late spring, then to blossom in a summer never to know autumn. . . . Seldom has Covent Garden Opera House been so beautifully solemnized as when Kathleen Ferrier flooded the place with tone which seemed as though classic shapes in marble were changing to melody, warm, rich-throated, but chaste.

Here is a selection of choice Cardusian imagery: "a face of vellum"; "a nose of considerable cellarage"; "picking themselves up bovinely"; "he would beam like the rising sun"; Cyril Washbrook's cap "so confident of peak"; "his violin did not produce, but rather *received* the music"; "the arabesque ornaments sparkled, not coldly brilliant but with life and animation, warm and sunlit"; "after hearing these performances

of the Cleveland Orchestra I am woefully made to realize
that many an orchestral run-through which we are subjected
to at London concerts is not much more than, so to say, a
paper-backed edition of the score of a masterpiece, abridged,
and not set in the clearest print".

All his writings are graced by modesty. Knowledgeable, he
made no parade of knowledge. Acutely sensitive of ear, he
never castigated a second-rate performance. A believer in the
values received by his highly-tuned aesthetic antennae, he
never tried to conceal his musical blind-spots.

Cardus not only wrote *about* music. His writing exhibits, in
every line and paragraph, the ingredients of music: rhythm,
grace notes, cadences. When he wrote about harmony, he
wrote *in* harmony. Cardusian prose is a living example and
enactment of Walter Pater's dictum that "All art constantly
aspires towards the condition of music."

The name *Cardus* has become part of the English language.
In books and in newspapers from all over the English-speaking
world, I have seen the adjective *Cardusian* used, meaning "grace
of language". His writing is so easy to read. By *read* I mean not
only with the eyes but also with the voice. One of the measures
of good prose is that it can be read aloud with ease, and be
listened to with ease. Cardusian syntax is always a very model
of lucidity. As an example of this, I invite you to read aloud the
following passage on Sir Thomas Beecham:

> In the fullness of his years he was best savoured in private
> with a few friends, the light winking on the wine glasses' brims.
> The smoke of his cigar, a sort of materialisation of his fanciful-
> ness, visible shapes of his wit, curled on the intimate air of
> the elegant room in which we sat, lost to measurable time.

One of the most distinctive features of the Cardus style is—
to borrow a musical term—its sense of line. Reading Cardus is
like driving along a great highway: there are no verbal detours,
no road blocks, no pauses, no lay-bys. The traffic—the flow of
words, ideas, and insights—is continuous.

Neville Cardus numbers among his readers not only musicians and music lovers, cricketers and cricket lovers, but also
many thousands of people, of all ages, who have never been to
a concert, never seen a cricket match. They and I would
avidly read Cardus on *any* subject: sixteenth-century place

mats or the insect life of the Sahara or the comparative size of car luggage-racks.

The most wonderful quality of the writing of Neville Cardus is its readability. Of how many critics can we say this? Very few. Most writers on music fall into one or more of the obvious traps. The trap of jargon: choking sentence after sentence with abstract words and technical terms, unrelated to life, to beauty, to art in the widest sense. The trap of over-seriousness. The trap of acting like a sort of musical traffic-warden, noting every tiny transgression from absolute accuracy. This is the type of traffic-warden who is capable of recording in his little black book that a Rolls-Royce is parked askew, without delighting in the beauty of shape, line, and colour of the car itself. Neville Cardus is one of the great critics of this century not only because of what he wrote, and wrote gloriously, but also because of what he did *not* write.

Cardus, throughout the whole of his career as a critic, was a fearless champion of the new music that he felt to be of value: the current vitality of Mahler in this country, after years of neglect, owes much to Cardus's persistence and soundness of judgement. But, for all his geniality, Cardus was equally fearless in questioning the worth of the bogus note-scribblings that some present-day "composers" have tried to foist upon the public in the name of new music.

Many—too many—music critics listen only with the outer ear. Cardus listened also with the inner ear. His insight told him about a performance in terms of the music itself: its nature, its purpose, its significance, and its aesthetic value. When writing about music, he showed a musician's gift for penetrating to the core and inner being of a composer and a composer's intentions.

Cardus was never content to listen, or write, only in terms of modulations and bar-structures. These technicalities—he always contended—represent only the language of music. Cardus saw his rôle as critic as being that of a middle-man, a medium, whose duty was to help his readers to see and feel and hear what lies *beneath* that language. Music is more than notes, rhythm, and counterpoint, just as a beautiful flower is more than stamen, pollen, and petals. Neville Cardus was more than a music critic; he was a critic of life.

*

Neville Cardus had the great artist's ability to take, lead, lure, his audience into his own world. His romanticism becomes our romanticism; his love becomes our love. No one can measure Cardus's influence. He has enriched the lives of thousands, helping them to feel—not only cricket and music, but all of life—with deeper awareness. A great teacher does not impart facts; a great teacher instills an attitude, an approach, a way of observing, a way of responding.

A writer, a broadcaster, a conversationalist—any communicator—is at his most perceptive and most provocative when he is speaking autobiographically. Many critics lack the self-confidence to be autobiographical. They attempt to hide themselves, and their ideas and opinions, under a cloak of pontification, as if forever making *ex cathedra* statements. Not so, Cardus. Neville was always content to *be himself*, and he enjoyed being himself, and his readers enjoy him as he was and for what he was. His writing is natural, unpretentious. He wrote from the depth of his feelings. And so we, his readers, as he tells us of his renewed pleasure at hearing, say, the G minor symphony of Mozart, can almost *hear* the Cardus heart-beat.

It is fitting that I should write this tribute to you, Neville, because with you, always so generous towards others, I studied the art of the written appreciation. For as long as Lancashire play cricket, for as long as music criticism is written and read, and for as long as people enjoy majestic English prose, your name and your legacy of writings will be individually and universally respected and loved.

R. D.

CONVERSATIONS WITH CARDUS

I

MUSIC-HALL

RD: Neville, I imagine you still mourn the death of the music-hall.

NC: Yes, very much. Every big city had its music-hall, and a city the size of Manchester had five or six. Music-halls weren't situated only in the centre of a big city. In London, for example, there would be a chain of music-halls, stretching from Holborn right out into the suburbs.

This form of popular entertainment was a communal one. People gathered together in a theatre and they saw what we now call "live" entertainment: comedians, singers, jugglers, conjurers, dancers. In each city, different audiences were listening to and watching different forms of entertainment and different artists. I find it very depressing to think that, every evening at about 8 o'clock, millions of people in this country are watching the same programme. Television is a splendid technical achievement, but it is not "live". Television cannot convey the full impact and spontaneity of an artist's personality.

When you went to the music-hall, you'd get a transcript of life. The comedians expressed the life of the pavement, the life of the boarding-house, the life of the family—particularly the mother-in-law. Great artists like Marie Lloyd expressed and sublimated the lives of the people—the pub, the dance palace, and indeed every aspect of life—and it was all done with vitality and a common touch, and often with the sort of vulgarity that makes all the world kin.

But the music-hall wasn't only Marie Lloyd with her wink, and George Robey with his innuendoes. You had a great range of artists putting over a picture of English life. I have seen Sarah Bernhardt, in the Manchester Hippodrome, followed by a comedian such as Wilkie Bard.

It is a great loss to the national life of this country that the music-hall has disappeared. People were entertained by an art-form in which they could better appreciate themselves, and see that ordinary life had its humour and its compensations. You must remember that, in the days when I used to go to the music-hall, there was no such thing as social security and welfare. We didn't have the Rent Act. There was no security at all: you could be thrown out of your house in ten minutes. And one of the most popular jokes in the music-hall was the moonlight flit (the departure of a whole family overnight to avoid paying rent). I lived in a slum. The richest people in Manchester, millionaires, lived within three-quarters of a mile of my house.

The whole complex of life was enshrined in the music-hall. People would go, not knowing if they'd be in a job next week. In the music-hall, they felt part of a large, friendly family. They used to come out transformed.

Morny Cash would sing:

> I live in Trafalgar Square,
> With four lions to guard me.
> Fountains and statues all over the place,
> And the "Metropole" staring me right in the face!
>
> I'll own it's a trifle draughty,
> But I look at it this way, you see . . .
> If it's good enough for Nelson,
> It's quite good enough for me!

The music-hall comedian had an accepting attitude to life. The tramp wasn't jealous of the rich: he was quite happy to sleep in Trafalgar Square. And so the music-hall had a strong sociological influence on people's lives. They went there feeling depressed, or feeling lonely, or afraid that they were going to be thrown out of their house next week, and then a comedian on the music-hall stage would put those fears into the perspective of human nature, human vicissitudes, human ups and downs.

From the years leading up to the Depression I remember one of the greatest of Lancashire's comedians—not George Formby junior, famous for his playing of the ukulele, but George Formby senior. Today, when I hear people talk about "depressing times", I don't think they know what "depression" means.

Today there is a National Health Service and social security. Between the wars, millions of people were out of work. They were on the dole. They weren't sure where their next meal would come from. And so, what did George Formby do? On the stage, he depicted the life of the down-and-out Lancashire mill-hand, with his scarf and cloth cap, finding a touch of humour amid all his problems, and he made the members of the audience say to themselves, "Well, we may be down and out, but we are not nonentities."

George Formby gave individuality to those who were down and out. And the music-hall brought strangers together. You'd sit next to somebody you'd never seen in your life, and you would come out talking to him. Sometimes, in a fit of laughter, your neighbour would embrace you. These people were not sitting in a dark room watching an imitation of life, being duplicated to millions of houses. Every music-hall audience was getting its own transcript of life.

And there was a romantic side to music-hall entertainment. People who were on the dole could dream their dreams when they watched an accomplished dancer. Take, for example, a wonderful artist such as Eugene Stratton. He played the part of a poor Negro in the days of slavery in America. He was quite unlike the singers you see nowadays, with their faces painted black, trying to be funny, trying to give an impression of gaiety and happiness. Eugene Stratton conveyed the pathos and the romance of the Deep South. He sang songs such as "Lily of Laguna" and "Little Dolly Daydream". Here was the enslaved Negro in a romantic apotheosis.

If any would-be highbrow says that that was escapism, he is talking nonsense. George Formby and Eugene Stratton brought to the music-hall stage the very aspects of life that people would normally want to get away from. So why should so many people want to go to the music-hall to see George Formby, who was mirroring their own lives, with all its struggles? Why did they go? Because his genius revealed a vein of acceptance and humour beneath the troubles of everyday life. In those days no other country had a greater sense of sympathetic humour.

These days, what is missing from the nation's entertainment is the reconciling and embracing humour that brings people *together*. I'm not talking about the higher grades of entertainment. I'm not talking about concerts or plays. We used to have them in those days, and we've still got them now. What is missing now is entertainment for the masses in theatres: today there are no music-hall artists to put the lives of people into a humorous and sympathetic apotheosis.

A whole tradition of humour is dying. How many *comedians* are there in this country today? There's only one I can think of who is worthy to be included in the company of the great music-hall artists. Only one—and that is Frankie Howerd. Most of today's comedians giggle at their own jokes. But artists such as Wilkie Bard, George Robey, George Formby, T. E. Dunville, and Dan Leno—they didn't laugh. They were very serious. In fact, George Robey used to *object* to laughter. When he got a guffaw from the audience, he would raise those celebrated eyebrows and say: "I am not here to be an object for public merriment. I will not be made a laughing-stock." Then he would point to some poor innocent woman in the stalls who was laughing, and say, "I'm *surprised* at you, Ag-er-ness."

Wilkie Bard used to come on to the stage dressed as a char-woman, carrying a pail of water and some cloths. He got down on his knees, dipped one of his cloths in the water, wrung out the cloth, and then made a big wet circle on the floor, showing his sphere of cleaning operations. Wilkie Bard then got up, picked up his (or, rather, her) skirts, came up to the footlights, and, in a very melancholy and aspiring voice, began: "I want to sing in opera." That was very moving: a charwoman who wanted to sing in opera. Here was a comedian giving expression to the deep-down subconscious ambitions we all had, whether we were on the dole or doing a job for the princely salary of 30 shillings a week (which in those days was what a bank clerk earned). We all found in the music-hall something that was more than entertainment. Music-hall was a communal expres-sion of the life of the working class. Nowadays we don't speak of the lower-paid as the "working class". Is it because they don't work as hard?

RD: The TV star of today is protected—far removed—from his audience, but a music-hall audience could show its pleasure and displeasure.

NC: The music-hall audience was often unruly. They had their standards and their expectations. They had each paid sixpence or a shilling to go into the gallery or the pit. That sixpence or that shilling would have been hard-come-by, and the audience expected to see something worth-while.

When I was a boy, I used to go to the Tivoli Theatre in Peter Street, Manchester. I'd go in the gallery for sixpence. My friends and I used to subscribe to an egg-buying fund. That great comedian, Dan Leno, once defined eggs as being in three categories: new-laid, fresh—and "eggs". We used to save up for about a week. Then we'd go to a shop and buy 24 "eggs", which cost about a shilling. We'd smuggle them up to the gallery of the Tivoli Theatre, and if an act was very bad—nowadays we'd use the word "phoney"—we would throw some of our "eggs".

I remember one night having to listen to a really awful *Lion Comique*. A *Lion Comique* was a type of singer, a rather heavy baritone, who would usually be dressed in a fur coat—with an astrakhan collar—and a trilby hat. He would sing sentimental songs about a day at the workhouse or "Give my love to mother".

I was then about 18. I was a keen cricketer, and I could throw straight. I threw an "egg" at this *Lion Comique*, and it hit him right in the middle of his dress-shirt. I felt absolutely no remorse at all! Often the curtain used to be brought down if there was too much commotion from the audience. A lot of television screens should be splattered with "eggs". The present-day equivalent is to turn off the set. And that doesn't hurt the artist until he sees his audience-ratings.

RD: Please tell me about Marie Lloyd. I have the impression that her suggestiveness was not so much in her lyrics, but in her whole being, her gestures, her wink.

NC: I only saw Marie Lloyd once, and that was when I was about 17 or 18. I wasn't sophisticated enough at that age to appreciate her fully. She had a very effulgent personality. She was the apotheosis of the barmaid. In the words of the Rossetti poem:

> The blessed damozel leaned out
> From the gold bar of Heaven.

Marie Lloyd would be very good at that. If there is a bar in heaven, it *would* be made of gold, and I can picture her leaning over it, almost haloed—because she expressed vulgarity mingled with refinement. I hope I can get this apparent dichotomy over to you. If you can imagine a refined vulgarity, that is what she had, because she was not blatant.

She used to express what we now call permissive things, simply by her personality and a final wink. For one song, she presented herself as a girl of about 19. And it is amazing how convincingly, by some sort of alchemy, Marie Lloyd could make herself look a very buxom overblown 19. This was her song:

> Our lodger's such a nice young man,
>   Such a good young man is he;
>   So good, so kind, to all our fam-i-ly!
>
> He's never going to leave us—
>   Oh dear, oh dear no!
>
> He's such a good, goody, goody man,
>   Mamma told me so.

Her wink, as she sang "Mamma told me so", gave the audience a hint of the permissiveness that was going on in the house between her mother and the lodger.

In those days there was a Manchester Watch Committee, a masculine version and forerunner of Mrs Mary Whitehouse and her band of porn-hunters. The Watch Committee had to guard the morality of what went on at pantomimes. One year, the Theatre Royal was featuring *Sinbad the Sailor*. George Robey was in the cast; and the principal "boy", who, like Marie Lloyd, absolutely personified the art of refined vulgarity, was named Maggie Duggan. She had thighs that could only be called Corinthian.

During this pantomime, there was a 30-second pause when George Robey was due to make his entrance. To an audience—waiting for the star of the show to appear—30 seconds is a long time. Maggie Duggan was standing in the middle of the stage. The seconds ticked by. "What's happened?" whispered the audience; "has something gone wrong?" Then Robey (Mrs Sinbad) arrived, in great agitation, and said to Maggie Duggan: "I'm so sorry I'm late, but I have been detained. In fact, I've been blocked in the passage." Now, in those days, there was only one slang meaning of the word "blocked" and that was sexual intercourse. George Robey crowned the joke by putting the word "passage" into bogus French: "I have been blocked in the pas-sahge." The Manchester Watch Committee demanded changes in that scene. But they didn't intervene over Marie Lloyd's wink, which was *much* more suggestive.

RD: You occasionally wrote music-hall notices, didn't you? And you came under the influence of Haslam Mills.

NC: When I first became a reporter on the *Manchester Guardian*, I had to do ordinary humdrum anonymous work, such as going to Manchester Town Council committee meetings. I had to do all the routine work of a reporter. Then one day Haslam Mills asked to see me. He was one of the most fascinating men I have ever met in my life, handsome, witty, a brilliant conversationalist, always suavely dressed, an excellent Chief Reporter. If he were alive today, he would make all the TV personalities seem crude and inelegant.

One Friday he told me he was going to send me, on the following Monday afternoon, to the Manchester Hippodrome, where a great comedian, Little Tich, was appearing. In those days, to be told in the *Manchester Guardian* reporters' room that you were going to review music-hall was like being elevated to the peerage—because you were allowed to sign a music-hall notice with your initials.

Haslam Mills gave me a few seconds to come back to earth, then he said, "Cardus, this being your week-end off, and in view of the fact that you will be going to the Manchester Hippodrome on Monday to write about Little Tich, I don't want you to have any social engagements on Saturday or Sunday." He was talking to me as though I were a member of society. My social engagements in those days involved a poached egg on toast and a cup of coffee in Lyons Corner House. "No, sir," I assured him, "I won't have any social engagements." "No," he said, "I want you to be alone. Tomorrow, Saturday, if it is a fine day, I want you to go for a walk. Go to the fields of Cheshire. Go alone, Cardus, and meditate upon Little Tich." He was prescribing a period of meditation 48 hours before a music-hall performance! I'm sure I must have done what he told me, because we used to take

B

those music-hall notices very seriously and we would write them with a most self-conscious sense of style. Arnold Bennett once said that he read the *Manchester Guardian* primarily for its music-hall notices. I have often wished that somebody would make an anthology of them.

2

ORIGINS

RD: What are your very first memories of listening to music?

NC: My very first memories have got nothing to do with what is loosely called "classical" music. I was brought up in a home in which we used to sing the music-hall songs of the day. The popular music at that time was very melodious. The first time I realized that I had in me an apparatus to receive music was when I went to the very lovely theatre in the Midland Hotel, Manchester. It held only about 800 people; you could get in at the back for a shilling. I went to see Pellissier Follies, with Fay Compton in the cast. In the interval, a string orchestra, conducted by Herr Drescher, began to play the "Vilja" song from *The Merry Widow*. *The Merry Widow* was just becoming well known: I'm going back to around 1908. When I heard that song, something *moved* in me.

Then I went to a musical comedy called *Florodora*. The music was composed by Leslie Stuart, who was organist of the Church of the Holy Name in Manchester. He was the George Gershwin or the Jerome Kern of his day because he wrote Negro songs for Eugene Stratton. In *Florodora* there is an octet, "Tell me, pretty maiden", and it begins with a long phrase, rather like the opening bars of a Brahms symphony. It is extraordinary to find music such as this in a musical comedy, sung by a chorus, four men and four women, dressed as mashers, the men with their morning-coats and walking-sticks, the women with their big hats and long dresses (not an inch of leg showing). No matter where a scene was set—whether it was Hong Kong or Honolulu—mashers were always dressed as though they were going to Ascot.

The difference between the pop music of 70 years ago and the pop music of today is that the music of Leslie Stuart and of Edward German, *Tom Jones* and *Merrie England*, would lead you eventually to Mozart and Bach. I don't think young people are led to Mozart and Bach by much of the pop music of today. Nowadays the process has been reversed. Whereas we used to rise from Leslie Stuart to Mozart, today they reduce Mozart, the G minor symphony and *Eine kleine Nachtmusik*, to the level of the latest pop music, all percussion and electric guitars, noise and wailing.

My love of music came from simple beginnings. I remember in particular a song that Eugene Stratton used to sing. Eugene Stratton was a wonderfully convincing "coon" comedian, acting the part of the coloured man from the plantation, and he had many imitators such as G. H. Elliott. That song, "Is your Mammy always with you?", was composed by Leslie Stuart. James Agate once wrote in the *Sunday Times* that if someone found in an old drawer the manuscript of this music, he would think it was a German song by Brahms, "Bleibt die Mutter bei dir immer?" I feel very much indebted to Leslie Stuart and to Franz Lehár: they were the first composers to awaken in me a feeling that music was going to play a big part in my life.

I used to go to all the musical comedies, and then I graduated to the Hallé concerts. I say "graduated", because a boy from the working classes, who lived in a back street and played cricket on the brick crofts,* risked being called "a sissy" if he went to a Hallé concert. I used to go alone and in disguise. I remember very vividly one of the first Hallé concerts I went to. I was then working in an insurance office in Bridge Street, Manchester. I walked all the way from Bridge Street to Rusholme for my evening meal—it was probably a Welsh rarebit—and then on that foggy night walked all the way to the Free Trade Hall.

In those days, there was a limited amount of space in the Free Trade Hall for the *hoi polloi*: there was room at the back for about 300 of the lower orders. We had to pay a shilling to get in, and we were positioned over what was called "the grid", a primitive heating apparatus. Steam used to come up from the

---

* A brick croft was a piece of wasteland on which houses would one day be built. Our "wickets" were hard, bumpy, and grassless. The ball shot off the pitch at unexpected angles, making batting a nightmare. I could have bowled Don Bradman middle stump, on a brick croft; I could have bowled out the entire England XI for less than 100. When I first bowled on a really good wicket, I wondered why I couldn't spin the ball.

floor, and, if we had got soaking wet while queuing in the rain, we'd soon feel warm as we dried out inside the Hall. Apart from those of us at the back, the whole of a Hallé audience of those days would be in evening dress: white ties and tails. There were vast numbers of Germans. Before and after a Hallé concert, you heard as much German spoken as you heard English.

In December 1908, I heard the first-ever performance of the A flat symphony of Elgar. It was conducted by Hans Richter. Something happened at that Hallé concert that had never happened before and I doubt if it has ever happened since then. At the end of the slow movement, the audience applauded passionately, and it seemed quite a while until—after a lot of shushing—the orchestra could continue. I read somewhere that the *adagio* was actually encored, but I don't remember that, and I'm sure Richter wouldn't have allowed it.

That A flat symphony made a tremendous impact, especially on young people. Never before had an English composer written a symphony of such stature. Hans Richter said it was worthy to go into the company of the Brahms symphonies. That first symphony of Elgar was played a hundred times in its first year. It lifted English music out of provincialism and into the international repertoire. We thought it was a good thing that an English composer should borrow some of his colour and technique from Brahms and Wagner. Only a second-rate composer can avoid being derivative.

Elgar had put English music on the map. I was 19 then, a member of the musical *avant-garde*, and I was determined to have a long love affair with music. In those days, there were few gramophone records. Records were then cylindrical things, with an awful quality of reproduction, and they usually began with a voice saying, "This is an Edison Bell record." You could buy records of popular music and musical comedies, but very little of Beethoven or Mozart, so if you heard a wonderful piece of music at a concert, and you went home, as I did that night after the Elgar, haunted by the lustre of the music, you were filled with sadness at not being able to afford to go and hear the piece again, for months or even years.

Around 1910, when I was 20, I used to sing at concerts. I had a friend who could play the piano. To have an upright piano in the house was then a sign of social status. My friend had gone to Hulme Grammar School, whereas I went to a board school. We were given a very elementary education: the three Rs and a bit of English history. In those days you had to pay a weekly education fee. So every Monday morning I brought my "school money"—2d. I was at school well before the advent of Women's Lib: all the boys were herded to one side of the classroom, and all the girls to the other.

With my friend at the piano, I used to sing all the popular songs of the day. Since there was no radio, no television, and no cinema, people used to go on Saturday nights to concerts: smoking-concerts, Grand Concerts, Freemasons' Concerts, Chappell Ballad Concerts. The organizers would engage a baritone to sing; sometimes I got paid as much as a guinea. I used to sing "Trumpeter, what are you sounding now?", "Glorious Devon" by Edward German, Amy Woodforde-Finden's *Indian Love Lyrics*, and "Grey days are your grey eyes" by Noel Johnson.

I got as far as singing Schumann's *Dichterliebe*—but not in public. Then somebody said that I should have my voice trained. So I went to a singing teacher's studio. He took me up the scale, and then he said, "You are not a baritone." I said I thought I was. "No," he said, "you're a natural tenor." Well, I didn't want to be a tenor. I'm not particularly keen on the tenor voice even now, unless it's the voice of a Gigli. This teacher put me on to the Behnke method. A lot was written in those days about "placing" the voice. In order to "place" the voice forward, I had to sing: "Koo-koo-koo, oo-oh-ah, koo-koo-koo". Then he told me that when I sang "ay" or "ah" I must make sure not to lift my tongue. I had never thought about my tongue before, and of course, as soon as he gave me that warning, my tongue came up every time!

After three months or so I was almost swallowing my tongue instead of singing, so I left this teacher and went to another one. As soon as he had heard me sing one or two notes, he said, "Ah, you have come to me just in time." That's exactly what my first teacher had said. As before, I was taken up the scale. Then my new teacher said, "You are not a tenor." And I replied: "I know I'm not a tenor. I'm a baritone." "Oh dear, no," he said, "you're a *bass*." He made me practise nasal resonance: "Naa-naa-naa, no-naa". After a month of that, I decided to give up singing lessons. I was afraid to go to another teacher. One had said I was a tenor. The other said I was a bass. And

I thought I was a baritone. I feared that if I went to another teacher, he might say I was a contralto.

So I gave up my career as a singer. To this day, I often wonder how much you can really learn from a singing teacher, because singing is such an individual thing. A piano can be tuned. If you break a violin string, you can replace it. But the vocal chords and the whole art of singing are matters of inner physiology and psychology. If you haven't been *born* with a beautiful voice, no teacher can help you to make it sound beautiful. I don't think any teacher can transform an indifferent voice into even a moderately good one.

I used to know a famous laryngologist to whom Kathleen Ferrier went when she was having some slight trouble with her throat. He told me that, when he first looked at Kathleen Ferrier's throat, through one of his special instruments, he experienced aesthetic ecstasy. He said it was so beautiful an example of vocal architecture that anybody could have taught her how to sing.

RD: Did you ever study an instrument?

NC: No, I never did. My voice training—even though short— gave me what I needed: even if you've only had a glimpse of the creative forge, you've learned something. Even if you've only bowled in a village cricket match, you are in a better position to know what a bowler is thinking and feeling like, when he is playing in a Test Match at Lord's.

There used to be a very helpful instrument in the old days called a piano-player. Newman wrote a book about it: *The Piano-player and its Music*. The keys were depressed by air pressure supplied by pedals. This air pressure passed through perforations on a paper roll. The roll played the notes, leaving you to control the expression and the tempi, as though you were a conductor. This was an amazingly quick way to learn music. I went through all the nocturnes and preludes of Chopin, and the impromptus of Schubert, without having to worry about my fingers, which were never nimble enough for the piano.

About 30 or 40 years ago, with the advent of broadcasting, the piano-player vanished. This was a great loss—even though it had been rather expensive for the average person to buy. The piano-player was a tremendous help to my musical education. It taught me the technical and aesthetic problems not only of a lot of piano music but of many orchestral works (in keyboard transcriptions). Bernard Shaw was another who learned a lot of his music from the piano-player.

RD: When did you first have the ambition to became a music critic?

NC: Ernest Newman was music critic of the *Manchester Guardian* until 1905, and then he went to Birmingham. When I was in my teens, I used to go into the Free Library in Rusholme and read Newman's column in the *Birmingham Post*. At around this time, he brought out a book called *Musical Studies*. That book made me wish to become a music critic. I sent articles to newspapers, and got them back with "The editor regrets . . ." My first piece of writing to appear in a music magazine was in 1916 when *Musical Opinion* published "Bantock and Style in Art". I got 7/6d for it. I was thrilled when I saw it in print.

At that time, there was a tendency to place Bantock before Elgar. The kernel of my article was that Bantock had a synthetic style. I think we should hear some of his music now. It is not entirely original: he was a very assimilative composer. Parry and Stanford were writing four-square English music, but Bantock's music had echoes of Debussy, Strauss, Ravel, and, in particular, Rimsky-Korsakov. Bantock was probably the first English orchestrator to use a really big paint-box: he flashed his colours about.

Newman, who was very hard to please, once paid an extraordinary compliment to Bantock. He wrote that *Omar Khayyam*—for the way it deals with issues of life and death—could be mentioned in the same breath as the B minor Mass of Bach. We may wonder how Newman could possibly arrive at such an opinion, and so we ought to try to discover what there is in Bantock's music that Newman found so alluring.

Newman always described himself as a scientific critic. He used to say to me: "You write well, Cardus, but I'm not really interested in your views or your opinions, because they are merely subjective reactions. I want to get *beneath* personal judgement—to the truth." Having developed his great system of objective, rationalistic criticism, he compared Bantock to Bach! Around 1910–11, when Strauss was at his peak, Newman said that the symphonic writings of Joseph Holbrooke were probably the most important in the whole of Europe at that time. And Newman said that the greatest English song-writer was a composer whose music I confess I have never heard to this day—Frederick Nicholls. Newman wrote: "He is creating a new type of English song. . . . His piano writing conveys the soul and the idiom of the instrument." Newman stopped just short of comparing Nicholls to Hugo Wolf. I have no objection to Newman having these opinions, but it is rather ironical for him to put forward such highly subjective views at the same time as he was claiming that he was inventing and evolving an objective and scientific approach to music criticism.

RD: Newman not only over-rated several minor composers; I am astonished at his blind-spot for Mozart. He once wrote of Mozart's many "exercises in the art of saying next-to-nothing to perfection".

NC: We must be careful not to belittle Newman. We *all* have blind-spots. But one notice he wrote really took my breath away. At a Queen's Hall concert, after the performance of one of Mozart's last great symphonies, a pianist played, not the "Emperor" concerto, not the B flat or the D minor of Brahms, but the Burleske which Strauss wrote when he was a young man. It is lovely café music. Newman said that, coming after the Mozart, the Burleske took us a few floors higher in our intellectual elevator. And he once described Mozart's *Figaro* as music for the kindergarten, claiming that it didn't get near to the depth and cynicism of Beaumarchais.

Newman objected to my way of writing about music: in the most friendly terms, of course, because we were very great friends. Now I personally have no objection to Max Beerbohm telling me he found Eleanor Dusé a limited actress, because he wrote in such an individual way, and it is interesting to know what Max Beerbohm *did* think about Dusé. I have no objection to Bernard Shaw saying that Sarah Bernhardt was a rather melodramatic actress and not in the same class as Dusé. These judgements, if they are original, if the man making them is himself an artist, are very interesting to most people. But not to Newman. He wanted to get to *Das Ding an sich*— the thing in itself.

I don't believe there can be any objective tests of criticism.

You can't get away from the personal equation. You can't get away from your own skin. You are conditioned by your temperament and your background, and by the climate you live in. You can't get away from the subjective, and no artist wants to. What would Beethoven have said if he were told he mustn't compose like Beethoven but instead should have a concept of music as an objective art?

It is only from personal experience that *anything* can be demonstrated. And to be interesting you must be personal. From the reader's point of view, Newman was at his most fascinating when he forgot all about his method. I remember going to the library, as a boy, and reading Newman's notice of a Gerhardt recital in Birmingham. He began something like this: "Almighty God in His omnipotence could probably create a lovelier and sweeter fruit than the strawberry, but so far He hasn't. And God in His omnipotence could no doubt create a lovelier and sweeter *Lieder* singer than Elena Gerhardt, but so far He hasn't." I'd never heard Gerhardt. Newman made me want to walk *miles* to hear her sing. I wouldn't have wanted to walk two yards if he had told me that Gerhardt had modulated smoothly into B flat.

Newman, at his best, was one of the wittiest of all writers on music. That's one reason why so many people read his column. "Imagine," I said to myself; "he is paid to do a job he enjoys." Many years later, as Newman approached his 80th birthday, I was asked by the *Sunday Times* to write his obituary. On a foggy winter afternoon, suffering from a chill, I wrote the obituary. I then went out and, on my way to Covent Garden, I met the man himself. "Good heavens, Newman," I said, "what are you doing out, on a night like this?" "I'm going to the Albert Hall to see a boxing match," he replied. The next day I wrote to the Editor of the *Sunday Times*, telling him that my Newman obituary would probably be published among my *posthumous* writings.

RD: Your other music-critic mentor was Samuel Langford.

NC: Sammy Langford didn't just write music criticism, he produced literature. So did Bernard Shaw and Beerbohm. They were artists. They knew how to write and they had something to say. They were not just music and theatre adjudicators or reporters.

Sammy was a peasant—in the best sense of the word. By "peasant", I don't mean he was uneducated. I mean that he had a countryman's outlook. His father was a market gardener—they used to grow the most beautiful flowers. Sammy joined him for a while, but he wasn't a businessman at all; instead he showed a lot of talent for music. He was a fine pianist, and when he was still quite young he became an organist and choirmaster. So his father sent him to Leipzig to study piano with Carl Reinecke. Langford came back to Manchester, but never quite made good as a pianist. When Newman left to go to Birmingham, one of the chief leader writers of the *Manchester Guardian*, Herbert Sidebotham, who knew Langford, suggested that he (Langford) should be appointed music critic. Sidebotham, who was a most unwarlike man, later became Student of War on the *Sunday Times*. When he left the *Manchester Guardian* it was as though the Pope had left the Vatican. I went into C. P. Scott's office to commiserate with him, and he replied gravely, "No man is indispensable."

Langford had never written music criticism in his life. After a month or so, he began to write with extraordinary ease. I don't think any music critic has written so perceptively about piano playing. He became, in my opinion, one of the most penetrating and most beautiful writers on music of all time, and yet today he is very under-rated. Few people who read about music have ever heard of him. In 1929, I published an anthology of his writings. Anybody who can get hold of a copy of that book will immediately see how marvellously well he could write. He often said to me, "Always write for the best-educated layman, and don't use technical terms unless absolutely necessary." He never wrote about a performance without relating it to the music. His writing went right into the heart of music and life and philosophy. Langford wrote with so much insight that he might have been the composer himself writing about his own work, and he wrote in such a way that the readers who hadn't been to the concert wished that they *had*. He could summon up the most apt metaphors—often from nature—and yet he never wrote round music. He always had his mind's eye on the notes.

One of his most memorable pieces was a notice for the *Manchester Guardian* of a performance of the B minor Mass, given at a Hallé concert in March 1924. I'd like to read you some extracts:

> The sublime Sanctus was once more the finest and most perfect movement of the whole. . . . In this movement we have the original prototype of how many Lisztian and other symphonic poems in which the heroes are crowned with eternal garlands, in the most tedious ways. Bach's garlands of divine harmony are neither tedious nor obviously descriptive, and perhaps they escape the one thing because they are not the other. . . . "He planteth His footsteps in the sea", says the Psalmist, but, though such an expression carries us far, it is by no means adequate as a description of this divinely moving bass part. The notes in their octave leaps are like vast pillars, not sunk into the deep, but embracing in their height and depth an imagination of both heaven and earth, and, if we add the sea, the combined images will not complete what one feels from the music. . . . Everything passing is but a symbol, says the wise Goethe, and music, in one sense the most swiftly passing and intangible of all mortal things, is in another the essence of the imperishable. . . . It should not be forgotten that all religious experience is in its nature miraculous, and that unless such music as this Mass makes a prophetic and miraculous impression it is not adequate to its purpose.

RD: Please would you describe Langford's outward appearance.

NC: "Old Sammy"—as we used to call him—was only about 64 or 65 when he died. When I first met him, he was in his mid-fifties. In appearance, he was a combination of Socrates and Mussorgsky. He had a great shaggy beard and an enormous dome of a forehead, and—well I hardly know how to describe his dress. He wore his clothes with an elephantine looseness of fold. He was almost always unkempt. It was the custom in those days to go to Hallé concerts in evening dress. Langford in evening dress was Langford *transfigured*: he became almost unrecognizable.

RD: He was a very fast writer, wasn't he?

NC: His handwriting was rather like Shakespeare's, but larger. He wrote in big sprawling letters, and for a music notice he'd use 20 or 30 pages of copy paper. He used to come back from a Hallé concert at half past ten, and he always caught the 11.50 tram. In an hour and 20 minutes, he'd produce 1,000 words. He never paused to reflect. He never re-read his "copy". Often he didn't number the pages. Writing became for Langford a kind of inspired conversation.

He was an extraordinarily versatile man. He caused a minor sensation one night at the *Manchester Guardian* when, in the Twenties, Einstein came to Manchester University to lecture on Relativity—in German. Few people in those days knew anything about Relativity in *English*, let alone in German. So who was going to report on Einstein's lecture? It then occurred to Crozier, the news editor, a brilliant man, that Langford, who was a good German scholar, might be able to write a *précis* of the lecture, and Langford undertook to do it.

We were all in a state of great excitement, wondering how he would cope with the formidable task of listening to, and reporting on, a lecture on Relativity, given in German. So we waited in the Thatched House, which was a pub just near the offices of the *Manchester Guardian*. At last, Langford came shuffling in, looking more like Socrates and Mussorgsky than ever, and asked for a glass of ale. By this time, we were all in a state of unbearable tension, anxious to know how he had got on. "How did it go, Sammy?" I asked. "Did you find it difficult?" "No, no," he replied, "Einstein speaks very good German!" Well, of course, we knew that. "What about his Theory of Relativity?" "I think I'll be able to write half a column. A very interesting evening, but *all* platitudes, *all* platitudes." That was typical Langford—the most light-hearted remark ever made about Einstein. Needless to say, Langford wrote a very fine account of the lecture, and he caught his tram home at the usual time.

He wrote beautifully about roses. He could have written about almost any subject. And he was a wonderful conversationalist. We used to sit in one of the underground cafés in Manchester and he would expound—never in a condescending way. He spoke as naturally as if you and I were discussing a football or a cricket match, or describing an early-morning walk. He would talk about *Faust* and Goethe and German literature in a most absorbing way: no professor at any university could have been so enlightening.

I was very lucky in my education. There was Newman, the Aristotle, with his rationalist feet on the ground; and there was the Platonic Langford, who also had his feet on the ground, but his head was in the world of ideals. I had the combination of Langford, the poet and artist, and Newman, the thinker and rationalist, who distrusted primary emotional reactions.

My two mentors made a synthesis. It was the biggest stroke of luck that any young man could have had. I learned the clinical side of music criticism from Newman, and then from Langford I learned the aesthetic, the creative, the inward, side. There is never a day when I don't go down on my knees and thank Newman and Langford for what they taught me.

3

AUSTRALIA

RD: As you look back, how do you feel about your stay in Australia?

NC: If, on my death-bed, God Almighty asked, "What have you done in your life?", I would be very humble, but I would ask Him if he would put my visit to Australia on the credit side, to be set against the things I had not done well. We all will go with some trepidation to the Judgement Seat, because of the mistakes we've made and the time we've wasted.

I went to Australia in wartime, 1940, and I had seven of the most wonderful and happy years I've ever known. I tried to sow some seeds in the country's artistic life. There had already been musical pioneering work in Australia: in the Thirties, Hamilton Harty went out there, to conduct concerts in Sydney and Melbourne, and some very well-known artists had been out to Australia—Chaliapin, for example. I think Paderewski went out to Australia, but he and many other musicians used to go there, play in one or two concerts, and then return to Europe or America. There were several colleges of music in Australia, but, when I arrived, there was no established standard of musical opinion or music criticism. There were some good performers and some very second-rate ones.

RD: A lot has been written about the architecture and the acoustics of the Sydney Opera House, but not so much has been said about the artistic climate in which the project originated.

NC: Quite so. The Opera House wasn't a mushroom that suddenly grew in the middle of the night. There has been a great deal of publicity about the fact that operas such as *War and Peace* and the *Magic Flute* have been performed at the new Opera House, but it seems to be forgotten that many years ago the British National Opera Company went out to Australia and performed *The Ring*.

Music in Australia was an untilled but very rich soil. I remember the very first concert I went to, as music critic of the *Sydney Morning Herald*. A critic, like any other performer, wants to make a good impression on his first appearance. I looked at the programme: Weber's *Oberon* overture, the fifth symphony of Beethoven, and some other work that I'd heard a thousand times. I thought to myself, "How can I produce a notice about music I've written about hundreds of times in England?" When the performance of the fifth symphony began, I realized that 50 per cent of the audience were hearing this marvellous work with the ears, the sensibility, and the imagination, with which I had first heard it 30 years before. To these Australians, in the Sydney Town Hall, the fifth symphony was a revelation. I found this a *tremendous* inspiration. I sent myself back to school, as it were, to find new meaning in the established masterpieces of music. I was in a virgin world. I became aesthetically young again.

RD: You used to do a Sunday-evening radio programme. Was this broadcast only in New South Wales or throughout the whole of Australia?

NC: Throughout Australia. I soon found a response from the public such as I have had in no other country. One night I decided to please myself, with my hour's broadcast about music—and never mind the public. I found a recording of the *Song of the Earth* of Mahler, with Bruno Walter conducting. I doubt, if, at that time, this work had ever been heard in an Australian concert hall, so I was taking a risk. I played the record, and then talked about the music. Ten minutes after the programme was over, I received a telephone call at Australian Broadcasting House in Pitt Street, Sydney. The call was from Alice Springs, which is in the remote bush: about as far from Sydney as Bucharest is from London. A man, with a broad Australian accent, was obviously overcome with enthusiasm. "Ah, that was marvellous music," he said, "wonderful music." No compliment that Mahler ever received would have pleased him more than to hear such heartfelt praise from someone in the Australian bush. Something in Mahler's music, with its nostalgia—"O Sun of Love, will you ever shine again?"—

and its delight in nature, blossoming anew every springtime, had touched the heart of a simple man living in the outback.

That is one of the many deeply moving experiences I had in Australia which rejuvenated my heart and mind. I wish that some of London's rather bored critics could have similar renewing experiences. The worst, the most destructive, thing in the arts is sophistication. I deplore the idea that everything in music can be systematized, analysed, familiarized, as if all you had to do was go into a big supermarket, and find Beethoven on one shelf, and Mozart on another; as if their masterpieces were easy-to-buy items, in a standard range of packaging. They are not. They are constantly rejuvenated by the sensibility of the listeners.

All art is a collaboration. A materialistic society—such as we have in many parts of the world today—will be reflected in the arts. A society gets the art it deserves. We are living in an age of amazing technology. This is the age of the computer, the spaceship, and the Skylab. Anybody who died as recently as 40 or 50 years ago, if he were born into the world of today, would be astounded at the progress of technology. But some aspects of this "progress" are destructive to the human spirit, and many *avant-garde* composers are expressing these aspects in their music. They will suffer, I think—or, rather, I very much *hope*—a powerful reaction. I believe that human nature fundamentally does not change. Within the next 50 years, there will be a series of reactions against the more ridiculous concepts of life today.

The aesthetic atmosphere is as fine as it ever was. Young people, in ever-growing numbers, are becoming familiar with Beethoven and Mozart, Bruckner and Mahler. In this age of contradiction, between the materialistic world and the higher, spiritualized world, I'll put my money on the spiritualized world. It will win in the long run.

RD: For your weekly radio broadcast in Australia, did you have any overall plan?

NC: No, I had no plan. I just said to myself, "Well, this week we'll have *Lieder*" or "This week we'll have opera." I chose the works that I wanted to talk about; if you are not *passionately* interested in a subject, you won't get anyone else interested in it. I varied the programme; it never became routine. I felt like a gardener planting seeds in fertile soil. I had to pluck out a lot of weeds. A lot of lovely roses have now developed: there's hardly an opera house or a concert hall anywhere in the world where an Australian artist has not appeared.

A culture doesn't grow overnight. Australia is now enjoying the fruits of the pioneer work that has been going on since the days of the all-but-forgotten English professor of music who lived and worked in Melbourne—Marshall Hall. Then, just after the Second War, came Eugene Goossens. They had their own Australian-born Professor, Sir Bernard Heinze; an Englishman, Dr Edgar Bainton, who came from Newcastle upon Tyne; and a Belgian, Henri Verbruggen, who was once first violin of the Scottish Orchestra and later went to Sydney as Principal of the State Conservatory. They were all gardeners, and they should not be forgotten now that Australia is about to reap a bountiful harvest.

If you forced me into a corner and asked me who was the greatest musical artist ever to come out of Australia, I would not say Melba, nor Barry Tuckwell, one of the greatest horn players in the world, nor even the incomparable Joan Sutherland. For me, the finest musical artist ever to be born in Australia was Marjorie Lawrence. Here in Europe, she is all too often forgotten. An attack of polio interrupted her career, but she managed to continue singing in public.

We shouldn't talk only about Australia's musical conquests. For example, the 1973 Nobel Prize for Literature was awarded not to an Australian-born writer, but to a man who has lived a good part of his life in Australia—Patrick White. And we shouldn't forget Ethel Florence, whose pen-name was Henry Handel Richardson. Her epic trilogy, *The Fortunes of Richard Mahoney*, very popular in this country in the Twenties, was one of the seeds of Australian literature. A lot of the seeds of Australia's artistic life have yet to attain full bloom. This is her summertime; the harvest has still to come.

RD: One of the most important advances is that Australia can now offer scope to its own artists.

NC: At one time, they all had to come to England. Now, as well as the new opera house in Sydney, there is a new concert hall in Perth, a new Arts Centre in Adelaide, and the Victorian

College of the Arts in Melbourne. There isn't any longer a
necessity for every young Australian artist to come to England
and be adopted by our music-loving public. Australia has had
promising writers and musicians in the past, but they were
ahead of their time. Australia used to be—first and last—a land
of sport: they only knew their Bradmans and their Keith Millers.

What Australia needs—and I don't think they've got it yet,
although there has been a great improvement—is enlightened,
cultured, and experienced, critical opinion. Whatever people
may say about critics—and, God knows, we have our faults—
we do contribute to the maintaining of artistic standards.
People, whether or not they know it consciously, do take notice
of what they read in newspapers. There are one or two young
critics in Australia who have had experience in England: they
have gone home with a set of standards by which to judge
what they hear and see in Australia. Australian critics are
gradually forgetting the notion that an artist has to come over
here, and get favourable notices in London-based papers,
before he can be recognized. Australian critics must make up
their own minds about the standards attained by their local
artists.

A lot of young artists in Australia are not as well known as
they deserve to be. I could name half-a-dozen very gifted
Australians, who, if they had been given proper encouragement
and training at the right time, would have become widely
known as first-class artists. If I were asked, "Who are the six
best women pianists you've heard in the last 30 years?", I
would reply: "Myra Hess and Moura Lympany—both of
them English—Muriel Cohen, Joyce Greer, Eileen Ralfph,
and Joyce Hutchinson; the last four, all Australians, being
pianists of the highest class."

If I were a millionaire and I wanted to spend an evening
with some friends, we'd have some wine and some dinner, and
then we'd retire to my music room. Now, if *you* were a millionaire, which famous pianist would you invite? I would ask
Artur Rubinstein to come and play. And, if he couldn't come,
I would ask Muriel Cohen.

RD: You've been talking about the need for informed music
criticism in Australia. During the Forties, at such a formative
stage in Australia's artistic life, you must have felt a great sense

of responsibility in your position as the country's senior music critic.

NC: That is true. I felt that acutely. If you're a critic in London, and you write a concert notice, you know that four or five other opinions will be published next morning. But in Sydney I suddenly realized that I was in a position of greater responsibility than ever before. I could destroy a young artist's career, if I was not careful. And, if I was not critical enough, I could perpetuate low standards. So I had to be very conscious of what I was writing. It wasn't a case, as in London, of just going to a concert and then writing a notice to entertain my readers. For the first time, I was taking part in the building up of a musical culture. England's artistic and critical standards have been established by hundreds of years of civilization. But Australia was, and still is, a young country. I had a column in a very influential paper—in those days it was the *Manchester Guardian* of Australia—and I did a weekly radio broadcast. Music criticism suddenly became a serious matter for me, but that didn't mean I had to write, express myself, in a serious way. The Australian public will never allow itself to be talked down to by an Englishman. I had to inform them by wit and humour. Your Shaws and your Newmans, your Max Beerbohms and your Agates, were influential only in so far as they could *entertain* their readers.

I learned not to patronize the Australians. I couldn't say, "Oh, we don't do things *that* way in England." And I didn't want to appear to be patronizing in another way by saying, "You are the best", because Australians on the whole are very shrewd and honest people. So the only thing to do was to educate them without their knowing I was educating them, and to do this I gave them every day something to laugh at. No one man, and certainly no one music critic, could build a musical culture. There had to be active and able people in the musical world: men like Bainton and Goossens at the State Conservatorium in Sydney.

And I had the utmost co-operation from the very enlightened music-broadcasts staff at the Australian Broadcasting Commission. I had no interference at all, and, what is more, I was given plenty of time: "air space" or whatever they call it. There was no radio when I was 20, but, supposing there had

been, I would have loved to have listened to Newman for an
hour every week, instead of simply going to the library and
reading 1,500 words in the *Birmingham Post*. To a young person,
the human voice is more vivid than the printed word. It would
have been like having lessons with a famous teacher.

The great thing for me in Australia was the combination of
the printed word and the radio broadcast. I had the opportunity to tend a garden, a musical growth. It was hard work.
Sometimes I felt there were Philistines everywhere. But when
Eugene Goossens came to Sydney from the United States, and
had the courage to conduct Mahler symphonies, then I felt
that the sowing season was over and that soon there would be
sprigs and buds and blossoms. It was Goossens who formulated
the idea of an opera house in Sydney, but he died before his
dream became a reality. I feel sure that the next ten years will
bring tremendous growth and development in the Australian
musical scene.

RD: Was the *Sydney Morning Herald* sold outside New South
Wales?

NC: No, the *Morning Herald* was a New South Wales paper. It
was sold mainly in Sydney. Some copies went to Melbourne, the
nearest state-capital, and no doubt copies were sent to libraries
throughout Australia. Now that more frequent aeroplane
services have revolutionized newspaper distribution, I would
imagine that these days the *Sydney Morning Herald* is sold over
a much bigger area.

Australia has its provincial newspapers, just as we have our
Yorkshire Post and *Scotsman*. The *Scotsman* is a great newspaper,
but people don't rush out into the streets of London to buy it.
There was a time, just before or just after the First World
War, when the *Manchester Guardian* had a circulation of only
about 3,000 in London.

There is a lot to be said for a paper that reflects a county or a
state personality and flavour. The *Morning Herald* expressed the
Sydney way of life, which is entirely different from the Melbourne
way of life, as different as Bradford is from Billericay.

RD: What else stands out in your mind from your years in
Australia?

NC: Late on Wednesday afternoons, at about 6 o'clock, I used

to give a 15-minute illustrated talk to children. It was broadcast on the radio, from a studio at the Australian Broadcasting
Commission. On hearing that the average age of these children
would be ten or eleven, I naturally began with music such as
the *Hansel and Gretel* overture and the *Nursery Suite* of Elgar. I
kept to this level of music for three or four weeks. Then one
morning I got two letters from these children: one of them from
a 10-year-old girl, wanting to hear some Bach; the other, not
only asking why I hadn't yet played anything of William
Walton, but also implying that I seemed to be talking down
to him and his fellow-intellectuals of ten and eleven! After that,
I put on more advanced music, such as Dvorak's "New World"
symphony and Schubert songs. I got extraordinarily intelligent
comments and letters from these young children. I was amazed
at the response.

To this day, Australians who are over here on holiday will
come up to me during the interval of a concert and say that
they used to listen to my talks when they were children.
Marie Collier, who died so tragically a few years ago, once
came over to me in a restaurant, after I had heard her in a
Covent Garden performance. I was both astonished and
delighted when she said she used to listen to my talks when she
was 12 or 13. In many ways, that gave me more pleasure than
to get praise for my books, which are for adults; and in any
case thousands of books are published every year. If I have ever
done any good in this world, it is the help I gave—especially
to young people—to make Australia what it is now becoming:
a musical community.

Australia will contribute to the musical world something
that is entirely fresh, because Australia is a young country
without the burdens of tradition. Tradition must not be thrown
overboard, which is what a lot of young people today are
attempting to do. A culture can't begin without the right soil
and the right roots, but, as Mahler once said, tradition can be
a hindrance. The ideal is for the past to continue to have a
subtle influence on the present, just as a flower continues to
owe its life to a seed or a bulb. This is what is happening in
Australia's musical and artistic life.

RD: Before your wartime stay in Australia, hadn't you been
over there to cover an England cricket tour?

NC: Yes, I first went to Australia in 1936 with G. O. Allen's team. I had always had an ambition to go to Australia, ever since as a boy I saw Victor Trumper batting at Old Trafford. I was only 12 or 13 when I first heard him.

RD: Neville, did you say "heard"?

NC: That was a Freudian slip. I often think of Trumper in terms of music. His bat made music. I again saw him, and heard him, when I was 19 or 20. Then I really knew something about cricket, for I was soon to become a professional cricketer at Shrewsbury School. I watched Trumper in the Old Trafford Test Match of 1909. He made only 48 in Australia's second innings, but I've never forgotten it. You'll always remember an innings of 200 or 250, or even 100, but if you can remember a short innings, from 1909 until the 1970s, then that batsman did something, had something, quite remarkable. I can see Trumper now, making those 48 runs with a grace and ease that has seldom been excelled.

There have been more lyrical batsman—Frank Woolley, for example—but Victor Trumper combined the grace of a panther with the power, the consummate power, of a lion. Trumper's batting could be dramatic and lyrical at the same time. If you asked me to give a description of Trumper, for the benefit of the young cricketers of today, I would say: "Try to imagine a combination of Denis Compton and Dexter." Even then I'd have to add a substantial, rock-like quality, because Trumper wasn't an easy batsman to get out. He never played the fool: he never threw his wicket away. I saw in him not only a combination of Compton and Dexter but also the basic soundness and quality of a Walter Hammond. A synthesis of Hammond and Dexter and Compton is, to say the least, a rare and gifted batsman. Trumper, when I was quite young, made me fall in love with Australia.

When I was 14 or 15, my chances of getting to Australia seemed as remote as my chances of becoming Lord Chancellor. But the wheel of life goes round and round, and, thanks to the work of destiny that we don't know anything at all about, I found myself on the *Orion* in September 1936. In those days, cricketers travelled to Australia by ship, a journey of four or five weeks, and they really got to know one another. These days, a cricket touring team is whisked across the world in a plane. Within hours, they find themselves in another climate. It is too sudden a modulation.

When we arrived in Fremantle, a number of reporters came on board. "What do you think of Australia?" they asked. I hadn't yet set foot on Australian soil: I'd only seen the country through a porthole! I told the reporters that I thought I would like Australia, but that I might miss music during the six-month tour. At that period of my life, the prospect of being without music for six months was as desperate as that of a traveller being in a desert without water.

This interview was published in Perth's evening paper and that same night I got a telephone call at my hotel from a doctor who lived in Cottesloe, a lovely suburb of Perth. He asked if I would like to join him for dinner, and he promised to arrange for me to hear some music. He got in touch with the University, and some female students entertained me by playing Chopin and by singing some Hugo Wolf songs. That was an incredibly moving experience: to arrive by ship; to tell some reporters that I feared I was going to miss music; to be tele-phoned a few hours later and invited to a doctor's house to hear music. That was one of the many kindnesses that endeared me to Australia.

I went into very few homes in Australia in which somebody could not play the piano: not like a virtuoso, but in a way that gave pleasure to everyone present. Just as the ethos and environment of musical life is entirely different today, compared with 40 years ago, so also has cricket changed and not always for the better. In the Thirties, there was not the scramble of one-day cricket. In those days, all Test Matches in Australia were played to a finish. Even if they lasted six or seven days— and two of the Tests on that tour lasted six days—Tests were played to a finish.

People today sometimes tell me that, if we had cricket matches without a time limit, the scoring would be slower. As a matter of fact, the scoring, when Test Matches were played to a finish in Australia, was probably the same as it is now, and perhaps even a little quicker. But the main point of interest about the Test Match played to a finish—and it struck me after I'd watched two or three—was that, from the very first ball bowled, one team was doomed. There was no escape. One team was going to be beaten. Every ball bowled was a nail in

the coffin of one team or the other. There was a dramatic sense
of inevitability about the match. When cricket was played to
a finish, there was no point in playing slowly. You had to make
runs; you couldn't play for a draw.

Without the time limit, a great responsibility was placed on
the groundsman to prepare a good wicket. You couldn't
play a match to a finish on a wicket that was prepared—as
some are today—as though schoolboys were going to play on
it. Those Australian wickets were like pavements: only on the
fifth or sixth day would cracks begin to appear. Either you
bowled fast—like McDonald or Larwood or Gregory—or else
you had to spin the ball. In order to spin the ball, on those
Australian wickets, you had to do it with the wrist. Off-spin
was no good, and so we had the great googly bowlers such as
Mailey and Grimmett and Bill O'Reilly.

The loss of the great spin bowler is one of the biggest losses
in cricket today. Nowadays we have the seam bowler, just
making the ball swing. I could teach any strong young boy of
17 or 18 or 19 to become a good seam bowler, in a year or two.
It takes longer to become a spinner. At St Peter's College, a
public school in Adelaide, I used to watch boys at the nets.
They were all emulating Grimmett and O'Reilly, learning to
bowl spinners.

The most recent great Australian spinner was Richie Benaud.
One-day cricket doesn't encourage the leg-spinner, because a
leg-spinner isn't going to bowl maiden overs all day. His
ability is to get batsmen out when the wicket is perfect, when
the ball doesn't swing, when you can't get the ball to turn by
bowling an off-break, when you can only get the batsmen out
by flighting the ball—by "flighting" I mean what the ball does
in the air, in addition to what it does off the pitch. That's
what great bowlers like Arthur Mailey did. In a famous match
in Sydney, during the 1903–4 England tour, Victor Trumper
made 185 not out. Australia made an enormous score,
just under 500, but Wilfred Rhodes, who could hardly turn
the ball at all in Australia, took five wickets for 94, not by
spin, but by curving and flighting the ball, giving the batsmen
questions to answer in the air. Cricket then was not just a
game; it was a fine art.

In those days, summer cricket was an absolute *passion* in
Australia. Horse-racing was too, but in another and smaller

dimension. Not only men in their thousands, but women also, went to cricket matches. 30,000 people would turn up for a match between Victoria and New South Wales, just as Lancashire and Yorkshire would attract a 30,000 crowd during the Twenties; just as at the Oval, in 1947 or 1948, when Surrey were playing Middlesex, the gates would be closed at mid-day.

Last summer, on the first day of the Surrey–Middlesex match, there were probably no more than 800 spectators in the stands. People ask: "Why has interest in cricket declined? Is it because most families prefer watching television or travelling about by car?" Well, when I went to Australia in 1936, people could have gone to one of the many wonderful beaches or to horse-racing. There are plenty of outdoor pleasures in Australia that we don't have to the same extent in England. But people didn't go sun-bathing when Bradman was batting. They didn't go to the beach when Alan Kippax was batting. They went to see cricket's great personalities. The sad thing about cricket today is that it has become *totally* competitive.

If I were allowed to repeat two periods of my life, I would choose my first five years with the *Manchester Guardian* and every day of my seven years in Australia. Mind you, there were moments when I wanted to get away; just as there are moments when I want to get away from London. When I'm in Paradise, I'm sure I'll want a fortnight in Hell for a change.

Australia and Australians were an inspiration to me. In Australia I was doing what everyone should always try to do: re-create himself. To do that, you must be among people who are not bored.

4

CRICKET AND THE ARTS

RD: You have always contended that the first artists to quicken your aesthetic sense were two cricketers: Reggie Spooner and A. C. MacLaren.

NC: Victor Trumper was like a comet that flashed into my ken and then disappeared for a few years, but, when I was a boy, I used to see a lot of Spooner and MacLaren. During the summer holidays I would go to Old Trafford and spend my sixpence. That sixpence, I want you to know, had to be saved up. As a schoolboy, you had to bring in the coal or do some- body's shopping to get your Saturday penny. It took several weeks to save up sixpence, so I could only go three or four times a year to Old Trafford.

When I was 15 or 16 I had a wonderful inspiration: I used to go and stand outside Manchester's Central Station, behind the Midland Hotel. The station is now closed. All the aristo- crats from London used to arrive there and go, from the station into the back-entrance-hall of the Midland Hotel, under an awning to protect them from the Manchester rain. I used to stand outside the station, and as the passengers came by I would say, "Carry your bag, sir?" One of them would let me carry his bag into the hotel, and I would usually be given sixpence. Then off to Old Trafford the next day.

There I saw MacLaren for the first time. He batted for only about ten minutes on a gloomy morning, with the clouds coming up. I had stood outside the ground, staring at a menac- ing sign: YOU ENTER AT YOUR OWN RISK. NO MONEY RETURNED. I chanced it, paid my sixpence, and went through the turn- stile. For the first time I was entering the place that for many years was to be my summer home. Lancashire were playing Gloucestershire, in those remote days around the turn of the the century. W. G. Grace had retired, but Jessop was there, and a quickish bowler named Roberts. MacLaren hooked him for four, with a majestic sweep of the bat. He did more than hook the ball to the square-leg boundary: he dismissed the ball from his presence. After MacLaren had made this majestic stroke, which was as sculpturesque as anything that ever came out of Ancient Greece, it rained and rained.

Everybody went home, except one small boy. He sheltered under a brick wall near the entrance to the pavilion, and prayed that the rain would stop. Little boys believe in miracles, and I prayed that the clouds would disappear and that the sun would declare itself. I waited and waited, and, when at last the rain did cease, I thought optimistically, "The players might come out again." And then, less cheerfully, I said to myself, "How will I get back through the turnstile? I've already spent my sixpence."

Out of the pavilion came a man in a blue serge suit, with a watch chain, and I recognized who he was even though he was in disguise. In those days, a cricketer who wasn't in flannels was to me disguised. It was the famous J. T. Tyldesley. He looked at this small boy, who was myself. "Good heavens, son," he said, "What are you doing here?" In a pleading voice I asked, "Aren't you going to play any more?" "Good Lord, no. The match was abandoned hours ago." I was about to burst into tears. He patted me on the shoulder and, handing me sixpence, he said, "Sonny, you go and enjoy yourself at the circus." I would never spend that sixpence. I think I've still got it somewhere. When I met all my pals the next day, I showed them my sixpence and said that Johnny Tyldesley had given it to me. Not one of them believed me.

RD: How did you become "Cricketer" of the *Manchester Guardian*?

NC: I joined the reporters' room as a very serious young man; I had no intention of becoming a cricket writer. My great ambition was to be either a music critic or a leader writer. In those days, under C. P. Scott, the first leader was very long— about 1,000 words—and it used to consist of three paragraphs, almost in sonata-form: exposition, development, recapitulation. I used to think to myself, "How wonderful to be a leader writer and *shake* governments, at home and abroad." But I was disillusioned one night when I went home to supper with one of the leader writers, a charming man by the name of Arthur

Wallace. At one point in our conversation during dinner, his wife said, "Oh *Arthur*, we've heard all this before. Don't talk such nonsense." I thought, "So this is all a leader writer counts for when he is in his own home." A young writer should beware of the hypnotism of print.

When cricket was resumed after the First War, they played two-day matches, eleven in the morning until half-past seven at night, and they played *real* cricket, not this limited-over "instant" stuff. I had not been well, and the news editor, a wonderful man named W. P. Crozier, asked if I would like to convalesce in the sunshine at Old Trafford and write one or two cricket reports. One or two!

I began writing in what was then the conventional manner. In those days, "So-and-so went on at the pavilion end *vice* (that is to say, 'in place of') So-and-so." The ball wasn't "driven for four"; it was "dispatched to the confines". My first cricket reports were full of phrases like this, but I didn't go quite as far as Jimmy Catton, of *Athletic News* and the *Manchester Evening Chronicle*, who used to refer to the ball as the "crimson rambler": "The crimson rambler sped over the greensward, dispatched from Frank Woolley's elegant bat." Jimmy used to write in that lyrical way when he was at Canterbury, but not when he was at Sheffield: he varied his style according to the setting. Today's cricket correspondents don't seem to be able—or to want—to do this. They write about a match in Sydney as if it were a match at Lord's or The Oval. They convey no sense of atmosphere.

In a Lancashire and Yorkshire match in 1919, the year in which I began writing about cricket, one of the great characters of that period, Cecil Parkin, took eight or nine wickets for next-to-nothing and won the match for Lancashire. I was so impressed by this terrific display of bowling that I went back to the office and wrote 1,500 words. The chief sub-editor said, "Good God, we don't have room for all that 'copy' ", and so my report was submitted to C. P. Scott, who didn't know a thing about cricket. As soon as he had read the piece, he said, "This must go in, without cuts." Not long afterwards I became cricket correspondent of the *Manchester Guardian*.

At first I used to sign my reports "N.C." Then Crozier said to me, "Your initials 'N.C.' won't do, Cardus. They already appear in the paper at the end of your arts-page notices.

We'll have to find you a *nom de plume*. Think up a suitable one over the week-end, will you." So I went home and on the Monday I had come up with nothing more original than "Mid-off", "Cover point", or "No ball"! Crozier's secretary, a very gifted girl by the name of Madeline Linford, overheard our discussion and she said to me, "Why not call yourself 'Cricketer'?" I said, "That's ridiculous. I suppose that if I were writing about football, you'd want to call me 'Footballer'." But Crozier thought "Cricketer" was a splendid suggestion, and so "Cricketer" I became.

The job of cricket correspondent was a very important one in those days. Today's cricket correspondents are only allowed about 500 words, but I used to write 1,500 words a day, 7–8,000 words a week. For the first month or so I conscientiously kept score, noting what time each batsman came in, how many fours he hit—and off which bowler and to which part of the field. We had no Roy Webber, no Bill Frindall, in the press box to help us with the statistics.

As I became more and more interested in writing about cricket, so the scoreboard became less important to me. I wanted to concentrate on the field of play. It was then that I began to see cricket as something more than a game. To me, Woolley and Hammond and Jack Hobbs were like actors in a play, and I wrote about them not only in terms of runs and strokes but also in terms of individual character. I found myself getting as deeply engrossed in cricket as in symphony concerts.

After about a year I felt I was becoming too literary; I was over-writing. And it was at this stage that I began to write about the humour in the game, as expressed by characters such as Cecil Parkin, Dick Tyldesley, and Emmott Robinson. For many years there have been rumours that I invented Emmott Robinson. He *did* exist, but he didn't say things exactly as I reported them.

I remember a very wet morning at Leeds; they didn't cover the wickets in those days. At 1 o'clock the sun came beating down and of course this meant that the wicket would become difficult for the batsmen. An hour or so later, Wilfred Rhodes and Emmott Robinson went out to inspect the wicket, and I went with them. Wilfred Rhodes felt the turf and said, "Emmott, it'll be sticky at 4 o'clock." Then Emmott bent down, pressed his fingers into the soil like an expert cloth-tester, and said, "No, Wilfred, half-past." What he really said was, "Aye, Wilfred." I'm certain that Emmott Robinson, when he read this story, firmly believed he had said what I made him say. But I didn't invent; my imagination drew out of him what was natural and germane to his character.

Then there's a story about fat Dick Tyldesley—no relation to Ernest and J. T. Tyldesley. Dick was a Lancashire man, round, red-faced, bulky but very nimble. He was fielding in the leg-trap during a Lancashire and Yorkshire match. Towards the end of the day's play, a Yorkshireman made a stroke on the leg side. Dick bent down and made what appeared to be a marvellous catch. Just as the batsman was about to depart, Dick told the umpire that the ball had touched the ground. In my report in the *Manchester Guardian*, I congratulated Dick for his sportsmanship: he had made an honest gesture not at all common in a Lancashire and Yorkshire match of that period. And when I saw him on the Monday morning I went over to him and said, "You showed wonderful sportsmanship in letting the umpire know that the ball touched the ground." Dick replied, "I thank you." What I reported him as saying was, "I thank you, Mr Cardus. Westhoughton Sunday School, tha knows."

In Lancashire and Yorkshire matches, the players tended not to conform to the Victorian standard of ethics. For instance, no batsman would ever dream of "walking", as we call it nowadays; he would always wait for the umpire's decision. And not only that—if there was an appeal for leg-before-wicket, the batsman would get away from the line of the stumps as quickly as possible. He would retreat to square-leg so that the umpire wouldn't be able to see where he had been positioned.

In the Twenties and Thirties there was a succession of Lancashire and Yorkshire matches at Old Trafford which didn't produce a result. The wickets were beautifully prepared by the ground staff and Ted McDonald told me that the wicket at Old Trafford was better than the wicket at Adelaide. Even he, one of the finest fast bowlers of all time, couldn't get the ball to rise stump-high. It was a batsman's paradise. I remember a Lancashire and Yorkshire match in which Lancashire had 500 runs on the board at lunchtime on the second day and still wouldn't make a declaration. I happened to meet Roy

Kilner, one of the Yorkshire players, and I said, "This sort of wicket is terrible. It's killing the game." Roy said, "Oh no, Mr Cardus. This is a different kind of wicket from pre-war days. You need educating up to it. What we really want in Lancasheer and Yorksheer matches, you know, is no umpire—and fair cheating all round!"

RD: How do you feel about present-day cricket—in no more than ten words!

NC: As a competitive game, I regard cricket as inferior to all the others. For example, few cricket matches can compare with a great singles battle at Wimbledon. If I want a competitive game, I take soccer; but I have no time for the player who plays chess in the middle of the field and forgets where the goal-posts are.

The great thing about cricket, as it was when I used to love it, was that it was not only a game with a competitive interest. As a boy (*and* as a grown-up!) I always wanted Lancashire to beat Yorkshire. But that was the long-term interest. As soon as a match began, I became absorbed by the different styles of the players. When Jack Hobbs came to the wicket to face the bowling of Larwood, it wasn't just Nottingham against Surrey; it was Larwood against Hobbs. Today, you have Dennis Lillee bowling at Boycott. This is the real fascination of cricket: the match *within* the match.

The public—influenced by the press and television—has become obsessed by the idea that cricket is just a matter of long-term victory. But, in the three-day or five-day matches, a lot of people go only on the first or second day and don't see the finish; and those who go on the last day didn't see the beginning. So they want to watch a match within the match. If I had to make one criticism about English cricket today, I would say: "The standardization of the players." People sometimes say to me, "You're one of the old fogeys who live in the past. You praise the past at the expense of the present." But I *don't* live in the past. I've repeatedly said that cricketers such as Sobers, Kanhai, Barry Richards, Mike Procter, Clive Lloyd, and those two other West Indians, Boyce and Julien, are as interesting, as personalities, as any cricketers I ever saw in the golden age. But they're not English! Why is it that I have to go to see an Indian or a West Indian or a

South African in order to feel the presence of a great cricketer's personality?

You could put Clive Lloyd or Sobers or Kanhai into the company of MacLaren and Spooner and Denis Compton, and they would be stars in the same firmament. But I can only name half of today's England XI. They are technically good, but you could select eleven others and you wouldn't notice any difference of style or technique. Where are the great players in English cricket? Is it a fact, as I've always maintained, that cricket, probably more than any other game, reflects the sociological climate and structure of society? Has our technological, standardized, Welfare State society caught up even with our cricketers? People tell me it's catching up with our footballers in the same way.

Cricket used to be a game in which there was time for a man to develop and reveal his personality. It was no accident that in the early 1900s we had opulent cricketers such as MacLaren and Jessop and F. S. Jackson. And not just amateurs—or Gentlemen, as they used to be called—but professionals such as Johnny Tyldesley and Frank Woolley. They played like millionaires. They didn't go on to the field to acquire runs, like sparrows picking up crumbs on a frosty morning. They came out as though carrying big bags of runs, to be spread about the field. I never felt that Woolley or Tyldesley or, in more recent times, Denis Compton—I never felt that they *made* runs, in the way that people invest money on the Stock Exchange. No, they *distributed* runs. They had a *largesse* of runs, and spread them plenteously all over the field.

When I came back to England, after seven years of "exile", the scars of war were everywhere. Many buildings were in ruin, and food was still being rationed: I could hold in the palm of one hand my week's supply of food. I went to Lord's one afternoon. There was a packed crowd, but it wasn't a Test Match. It was in the middle of the week, a Wednesday afternoon, Middlesex and Worcester, in front of 20,000 people. A lot of them looked as though they hadn't had a square meal for a very long time.

The thought came to me that, two or three years before, when the V-bombs were causing terror over London, every single person in that crowd was living from hour to hour. And now here they were, all happily cheering Compton. They were running his runs with him. They were all part of his largesse of brilliant cricketing skill. Compton's wonderful personality spread across the field like sunshine coming down from the heavens. That's what a great game can do, and I won't be satisfied until I see cricket doing that again—which it did, in 1973 for example, at Lord's, when the West Indians were there. I got that same feeling of old—of the game of cricket as not just a competition, with each team trying to beat the other, but a contribution to the *joy of life*, in summer.

RD: Apart from yourself, I can think of only one music critic who also wrote about sport, and that was Ernest Newman.

NC: Newman had an extraordinary range of interests. He was very keen on billiards. In his later years, he was president of his local cricket club in Surrey, but to the best of my knowledge he never went to a first-class cricket match. He was a passionate admirer of boxing. Newman was never a physically strong man, although he did live till 90. I could think of a lot of people, if I gave my mind to it, who have been attracted to violent sports like boxing, even though—or perhaps because—they were rather febrile and delicate themselves.

Newman wrote a 1,500-word description for the *Manchester Guardian* of one of Carpentier's fights. The only man today who has that same range is Alistair Cooke. His many interests include music and golf; he is a latter-day Ernest Newman. I'm sure Alistair Cooke could write a concert notice, and I know he did once describe a cricket match at Old Trafford for the *Guardian*.

Shaw had a great interest in boxing at one period, as he showed when he wrote his novel about prizefighting: *Cashel Byron's Profession*. And a less sport-minded man than Shaw you could never imagine. I couldn't imagine Shaw going to a football match or a cricket match. Never.

I can't think of any other music critics who have written about sport. I've known artists, actors, writers, and composers, who have been keen on cricket, but music critics don't seem to go to watch sport. They are too busy reading their scores. The wrong scores sometimes!

RD: Who are some of the people in the artistic world who have been interested in cricket?

NC: J. M. Barrie often went to Lord's. Lord Snow is a very keen cricket fan, and so is Harold Pinter. Then there was Arnold Bax, who I hope will soon again get the recognition he deserves as a composer. He may not have been a Beethoven or a Brahms, but in the Thirties he was as well thought of as many of our leading composers are today. He was a keen cricketer, and he had a brother who played.

I went up to Manchester some years ago for a Barbirolli performance of the ninth symphony of Mahler. Barbirolli wanted me to talk to the audience about the work. After the concert, I went back to his house to have a late supper with him, and I thought we'd discuss Mahler. Oh no; we talked cricket. A Test Match was being played in Australia, and he kept going to the radio to find out what the score was.

I often used to see Edward German at Lord's. He was not a composer of great symphonies, but a composer of very beautiful, what we used to call "light", music. We often used to hear the dances from his incidental music to Shakespeare's *Henry VIII*, though that's not the real Edward German. He has left us *Tom Jones*, one of the most beautifully orchestrated scores of all English light operas.

Many, many musicians have been keen on cricket. I just can't begin to name them all. Naturally, most of them have been English. I don't think I've ever seen a foreign-born musician at a cricket match. I can't imagine Kreisler or Menuhin ever having watched cricket, but I must try to persuade Daniel Barenboim to come to Lord's, because, as I once said, we've got our slow movements there too.

RD: What is there about cricket that attracts artistic people?

NC: Cricket has a lot of aesthetic appeal. Perhaps, for the artist, it represents not only the joy of life in summertime but also an extension of his aesthetic awareness. When I was music critic on the *Guardian*, and living in Manchester, I used to come down to London to write about opera at Covent Garden. At Lord's one afternoon in 1938, I wrote 1,500 words after seeing Wally Hammond make a wonderful double-century. When I went to Covent Garden that night, I felt a certain lowering of aesthetic temperature. Nothing I heard from those Italian tenors, bawling away in some Italian opera, could compare with the aesthetic uplift that I got from Hammond's marvellous innings.

It seems to me that artistry is not tied to any particular medium. If you are going to be an artist, it may be best for reasons of personal fame to express yourself in a permanent artistic form such as music, literature, sculpture, or painting. But sometimes this spark of creativity, this spark of personality, expresses itself through a medium that isn't in the strictest sense an art.

I have had aesthetic experiences from the cricket field which I mix and mingle, without any dissonance or discord, with all the pleasures I've had from music, from the theatre, from literature. If I were put into a corner by the Almighty and He asked me, "Did you get a bigger aesthetic thrill when listening to a well-known violinist than you got when seeing Frank Woolley bat?", I would say: "Not necessarily. I'd have to go to a violinist of the stature of Menuhin in order to find a musical experience that surpassed the thrill of watching Frank Woolley."

Music has enriched my life, ever since I was a boy in Manchester, but I can remember many times when I have been much nearer the core or the well-spring of beauty and creation, and spontaneous joy of life, when I've seen a cricketer like Dexter, or young Cowdrey when he first played in Australia. I was thrilled when Cowdrey got a century at Melbourne against Keith Miller at his most ferocious. Here was I, with a panorama in my mind of all the great cricket that had been played on that ground at Melbourne, from Trumper to Bradman. And here was this young man of 21 or 22, unrazored and fresh from England, on this famous stage, this Melbourne cricket ground, like a young singer appearing for the first time at the Scala, or Covent Garden or the Metropolitan. For me this wasn't just a sport-spectator's excitement; it was an imaginative excitement.

I have seen from time to time a performer on the football field who has given me the thrill of seeing a unique personality expressing himself by means of a leather football—or are they made of plastic nowadays? Footballers such as Bobby Charlton and Stanley Matthews have as much claim as any English tenor or violinist to be regarded as part of the British tradition of great personalities. The same spark is needed to excel in any calling. Any artist who has that spark is contributing to the great—what can we call it?—the great fire of life that warms us all and helps us through, in spite of the dead matter of materialism, in spite of man's fits of destruction.

I came back to England after the Second War, and I had not seen the storm and tragedy of the bombing. I remember one day when I was out walking in London. I came across a piece of wasteland that showed signs of heavy bombing. And out of the rubble was growing a flower. I'm not a botanist, so I don't know what it was called. That sprig, growing out of the rubble of war, wasn't an orchid; it couldn't have been put into the Chelsea Flower Show; but it was a sign of the eternal spark of creation. And that spark can be found in all the activities of life.

Don't misunderstand me. I know there are degrees of artist. Although I get the same essence of aesthetic pleasure from a really great cricketer or footballer as I get from a really great performer at a concert, note that I say "performer". I'm not telling you that Woolley or Victor Trumper gave me the same aesthetic pleasure that Chopin or a *creative* artist can give me. And I'm not saying that Bobby Charlton and Stanley Matthews are artists on the same plane as Menuhin or Horowitz or Schnabel, because they are not dealing with the same material. But *every* artist, in his own way, is a manifestation of the creative spirit.

That's my philosophy, which has taken me a very long time to develop. I can't relate my philosophy to any brand of theology, and even though recognizing the fact that these eternal sparks do manifest themselves—in games, in the arts, in a sprig growing out of post-war rubble—I have to say to the bishop, "I don't believe in your God"; and I say to the Buddhists, "I don't believe in your nirvana." And then, forced into a corner, I confess, "I believe in *my* God. No priest or bishop has brought me to Him. In my own way, I've found Him."

5

COMPOSERS

RD: Langford said: "Other men compose music; Mozart *is* music." And you once called Mozart "the most truly musical of all composers". Do you still feel that?

NC: Yes, but first of all I must amplify what I said. I regard Beethoven's mind as the greatest that ever expressed itself in music. He composed during a transition period, and he reached forward. He broke up the beautiful, almost-perfect, eighteenth-century patterns. Some of Beethoven's music must have sounded, in his day, as radical and as far-reaching as Stockhausen's sounds to us now. The development section of the first movement of the "Eroica" symphony was a tremendous stride forward for music.

In Mozart we have the *perfect* balance of two things: perfect form and perfect substance. Mozart uses trombones in *Don Giovanni* with dramatic effect. Here he is reaching forward, but he never strains, never becomes unmusical. Mozart wrote in a letter that even when a composer is expressing an ugly or tragic aspect of life, he must transform it—endow it with beauty.

Pianists, with any conscience at all, are always afraid of playing Mozart. His writing has little of the sophisticated harmony of a Debussy or a Chopin. In Mozart sonatas the left hand sometimes gives only the simplest tonic-dominant support to a poignant right hand consisting of isolated notes. Every note must be as individual as a star and yet at the same time related to the whole of the constellation.

When I was in Manchester I often used to hear Schnabel, especially when he came to play with the Hallé. Schnabel was not renowned for over-practising. Once, when we met in Manchester, he said to me, "Cardus, I'm going back to London, and I will now practise for a fortnight, four hours a day." "Good heavens," I said, "Why?" "At my next recital I have to play Mozart."

A wrong note in Brahms or Beethoven doesn't matter quite as much, but if you play a wrong note in Mozart it's like putting a star off-course—and there might be a collision, an explosion. So that's why I regard Mozart as the most musical of all composers. Strauss once said: "The melodies of Mozart are like platonic ideas: they are perfect." And Strauss once admitted that he would have given nearly everything he composed to have written the G minor symphony. It is not often that a great composer speaks so generously about another composer!

Hans Richter was once asked to name the greatest composer of all time. Without hesitating, he said, "Beethoven". The questioner was taken aback. "B-But, Herr D-D-D-Doktor, what about Mozart?" "Oh," replied Richter, "I thought you were referring to *the rest*."

RD: You have, I know, a deep affection for Mozart's clarinet concerto, particularly the slow movement.

NC: An incredible piece of music. It embodies, enshrines, all that I am trying to say about Mozart. The *adagio* contains some of the most profound music Mozart ever wrote, and yet a child could play it at the piano. The clarinet, in the second theme, has a figure containing five descending notes—just that—with a lovely accompaniment in the strings. Those few simple notes are as moving as anything else in all music. Why should five descending scale-notes bring all heaven to our ears?

There is no rhetoric, no over-emphasis, in Mozart's music. He never underlines: he doesn't need to. God forgive me, I'm not an anti-Wagnerian, but I feel that Wagner too often underlines. He puts so many phrases and passages in italics that I'm sometimes reminded of the letters of Queen Victoria! I know you have to take a composer warts and all, but often, after I've been to an intense performance of *Tristan*, say under Furtwängler—and I rate *Tristan* as one of the most amazing works of art that ever came out of the mind of man—I've gone back to my flat and listened to some Mozart, as a catharsis, to get myself cleansed.

RD: For a very long time you have been an advocate of Mahler. What is there about him—the man and his music— that so captivates you?

NC: I was first interested in Mahler many years ago, at a time when his music was anathema in this country. Newman wrote a favourable notice of the seventh symphony of Mahler as far back as 1913, after Henry Wood had conducted it at the Queen's Hall. This was only a few years after the first performance. Newman was then with the *Birmingham Post*. He came down to London to write this notice for the *Nation*, at a time when Mahler was virtually unknown in this country. Newman at once recognized him as a composer who was not only saying something original, but also, in his orchestration, was saying it in an original way.

Langford was one of the first critics to champion Mahler and, in the early Twenties, he opened my ears and mind to Mahler's music. But in those days we had very few performances of Mahler's symphonies, and not very good performances at that, and in some of my first notices I said that he was just a synthetic composer. When I had a chance to really get *into* Mahler, I found that he was absolutely individual. For example, the slow movement of his fourth symphony, beginning with plucked strings, reminds you of Schubert's string quintet, but the symphony is Mahler through and through, with his own fingerprints. Of course every great composer has to take his roots from the established language. Then he draws inspiration from the newest vocabularies and amalgamates them with the established ones. You cannot write a masterpiece in an entirely new language: the way-out *avant-garde* always vanishes 30 years after he has "advanced".

I have always been intrigued by the enigma of Mahler's short-circuitings. Some of his music shows a lack of good taste, and makes us wonder what went wrong. Debussy and Ravel once walked out of a concert during a performance of Mahler's fifth symphony. These two composers, with their French fastidiousness, simply couldn't take it: Mahler's music, if it is badly conducted, can sound rather schmaltzy.

I've often wondered what would have happened if Mahler had been born ten years later. He was born in a transition period in music, under the bulky shadows of Beethoven, Schubert, and Berlioz, but he managed to reach forward and provide the bridge over which Berg and Schoenberg walked, or rather *prowled*. In parts of the ninth symphony there are the beginnings of the escape from a key-centre.

What fascinates me about Mahler is the dichotomy in him: the fact that such a fine musical thinker could show traces of sentimentalism in his writing. But I emphatically reject the notion that Mahler was just a sentimental neurotic who used music in order to express his complexes. That is nonsense. If you compare the musical development in a late symphony of Mahler with the development section in a symphony of, shall we say, Brahms, the only difference is between what Ernest Newman used to call "tree" form and "table" form. "Table" form is like the four legs of a table, all four equal in height, forming a square, and keeping the table upright. "Tree" form in music is like the branches that grow from a trunk: they grow, seemingly, to no preconceived pattern—no two trees are alike —but they do make an aesthetic balance.

When people tell me that Mahler's music is virtually formless, I say "Don't talk rubbish", but I have to admit that sometimes he took his experiments with structure too far. For example the *finale* of the sixth symphony lasts as long as an average symphony. He indulges in some unnecessary repetition in this movement, but even in his repetitions there is variety of expression.

Sometimes Mahler was in danger of being trapped between two schools of composing: between the symphony as absolute music and the symphony as programme music—the symphonic poem. Mahler always swore that he was not a writer of programme music. He did introduce those ominous hammer blows into the sixth symphony to describe the downfall and death of the hero, but he didn't describe life as literally as Strauss, for example, describes windmills and bleating sheep in *Don Quixote*, and the hanging of Till Eulenspiegel. But we must not overdo these aspects. To me, Mahler's music at its best is in itself worth knowing and worth working for.

RD: The richness of Mahler's scoring has benefited from the enormous improvements in orchestral standards and in recording techniques, but there must be other reasons for his present popularity.

NC: That is something I've been thinking a good deal about. I believe it is because Mahler avoided the *bourgeois*, magisterial way of writing, so prevalent during his lifetime. Instead, he almost prophesied the coming of pop music. The beginning of

the sixth symphony and the march in the first movement of
the third symphony—here is Mahler the prophetic. He is, in
his way, a modern composer. He found the *Stimmung*, the right
wavelength, for the young people of today. He said himself he
wanted to write a symphony to the world. Mahler is one of
the most democratic of composers: he appeals to all ages and
conditions of men. At concerts of his music in recent years,
I've seen young people who the next day were obviously
going to go and hear the Beatles. And at the same time, the
most serious-minded musicians, the academics, who want to
know what music is all about, and how it is structured and
organized—they find Mahler a very fascinating and fruitful
composer to study.

RD: How much twentieth-century music is of lasting worth?

NC: That is a big question! I should have to be clairvoyant to
answer that one.

The history of musical development and music criticism
suggests that virtually every great composer was recognized
and valued by many of those who had access to his music. You
might counter by saying that Bach was in obscurity for years
and years. But Bach was writing in the little chapel of a small
provincial town, and for a while there was no means whereby
the general public could get to hear his music. As soon as his
music was widely propagated he was hailed as a great composer. Then there is the old story about Wagner not being
recognized in his time. Wagner was very *much* recognized in
his time. One of the reasons why for a long time his name
wasn't well known in Germany is because he was too often
abroad, but, soon after Liszt conducted the first performance
of *Lohengrin*, Wagner's operas were being performed in all the
leading opera houses of Europe. So I don't go along with the
idea of neglected genius.

What twentieth-century music will still be played 50 years
from now? If there were a Stock Exchange for music and you
could invest in composers, for futures, I should put some
money on Britten. I'd certainly invest in Elgar, because his
music will be played in this country, but I don't know if it will
played on the Continent. Some of Tippett and Walton will be
played. As regards foreign-born composers, there's a great
scarcity. There has seldom been a time when there were so few

Continental composers whom you could confidently invest in for futures.

I might be prepared to invest in some of the best of Messiaen and Shostakovich, but I'm not sure if I would risk much money on Stockhausen. I think Stockhausen is destined to go down in history as an experimenter. It has always been my conviction that the pioneers, the composers who change the language of music, are not the men who write the masterpieces. The master-composers of the present and the future will do what the master-composers did in the past. They will take what they need of new developments in music and incorporate them into their own style, their own palettes. In the 1880s and 1890s, Wagner was called "modern". Certainly Wagner pushed the language of music forward, but if you look at his music carefully you can see that it was a plant that grew naturally out of the soil of Weber and Marschner. Wagner's music was not a sudden, sporadic invention.

Fashions can change in music as rapidly as in any field of life. When I was a young man, Strauss was thought to be the anti-Christ of music. *Elektra* was one of the biggest bombs that ever burst on music—a nuclear bomb—and Stravinsky's *Le Sacre du Printemps* was soon to follow. But today nobody thinks of *Elektra* as particularly modern, and Strauss is now seen to be the last of a long romantic tradition.

I can remember seeing the old stagers at a Hallé concert walk out in outrage during the battle section of *Heldenleben*, a work which today is almost considered old-hat. Some of them wrote to the *Manchester Guardian* saying they wanted to hear more Haydn at Hallé concerts "to wash ourselves clean after Strauss's infamous barbarities". In a speech made by Strauss he said that somebody had described him as "the Buddha of music". "I don't know," he said, "who is the Buddha of music, but I think I know who is the Pest." He was referring to the critic who had made this extraordinary statement.

So, although it is very difficult to prophesy, if you assembled a jury of twelve of the most learned musicians of the present day—I don't mean academic musicians, I mean active musicians: conductors, singers, violinists, pianists, people who are qualified to talk about music as a living art—I don't think one of them would doubt that Britten's music has lasting qualities. And, so far as other English composers are concerned,

I think a good majority of this jury would vote for Tippett.

RD: Would you invest in Schoenberg and Berg?

NC: Berg, I think, will last. Opera houses, for a long time to come, will always be reviving *Wozzeck*. Berg, a student of Schoenberg, claimed that he could hide a tone row in a composition and defy detection. And he incorporated other composers' influences and absorbed them into his own style and methods. For example, he took some of his colours from Mahler's palette.

Schoenberg to me is a paradoxical composer. He extended the language of music and I think he will go down in history as a sower of seeds, but he didn't reap the harvest; other composers did that. As an artist, and in temperament, Schoenberg was a romantic. To verify that, you have only to hear the *Gurrelieder*—which he wrote when he was about 26, an incredibly young age—and *Verklärte Nacht*. You can imagine the predicament of this far-seeing young composer, after he had written the *Gurrelieder*. He knew he couldn't go on writing in that idiom for the rest of his life. By striking out on new musical paths, he denied certain aspects of his temperament. Intellectually he was *avant-garde*, but I maintain that he was not *avant-garde* at heart.

I believe Schoenberg will be remembered not so much as a great artist but rather as a great theorist. I hope I'm proved wrong because I have a great admiration for so courageous a composer. Had he wished, he could for years have gone on writing in the beautiful idiom of his youth. But no, he had to do something different. *Moses and Aaron* is not very often played nowadays. It will always be a curiosity piece, but it will never be ranked alongside operas such as *Meistersinger*, *Tristan*, *Figaro*, *Otello* and *Falstaff*, or *Pelléas*.

Having spoken earlier about changes in musical fashion, *Pelléas* reminds me of the long period in England when French music was almost completely neglected. For much of the nineteenth-century, and in the early years of the twentieth, England was under the musical domination of Germany: Brahms and Beethoven, Wagner sweeping over Europe in a great wave of popularity, and then Strauss. Manchester was like a German city. As in London, music in Manchester was more or less controlled by German Jews. I'm not saying they didn't use their patronage wisely; indeed they acted with great generosity. But naturally they gave concerts a strong German bias, and Oscar Wilde said, "Music is beginning to speak with a German accent." The result was that a lot of the early Italian composers, and most of the contemporary French composers, were absolutely unknown to the general public.

When I was 18 or 19 I was a rebel, and I wanted to change this state of affairs. Every young person, of every period, is in the *avant-garde*. It is not a modern invention. There has always been an *avant-garde*. There has always been a permissive society. We didn't go about with long hair, as so many young men do today; we went to the opposite extreme and wore short hair. Our main way of protesting against the Establishment was not to wear a hat, and we were called the "No-Hat Brigade". To be a "no-hatter", to walk without a hat down even the streets of Manchester—never mind Bond Street in London—was as daring as being a streaker today.

As one of the *avant-garde*, I took part in a deputation to a friend of Wagner, the great Hans Richter who was then conductor of the Hallé. We wanted to hear some modern French music and we wanted Richter to conduct it. By "modern French music" we didn't mean Boulez or Messiaen: they probably hadn't even been born then. We wanted to hear Debussy and Ravel. Richter replied, in his heavy German accent. He was not a German—he was born in Hungary—but he spent some of his formative years in Austria. All he said to us was: "Zer ist *no* modern French musik."

When *L'Après-midi d'un Faune* was first played, a few years after I was born, that was modern music. But twelve months later it was no longer "modern" music. When we had heard this work three or four times, it became intelligible. My objection to some of what is today called modern music is that, even if I heard it *40* times, it would still be unintelligible.

RD: How do you react to electronic music?

NC: I can't follow it. My musical receiving-set was not built for electronic music. Musically, it doesn't mean a thing to me. Not a thing.

RD: Would you go so far as to call it bogus?

NC: No, I wouldn't go so far as to say that electronic music is bogus, because the men who are composing—or rather *producing*—it are probably very sincere. They no doubt think they've found a new path. And, after all, critics have often been wrong. Hanslick, who was a great critic despite his occasional short-circuitings, once came out of a performance of *Meistersinger*, and, on hearing a barrel-organ playing "O du lieber Augustin", said, "Thank God for melody." And composers are sometimes so obsessed with their own Muse that they cannot see the value in a fellow-composer's work. There are several well-known examples of this kind of myopia. Hugo Wolf didn't acknowledge Brahms as a great composer, but this was largely a matter of difference of temperament. But Wolf was positively tender-hearted compared to Weber, who, after hearing the seventh symphony, declared that the only fit place for Beethoven was a mad-house.

A jury of the leading musicians of today might differ about Britten's precise historical ranking, but they would be unanimous in regarding him as a composer of importance. But if this jury of musicians were to be asked for their verdict on the case of Stockhausen v. Music, I think there would be divided opinion. Stockhausen is experimenting in sound. I should be inclined to say that what he writes has more to do with acoustics than with music.

RD: Reverting back to our musical Stock Exchange, I'm sure you would buy shares in Gershwin and Jerome Kern.

NC: Both of them were men of extraordinary talent. I nearly said "genius", but that is a word to be used with the greatest moderation. I have a lot of time for much of the music that highbrows pooh-pooh, and I owe it to a composer of music-hall tunes, Leslie Stuart, that I ever became interested in music at all. On the plane of what is now called "the musical", a composer can be as fine an artist as Mozart was on his plane. An operetta such as *The Merry Widow* is in its own way as memorable, and as worth listening to and cherishing, as *Meistersinger*.

The real musician should have a very wide range and compass, but there seems to be a certain snobbishness in music—to a greater degree than in the other arts. For instance, few people—even cultured literary men—would scoff if I admitted that I read not only Balzac, Tolstoy, and Proust, but that I also get a tremendous amount of pleasure from P. G. Wodehouse. But if I told certain of my fellow-critics that I regard the octet in Leslie Stuart's *Florodora* as just as perfect a composition, on the plane of musical comedy, as is the quintet in *Meistersinger*, on the plane of grand opera, they would raise their eyebrows.

Twenty or thirty years ago, you wouldn't dare talk about even Franz Lehár to an academic musician. When I was out in Australia, Ormandy came over from Philadelphia, and he conducted the Sydney Symphony Orchestra. Even though the Orchestra had been depleted because of the war, and included a lot of students, Ormandy in no more than a fortnight made it *sound* like the Philadelphia Orchestra. One night, he concluded a Brahms and Beethoven concert with the Kaiser waltz of Johann Strauss, one of the most marvellous waltzes ever written. As I was leaving the concert hall, a very academic Englishman, who was then living in Sydney, said to me, "How *tasteless* to play the Kaiser waltz at a serious concert." "Good heavens," I replied, "Why not? It's a masterpiece."

That sort of snobbishness is disappearing, thanks largely to today's younger generation, who have been helped and influenced by the radio and the gramophone. When I was a boy in Manchester, very, very few young people went to concerts. Nowadays even if you go to a concert with a fairly demanding programme, you'll find the audience filled with young people. The third symphony of Mahler was played at the Proms the other night—it was a sell-out. The younger members of the audience listened to the Mahler with a degree of raptness not often found even at Covent Garden. This symphony finishes unsensationally, with a very long *adagio*, but all these young people clapped and shouted with delight and gratitude. As they left the Albert Hall, most of them were talking about the *music*.

RD: Do you have any musical blind-spots?

NC: We all have our blind-spots. Musical taste can vary as much as the taste for wine or the taste for food. I lived in Australia which is a land of salads, but I don't like salads. I can't explain why: there must be a deficiency in my palate. In the same way, I have deficiencies in my musical reception, and I confess that I have committed one or two grave sins of

omission which I shall no doubt have to account for in the
next world.

Bach, heaven help me, does not mean as much to me as
Mozart—nothing like as much. I could quite happily resign
myself never to hear another note of Bach, for the rest of my
life, but I could not bear never to hear Mozart again. I *know*
Bach is a great composer. My historical sense, my sense of
comparative values, my understanding of music—they all tell
me that Bach is one of the greatest composers of all time. But
I seldom get any real or lasting satisfaction from his music
because I find a lot of his music predictable. Contrapuntal
writing can be as predictable as a mathematical formula.

I was brought up in the nineteenth century and I have
witnessed during my lifetime the great *harmonic* development
of music. I am always deeply moved by a modulation in
Tristan or by a change from major to minor in Schubert, so
simple that a first-year student of harmony could have done it.
If I was an accomplished composer and I came across an
unfinished fugue of Bach, I would be able to finish it—because
the second half is implicit in the first—but I would never ever
be able to complete the "Unfinished" symphony.

RD: Do you have any blind-spots for specific works?

NC: Yes, I have one or two, even among my favourite composers. For instance, I feel a little bit iconoclastic about the last
movement of the ninth symphony of Beethoven. The first,
second, and third movements are for me marvellous music, as
is the beginning of the *finale*, with the great recitatives in cellos
and basses, but, when the chorus begins singing the Schiller,
the ninth seems to lose the mystery and the deep implications
of the earlier movements. I made an outrageous statement in
one of my books when I was writing about Delius. I said that
a listener would find much more beautiful choral writing in
the *Mass of Life* than he would ever find in the ninth symphony
of Beethoven.

When I reflect on that comparison, I realize that it would
have been more precise for me to have said "more sensuous"
rather than "more beautiful", and not only because of the
cruel heights to which Beethoven takes the sopranos. Beethoven
was breaking some of the bonds of musical form. Beecham
always used to say that Beethoven was really the first modern

composer, and the beginning of the wrath to come. Despite all that has been written since, I believe the development section of the first movement of the "Eroica" to be one of the most extraordinary revolutions that has ever been achieved in music. It makes a lot of present-day composers sound very limited in outlook and ability, because Beethoven's revolution was not simply a technical revolution; it was a revolution of symphonic and artistic creativity.

RD: If you could take only one piece of music to your desert island, what would you choose?

NC: Of which composer?

RD: Of all music.

NC: Oh goodness, how can I choose *one* from all the hundreds of works I like? It is a terrible dilemma. But if you force me to choose, and if I had the right singers—including Pinza—I think I might take *Don Giovanni*. My second choice—and it is a very close second—would be the *finale* of the fourth symphony of Beethoven. It is a wonderfully genial and witty movement, with none of the austerity, none of the high philosophy, of, say, the ninth symphony. But then I'd say, "What about *Tristan*? What about the G minor symphony? What about a lot of lovely piano music of Chopin?" It is an unfair question to ask me to choose only one work. It was bad enough, a few years ago, when Roy Plomley invited me to take part in his *Desert Island Discs* programme. Then I was allowed to choose eight records.

If you were to ask me which composers I first picked up on my receiving-set, which composers I am indebted to for initiating my lifetime's enjoyment of music, I would reply Lehár and Leslie Stuart. A few years later, I went to the Carl Rosa Opera Company's performance of *Tannhäuser*. It is no longer one of my favourite operas, but it was one of the first to make me realize that music would be more than a passing interest in my life.

And I must remember the debt I owed to Elgar when I was nearing my twenties. He had a great influence on me when I was young. I not only heard Richter conduct the first perform-ance of the A flat symphony, I heard Kreisler and the young Menuhin play the violin concerto. I don't know which of the two played it the more beautifully. Naturally Kreisler played the concerto with more maturity, because he was an older man, but I think Yehudi would be the first to admit that he has never played the work so beautifully since the time when I first heard him, when he was about 18. They both played the concerto in a way that, I'm sorry to say, we will never hear again.

Elgar meant a lot to us, earlier this century, because we were looking for an English composer who could make an impact on the Continent. We had been brought up on Stanford and Parry. They produced good work, but it was not *big* enough, and their orchestration tended to be rather black and white. We were beginning to hear Strauss and Debussy for the first time, and we were looking for an English composer who could write a symphony—a symphony we could listen to with the same devotion as we listened to Brahms or Tchaikovsky. And then we heard the A flat symphony of Elgar, which Richter said was one of the finest symphonies ever written.

RD: Did you ever meet Elgar?

NC: Yes, I met Elgar once or twice. There was one occasion in particular that I shall never forget. It was at Hereford during the Three Choirs Festival. Elgar, stooped and white-haired, was conducting *Gerontius*. I can't remember the names of all the soloists, but I think one of them was Gladys Ripley, a lovely angel of a singer, who, like dear Kathleen Ferrier, died when she was still only in her forties. I was with J. A. Forsyth who at that time was writing music criticism in London. He had been secretary of the Hallé concerts, and he knew Elgar very well. Before this performance of *Gerontius*—which was in the afternoon—he told me that afterwards we were invited to go to the Hereford Club and have a drink with Elgar.

Everyone in the audience was deeply moved by the perform-ance. I said to Forsyth: "We can't go round to the Hereford Club now. Elgar must be very tired. He won't want to see anybody." "An engagement is an engagement," Forsyth said; "you must meet Elgar." And so we went to the Hereford Club. We stopped in the doorway. There was Elgar in the middle of the room, only a short while after he had conducted a most moving performance of his own music. He had a newspaper in his hands, and he called out: "Jimmy, come in—and bring

Mr Cardus with you. We must have a champagne cocktail. I've backed the winner of the St Leger this afternoon."

Those were the words of a great man. They were proof that Elgar—like all other great composers—was not *just* a composer; he was first and foremost a human being, and he happened to be able to express himself through music. A lot of highbrows think it was shameful and degrading for the composer of *Gerontius* also to have written the music for "Land of Hope and Glory". In my opinion, this is proof of his range: the range of a large and protean personality. Every composer has written his share of popular music. If some of the highbrows had been living in Mozart's time—when there was no Glyndebourne for them to go to, in their evening dress—where would they hear his music? As they walked down the streets of Prague or Paris or Salzburg or Vienna, they would hear people whistling tunes from Mozart's works, just as people today can be heard whistling "Land of Hope and Glory".

And "Land of Hope and Glory" is "a damned fine popular tune"—that was Elgar's own view. It has been debunked because of the words that Benson wrote for it, but it was not originally written for that purpose. It was at Queen Alexandra's request that Elgar adopted the tune of the trio of his first Pomp and Circumstance march for the *finale* of the *Coronation Ode*. At the time of composing the Pomp and Circumstance marches, there was nothing in Elgar's mind about "Land of Hope and Glory": he was just composing military marches, in the way that Meyerbeer or Willie Walton or any other composer would.

I return again and again to my memory of this man who, no more than an hour after conducting a most moving performance of *Gerontius*, could be as gleeful as a schoolboy because he had backed the winner of the St Leger. It made me realize that Elgar was so much more than just a professional composer. He was an artist. He was a man, in touch with life in its heights and depths, who put his aesthetic reactions and his impulses, the whole of himself, into his music.

RD: Which other well-known composers have you met?

NC: I met Strauss several times in Salzburg and once in Vienna. I remember asking him why he seldom conducted *Rosenkavalier*. I said to him, "I have heard you conduct *Elektra*, *Salome*, and *Die Frau ohne Schatten*, but I have never heard you

conduct *Rosenkavalier*." "It is very difficult to conduct,"
Strauss replied, "especially the last act."

And I never had the good fortune to hear him conduct
Tristan. Every time I went to Vienna, Hofmannsthal and Berg,
and famous orchestral players such as Arnold Rosé, used to
assure me that Strauss's conducting of *Tristan* was one of the
most unforgettable experiences in music. You might wonder,
because of his undemonstrative style of conducting, how
Strauss brought penetration and passion to Wagner's music,
but everyone who remembers Strauss's performance of *Tristan*
says it was very intense and equalled in our time only by
Furtwängler.

I heard Strauss conduct many times, and he certainly
achieved some extraordinary effects without any rhetorical
gestures. He was as economical of gestures as Klemperer. And
he wrote ten golden rules for conductors. I can't remember
them all, but one of them was: "Never let the horns and woodwind out of your sight: if you can hear them at all, they are
already too strong." Two others have just occurred to me:
"When you think you have reached the limits of *prestissimo*,
double the pace." "You should not perspire when conducting;
only the audience should get warm."

I met Rachmaninov on one occasion. He had given a recital
in the Queen's Hall in Langham Place. Rachmaninov was
staying at the lovely old Langham Hotel. At the end of his
recital he was called back to the platform for an encore. He
immediately sat down and played his famous Prelude. I was
rather disappointed: I wondered why he wanted to play *that*
as an encore. So I took courage and went over to the Langham
to meet him. I said: "Mr Rachmaninov, everybody knows the
C sharp minor Prelude. Why did you play it for your encore?
I would have liked to have heard you play some Chopin."
And Rachmaninov replied, "Ven I play zat Prelude then I can
go home!" Of course he was right. Even if he played twenty
encores, the audience would still wait to hear the C sharp
minor Prelude. I found him to be a very engaging and charming
person—and I was with him for only fifteen or twenty minutes.
He is a rare man who can give an impression of charm and
courtesy in so short a time, such that 40 years afterwards you
can vividly remember the experience of meeting him.

He was a pianist of amazing ability and insight. He wasn't

a great Beethoven player, but he excelled in Chopin and in Schumann, and nobody who hears Rachmaninov's own piano music being played today can have any idea what *he* made it sound like. His piano music tends nowadays to be very much under-rated, but his performances elevated it to the top class. And the solo parts of his piano concertos are superbly written. Rachmaninov was one of the last composers to write for the piano as a *pianist* would write.

RD: For me, one of the miracles of music—perhaps unique in the history of any of the fine arts—was the half-century 1785–1835. How do you account for this astonishingly prolific 50 years: astonishing, not only for the quality of the music that was written but also for the fact that all branches of composition flourished—solo, chamber, choral, operatic, and orchestral?

NC: To find the answer to that question you'd have to go to a sociologist. A number of influences—political and economic, as well as cultural—contributed to this wonderful period in musical history. You could equally well ask why cricket enjoyed a golden age in the 1930s.

And of course there have been other periods rich in musical composition. Round about 1920 we had, at one and the same time, the flourishing of Elgar, the ripening of Delius and of John Ireland, and Arnold Bax, who for some reason that I cannot fully account for is now almost completely forgotten. On the Continent, there was Strauss, Bartók and Kodály, and the beginnings of the great revolution in music—Berg and Schoenberg.

Fifty years from now, music historians will look back to the 1970s with admiration. They'll say, "To think there was a period when, in England alone, Britten and Tippett and Walton were all active, as well as promising young composers such as the Australian-born Malcolm Williamson." We also have in this country the incredible Barenboim. Who can say what he will have achieved—and in what branch of music —25 years from now? I wish I could live long enough to know.

No one can say that musically this is a sterile age. In London in the last two or three months, the whole of *The Ring* has been performed, and it was a sell-out, and, in the space of a week or ten days, the Scottish Opera Company performed *Tristan* and *Pelléas*, conducted by Alec Gibson. No other conductor known to me—and I've known most of the great conductors from Richter to Klemperer—would have dreamed of conducting *Tristan* and *Pelléas* in the same week, because these two operas are poles apart. It is an achievement to conduct both of them in a lifetime.

Now you might argue that Gibson was rather too intrepid to conduct two such diverse operas. These performances may not have reminded us of Furtwängler's *Tristan* or of Monteux's interpretation of *Pelléas*, but they gave much satisfaction and pleasure to the audiences, and they attained quite a high level of technical accuracy, which is proof of the great advances that have been made in the technical presentation of music during my lifetime.

Orchestras are now more or less permanent, and many of them are subsidized. And they have much more rehearsal time. You have only to read Bernard Shaw's music criticisms of the 1890s to realize what used to happen at concerts that were given after little or no rehearsal. The technical control—not only of orchestras, but also of soloists—is highly symbolic of the technological age we live in. We've already got to the stage where we take it for granted that men can fly to the moon. And the prospect of flying from London to Sydney is less daunting than the train journey, when I was a young boy, from Manchester to London. As soon as your dearest relations arrived at Euston, they would send you a telegram: "Arrived safely."

RD: Members of today's *avant-garde* often forget that you have spent virtually the whole of your career—as music critic—championing new music.

NC: They call me "square" because I don't acknowledge Stockhausen as the greatest composer of all time. Decades ago, I was fighting the battle for Stravinsky and Debussy and Sibelius and Vaughan Williams, and for a lot of other composers who are not nowadays considered to be modern. I persuaded Harty to conduct Mahler. And I worked hard, even in Lancashire, on behalf of William Walton. He was born in Oldham, next door to Manchester, and yet it was ages before his B flat minor symphony was played in Manchester, conducted by Harty. Eventually we all become old and square and conservative. I think it was Stendhal who said that every conservative was a rebel in his day.

It may surprise you, and a lot of other young people nowadays, to think that Richard Strauss was once an *avant-garde* composer. I've always maintained that Stravinsky's *Sacre du Printemps*, which caused the great riot in Paris, was not the greatest bombshell in musical history. The discoverer of nuclear energy in music was Beethoven. And the biggest nuclear bomb in the world of music was dropped in 1909—it was *Elektra* of Strauss. That detonation was a shock to everybody.

When I was writing for the *Daily Citizen* for a penny a line, I argued the case for Strauss. I was then in my twenties. I raved and was highly adjectival and spoke of him in terms of the beauty of his music. But the young men of today who are plugging Stockhausen—they don't tell me his music is beautiful or exciting. They don't tell me his music makes their lives happier. But we thought in those terms about the *avant-garde* works of our day. I am astonished to think that when I was 18 Debussy's *L'Après-midi d'un Faune* sounded modern, but when we had heard it three or four times we knew it was a work of both immediate and enduring value.

If John Cage and Stockhausen and Messiaen are composers of rare genius, I want to know why the critics do not write glowing descriptions of their music. And why aren't present-day opera composers creating beautiful people such as the Marschallin and Octavian and Figaro and Isolde? With all respect to Benjamin Britten, the only genius we have in this country writing opera at the present time, there are no really beautiful and romantic women in his operas. No Salomes, no Carmens, have emerged from his creative mind. As a fact, no Englishman has given us a fine and beautiful creature in opera. We leave it to foreigners to produce the Carmens and the Mélisandes.

In the same way, England has produced any amount of wonderful light music, from "Early one morning" to Gilbert and Sullivan, and Flanders and Swann—but even Eric Coates never wrote any genuine *Kitsch* music. A lot of people seem to think that *Kitsch* means "vulgar". It doesn't. The Viennese idea of *Kitsch* is of something alluring but not quite pure, something not of the first order but something better than second-rate.

You wouldn't call a waltz by Johann Strauss *Kitsch*—because it is very well organized, very well put together. The Emperor waltz, for example, is like a little symphony: it has form and shape; it is aristocratic. Whereas a true *Kitsch* waltz, such as the one from *The Merry Widow*, curls round the heart and tickles the senses. The only genuine *Kitsch* waltz written by an Englishman is in *Bitter Sweet* of Noël Coward: it has the authentic sensuous curve, with a touch of sex in it. There's a waltz in Sullivan's "di Ballo" overture, but it is like a French waltz: fine and clear and sparkling, lacking the drowsy syrup of a *Kitsch* waltz.

I've often wondered why an English composer can't write a *Kitsch* waltz. Is it something to do with our personality or our climate or the food we eat? No English composer has produced an opera heroine that I would want to be in love with, and yet our novelists have created beautiful women. I fell in love, when I was a boy, with Beatrix Esmond. Thackeray described her thus, as she walked down the stairs: "She was a brown beauty; that is, her eyes, hair and eyebrows and eyelashes were dark; her hair curling with rich undulations, and waving over her shoulders; but her complexion was as dazzling white as snow in sunshine."

I fell in love with poor Tess of the D'Urbervilles and with many of the other women in Hardy's novels, one after another. When I was 16 or 17, I spent all my spare time in the Reference Library in Rusholme, reading fiction. I've lost count of the number of fictional girls I was in love with. At that time I never had any interest in real-life girls, because they were not half as enchanting as the lovely creatures I met in my walks through literature. After spending an evening with Beatrix Esmond, or after falling in love with Sophia Western in *Tom Jones*, or after having an affair with Bathsheba Everdene in Thomas Hardy's *Far from the Madding Crowd*, I went out into the street and I couldn't get interested in any of those ordinary-looking, pale-faced, Lancashire girls.

The heroines of literature were the first to awaken my emotional senses, and it has always been a mystery to me why we have so many attractive and desirable women in our novels, and yet there is not a single woman in an English opera that

I would cross the street to kiss. Not one. It is an extraordinary phenomenon. Now wonder the foreigners can't understand us.

RD: You have often spoken about the danger of too much formal education. This danger must apply to composition and to music criticism.

NC: You first have to learn the notation, the language, of music. Anybody can do that from a book within six months, but you should not treat the textbook as the last word. I remember, when I was 16 or 17, getting a book on harmony out of the library. It stated that you mustn't use consecutive fifths; you must do this, but you mustn't do that. But composers are always breaking these laws!

The biggest danger of formal education is that you may tend to fall into an academic way of looking at things: you put on blinkers, and then you can only see in one direction. Nowadays a composition has only a slim chance of being accepted by the critics unless it is atonal or serial or electronic. Take a case in point. The third symphony of William Alwyn is to me an extraordinarily fine piece of music, but it is quite unjustly neglected—mainly because it is not atonal. There is a lot of other good music that current fashion prevents us from hearing.

A critic should be wary of formalism, doctrines, fashions. He should try, so far as he can, to keep his mind open; but he mustn't let it become so open, so all-receptive, that he loses his personal censor. Shaw once said: "Prejudice? Of *course* I have prejudices. I wouldn't be worth my salt as a music critic if I didn't have prejudices, because they are the other side to your preferences." We each have certain types of music that bore us. We can't listen to every composer's music with equal attention. We all have at least one blind-spot, but nature usually compensates for this by giving us antennae that can receive other wavelengths. I see the musically receptive mind as a kind of wireless-set. I can receive clear messages from this, that, and the other, wavelength. But there are some foreign stations on any set: I can hear the sounds but I can't translate them. My musical intelligence can understand them, but my personal musical aesthetic, my inward sense, doesn't take them in.

Some of Stravinsky's music, of his later period, doesn't mean anything to me. Not because I don't understand it; but simply because it sounds to me like the music of a burnt-out genius. And I'm certainly not anti-Stravinsky: I lived in a period when we had to fight on Stravinsky's behalf. The first work of his I ever heard, when I was quite young, was the *Firebird* music. At that time, it was regarded as ultra-modern, but I can see the day rapidly coming when the *avant-garde* will be turning against Stravinsky and muttering "square".

A critic should be very much on his guard *against* the *avant-garde*, because, as Newman demonstrated beyond all argument in his book *A Musical Critic's Holiday*, the pioneers of music never live to see the fruits of their tilling. The great composers don't begin epochs; they consummate them. That's why a music critic should give the young composer every chance, and give him a fair hearing, but not be carried along by the crowd. A music critic has got to be very detached. He must keep *apart*.

The whole business of music is becoming so enormous. It is like a great big supermarket, and no one has time to visit every department. And a lot of present-day music is like self-service food, all manufactured and packaged. You go down the aisle, carrying your shopping-bag, and you pick up a couple of packets of Stockhausen and a box of Messiaen. The techniques of composing have become so standardized that I am certain I could produce a very good imitation of a modern atonal work. I could write *Twelve Pieces for Piano* (Op. 1), and I would guarantee to fool nine critics out of ten. But I could not for the life of me write anything approaching the G flat impromptu of Schubert.

RD: What are the essential differences between a period work and a work that survives changes in musical fashion, and seems to have relevance for mankind across the centuries?

NC: This depends to a large degree on the character and life-experience of the composer himself: some have seen farther and deeper than their fellow-composers. But it is not only a question of having a far-seeing mind like Beethoven's. Goethe made the very penetrating observation that even if you are a genius it might have made all the difference to your fame if you were born ten years earlier or ten years later. A genius composer needs not only the ability to crown and culminate an epoch; he needs to be born at the right time. He needs a recent

heritage of great or germinal music to draw upon and assimi-
late. And, just to complicate the issue still further, a great
composer needs not only ability; not only the good fortune of
having been born at the right time. He needs to have been
born at the right time *in the right epoch*. He has to do more than
sum up his period and stand at the summit; he has to be
standing on the right summit. It is astonishing to recall that
Meyerbeer summed up one of western Europe's empire
periods, with all its harshness and vulgarity and opulence, but
it wasn't a period that was destined to last. It was a transition
period and Meyerbeer sank with it.

All the fine arts are in a state of transformation. Composers
are sowing the seeds for a new epoch, 20 or 30 years from now.
Some genius will come along and take as much as he wants of
all this experimental work, and mingle it with older, more
established traditions. Revolutionary composers are usually
second-rate. It would surprise many people to learn the name
of one of the most famous composers in France at the turn of
the century. I'm not thinking of Debussy; I'm not thinking of
Berlioz, who had a long period of neglect—even to this day
the full genius of Berlioz is not recognized in France. The
composer I have in mind, Alfred Bruneau, used to be regarded
as the greatest of all French composers of dramatic music. He
wrote operas to libretti, some of which were written by Zola
and some of which were based upon the novels of Zola. Zola
at that time was *the* sociological realist. Because Zola was in
fashion, and because the public and the critics felt that Bruneau
was doing pioneer-work in bringing the language of Wagner
into French opera, Bruneau was elevated to the top rank—but
only for a few years. He is forgotten now. Many composers—
who were regarded as in advance of their time—have suffered
the same fate. The men who open up new paths seldom have
the chance to walk along them. They are too busy laying the
foundations.

It is hazardous to prophesy about the future of music, but I
believe that 50 years from now Stockhausen will be of historical
interest only. His pioneer-work will not be wasted: some
composer will have derived something from Stockhausen's
music that Stockhausen himself was not fully aware of. Music
has got to evolve and keep evolving. One aspect of musical
composition that is only vaguely understood by the general

public is that music lives off itself: unlike many of the arts, music does not often or so obviously cross-breed. Literature, painting, sculpture, all come from life itself. Literature is made up of the words of everyday speech. The dramatist is dealing with human nature. As you leave the theatre, you ask yourself whether or not the woman eventually leaves her unfaithful husband. You can relate the play to human life and experience. Painting is a representation of those aspects of the universe that we can see with our eyes. Even a surrealist uses the colours and the patterns of the external universe: he deals with symbols we can recognize—even when the picture is turned upside-down!

But music is a language *per se*. The language of music does not come from the external universe. You can't look up in a dictionary the meaning of a musical note, because it means nothing until it is heard in conjunction with other notes. And even then the meaning is subjective, because music is the most mysterious, the most abstract, of the arts. Music, like a golden spider, spins its own web.

So, when a composer introduces new techniques, we cannot say it is not good music, using the same system of values that enables us to say that a play is not good theatre because it is not true to life. We can only say it is not like the music that we have known up till now. It is nonsense to suggest that today's young experimentalists are all great composers who are not being recognized in their own time. Because of radio and television broadcasts, and the greater availability of musical scores, the theory of neglected genius is even less plausible than it used to be.

RD: Language itself seems to evolve in the same way as the language of music evolves.

NC: Yes. Certain temperaments can express all they have to say within traditional musical techniques, but the pioneers— to put it into literary terminology—find new adjectives, new word-orders, new rhythms. They feel the need to extend the inherited language.

The words we speak go through this same ever-changing process. Every day new words are assimilated into our language and old words take on new shades of meaning. Words are like coins. Every day some of them get so battered that we are forced to reject them, and we toss them over the counter in exchange for new ones. I hope we will soon throw out of our vocabulary such words as "involved", "escalation", and "arguably". When I was young, "fundamentally" was a much over-used word. It has been replaced by "basically", and now *that* word is over-used and due for replacement.

RD: Not only does language evolve; a great composer evolves. Only a second-rate composer remains more or less static, in quality and originality of output.

NC: There are certain composers who are confined, and are content to be confined, by the nature and limits of their medium. They don't try to reach beyond. If I had been listening to a work of Saint-Saëns, and you asked me when he composed it, for all I would know it might have been Op. 30—and it might equally well have been Op. 530. There would only be a development of technique. There wouldn't be any marked development of inner musical consciousness. Every great artist goes through inner as well as outer changes. I often wonder what might have happened to Schubert if he had lived longer.

RD: He was beginning to study Bach.

NC: Well, I don't think *that* would have done him any good! Schubert would never have become a primarily contrapuntal composer. He was studying Bach because he wanted to obtain a post as court organist. A Schubert who weighed up every note would not have been the Schubert we know and love.

And I have always wondered what would have happened to Mozart. You can see the hand of fate operating in timing the birth and death of great men. Mozart died only a few years before Beethoven came along and blew up the eighteenth-century classical style, that perfect synthesis, which we perceive in Mozart, of depth and power. Mozart achieved a perfect balance even in the second-act *finale* of *Don Giovanni*, when the Commandant, now a marble statue, arrives. His arrival is heralded by the most terrifying trombone chords in all music.

Beethoven blew up this eighteenth-century palace, this Versailles of music. Beecham used to say: "Beethoven was responsible for all the wrath to come." I don't think of Schubert as a *composer* in the same mould as Beethoven, struggling with his notebooks, with hammer and anvil, pounding the music into shape. I picture Schubert as just sitting down at his desk and writing music, like Mozart who wrote to his father: "I couldn't get the ideas down quickly enough." They came to him like children from God.

Wagner, on the other hand, was a composer in the way that another man is an engineer. I don't mean that in a pejorative way, but for some composers, such as Beethoven, writing music required much effort and much suffering. I can't imagine Mozart sweating blood, and Schubert probably found conversation more difficult than composition. As you once said, Robert, Schubert could have picked up a menu and set it to music. The Mozarts and the Schuberts are the rare gifted-by-God composers. I can't think of a single living composer who composes *by grace*. They write music only through very hard labour and very hard thinking. But one day the musical language of today will be firmly established and then someone will come along and compose by grace.

RD: Please would you discuss romanticism in music.

NC: Stendhal once said that romanticism is the art of the day; classicism, that of the day before. All art of lasting worth is first romantic, and then, with the passing of time, becomes classical. Bach at one time was considered a romantic. The B minor Mass, for example, is full of emotion, full of feeling, taking into account the period idiom of baroque contrapuntal writing, which had few of the esoteric harmonies available to Wagner. Some people regard Mozart as a purely classical composer. But such works as the G minor symphony and the clarinet concerto are much more than so-called absolute music—they are full of pathos and romantic undertones. And then you turn to *Don Giovanni*, to *Zauberflöte*, and to *Così fan tutte*—there is romanticism.

Every artist should aspire to have a combination of both romanticism and classicism, feeling and form. He can't express himself as a romantic, or as *anything*, unless he can so in a structure, a form, which is immediately intelligible. At one period *Tristan* was seen as the fullest bloom of romantic feeling in opera. But if you examine the score, you will see that it is as carefully organized in structure as any fugue of Bach. Wagner said that when he was composing *Tristan* his feelings were intense, his imagination hyper-active, but that at the back of his head was his critical observer, cold and calculating, watching the effects so that he didn't overdo them.

The word "romantic" is a useful one in describing music, but it has to be used with care. Weber's *Freischütz* can be called the beginning of German romantic opera, but I wouldn't use the word "romantic" to describe Debussy's music; I would prefer words such as "fantasy" and "impressionism". Romanticism is inclined to be uninhibited. Debussy's colours are pastel; there's no excess of feeling. Romanticism is an overflow of imagination, and requires a very strong intellectual control to keep it within bounds.

Romanticism in music is a phrase applied mainly to German composers. You wouldn't call Puccini "romantic". Puccini was Italian, picturesque, sentimental, a miniaturist except in *Tosca*. *Butterfly* and *Bohème* are perfect miniatures of domestic life and the old idea of the artist in his attic. This is music of charm and sentiment, but it is not the poignant romanticism of Schumann or Weber or Wagner.

Full-bloomed romanticism in music expressed a feeling of an epoch passing. Composers, from Schumann and Wagner to Hugo Wolf and Mahler, sensed that nineteenth-century civilization was passing away. They had a prophetic instinct, and they incorporated in their music the kind of poignancy of farewell we find in the *Song of the Earth*. And romanticism in English poetry can be very intense. In some of the best of Tennyson, for example, there is this same feeling of things passing.

RD: For several decades you have been looked upon as the arch-romantic among English music critics.

NC: To some people, romanticism is a very broad-spread word. It can be applied to Bach; it can be applied to Purcell's *Fairy Queen*. I would contend that you can't *be* an artist unless you are a romantic. To me, romanticism means imagination—imagination with a sunset touch.

The youngsters of 17 and 18 who fill the Albert Hall to hear Bach or Bruckner at a Prom concert, know much more about music than I did at that age because music is so much more accessible now. You only need to turn a knob, and you can hear a quartet or a symphony or an opera at any hour of the day. My generation didn't have that opportunity. We had to go to the Free Library and try to find the score of a piece of music we liked. But what about those who hadn't been taught to read music? What did they do? They had to wait for a concert performance. We would look forward to a concert for weeks or even months. We might only be able to hear, or perhaps could only afford to go and hear, two performances in two years of a particular work.

Young people of today are incredibly lucky in being able to hear so much music, but I sometimes wonder if maybe they are too lucky. When I was young I often used to go to the theatre. I went to see Shaw's and Galsworthy's plays, and I regarded them as a picture of life. But music to me was a *miracle*, and when I went to a Hallé concert it was an experience altogether different from going to the theatre. When going to a concert I was entering into an experience that was other-worldly. I didn't look at the orchestra; I listened. I was hearing Mozart or Beethoven and their wonderful emanations of man's spirit expressed in music. I hesitate to use extravagant language but to me to be present at the playing of music was like a Eucharist: I was tasting the body and the blood of the composer. To this day, the music of Delius comes to me as the *essence* of him. His music becomes a disembodied medium of the man himself.

If I see a play in which there are six or eight characters all speaking everyday language, I'm getting a mirror of life, but I don't feel that I'm in touch with the body and the blood of, say, Galsworthy or Shaw. There is only one dramatist who affects me in the same way that music does—Chekhov. Chekhov speaks through all his characters. Every one of his characters is an emanation not only of Chekhov himself but also of human nature. You don't come away from a Chekhov play talking about the plot or about the message. He is not a philosophical playwright. He didn't inspire any social reforms as Galsworthy did: his play *Justice*, for example, helped to bring about reforms in prison life.

Two people in a Chekhov play will come on to the stage and one will say, "I've got a bit of a headache this morning." And the other will reply, "Oh well, we all get headaches from time to time." I am always very much moved by one particular scene. Two men are talking about nothing whatever: about the weather, how close it is, and "there are such a lot of flies about". Then one of them asks, "Have you been reading any poetry lately?" "No, but when I was young, when I was working in a bank, I used to write poetry." It is so simple. Chekhov is not trying to express any great, universal ideas, but he does express great, universal themes. If you asked me to say who the most lovable composer is, I would answer "Schubert". And the most lovable dramatist—Chekhov.

Mozart created Don Giovanni. He created Pamina and Blonde and the Commandant. He could write a clarinet concerto like an angel. He was a human being and he was a god. Beethoven could be as human as a peasant in the "Pastoral" symphony, and yet he could also write the "Eroica" and the ninth: he was more than life-size. Wagner was like a great volcano erupting. There is something in Wagner that makes us afraid. We cower in front of him. But you feel like embracing Schubert, and the same with Chekhov.

Chekhov had the kind of genius that can make an immortal and beautiful thing out of nothing whatever: a man talking about his headache; a man remembering that he used to write poetry years and years ago, when he was working in a bank. To me that is much more moving than volumes of rhetoric about "We are such stuff as dreams are made on"; just as the figure of descending notes in the slow movement of Mozart's clarinet concerto touches me more deeply, because of its innocence and freshness, than the eloquence of Wotan's *Abschied*.

The really great artist can do two things: he can take you to the summit, the snowy peaks of the mountain-top; and he can take you down to the dales, where wild flowers grow. Beethoven can do this, and so can Shakespeare. Shakespeare gave us Hamlet and Othello; he also gave us Falstaff, Caliban, Beatrice, and Bottom. The number of artists who can achieve this range can be counted on the fingers of one hand. I'm not suggesting for one moment that Chekhov is in this class, but like Schubert he has a lovable simplicity that goes straight to the heart. Chekhov does not talk sociology. He does not contribute any new statement about mankind. In his own way he gives us the greatest of all messages, and it is simply that we are all human beings and we are all liable to have headaches.

D

6

SINGERS

RD: You have always had a deep affection for Lotte Lehmann. I'd be glad if you would describe her presence and sense of theatre as the Marschallin in *Rosenkavalier*.

NC: Lotte was the most lovable of all the Marschallins I have known; she was not the youngest, because I didn't hear her sing until she was about 35. Strauss always said that the Marschallin must not give the impression, in the last act, that she is finished with love and with life—she is young enough to have affairs with other men. But Strauss contradicts this view when the Marschallin in monologue talks about getting old. She is afraid of time. She fears that time is flowing away from her "like sand in the hour-glass", and she gets up in the middle of the night to stop the clock. No girl of 28 or 29 is so pessimistic about the passing of time, and yet Strauss in an almost onomatopoeic way gives you the impression of time quickly ebbing from her: it is the music of resignation.

Lotte made the Marschallin mature and gracious. Her final "Ja! Ja!" was an *Abschied*, a farewell to young passion. Lotte was extremely moving at this point: although this would not be the Marschallin's last affair, she was never again going to feel that same bloom of love. But it belittles the work if you imagine that the Marschallin has a great many love affairs to come: this contradicts the poetic side of the opera. When it was first performed in this country—I was only young then and I adored *Rosenkavalier*—Ernest Newman shattered me by saying that it was 40 per cent German horse-play, 40 per cent second-rate Franz Lehár, and only 20 per cent genuine Strauss. This view can be justified up to a point—there is a lot of knock-about music, especially in the third act—but for me what makes *Rosenkavalier* more than merely a superior version of a Johann Strauss operetta is the character of the Marschallin.

Lotte Lehmann brought out the pathos of a woman who was

going over the meridian. Lotte gave us *all* of the Marschallin: her breeding, her understanding, her wit, her willingness to accept fate with pressed lips. Lotte was such a very fine actress. I remember a meeting in the Savage Club with Jimmy Agate, drama critic of the *Sunday Times*. He said, "I'm in the middle of writing an article and I'd like your opinion. Who are the three finest actresses you've ever seen?" "Oh," I replied, "that's a very hard question to answer. Peggy Ashcroft and Edith Evans would certainly be near the top of my list, but my all-time favourite is Lotte Lehmann." "No," snapped Jimmy, "I'm not talking about opera singers; I'm talking about actresses." "So am I!" I said, "Lotte is as great as an actress as she is as an opera singer."

I shall never forget her entrance in the first act of *Die Walküre* when as Sieglinde she comes down the stairs and sees Siegmund lying down, having come in out of the storm. She says "*Ein fremder Mann*"—a strange man. No one else in this part has conveyed quite the same mixture of curiosity and apprehension at finding a stranger in the hut. And with the whole woman of her, as she leaned forward, she gave you a prophetic hint that she was going to mean something in the life of Siegmund. Everything she did, by voice and by gesture, seemed so natural.

I saw Lotte in *Die Frau ohne Schatten* in Vienna in 1924 or 1925, with Strauss conducting. This is an opera not often performed in England; Strauss told me that *Die Frau* was his *Meisterwerk*. Lotte was superb in it. She always said to me, "I never regard myself as a vocalist." This was an incredible thing for her to say, especially if you have heard the record of her singing in that wonderful and tender trio in *Rosenkavalier*.

Lotte now lives in Santa Barbara, California. She is suffering a great deal from arthritis. She wrote to me some years ago and said, "There is a wheel-chair in the hall of my house and I give it disdainful looks, but I'm afraid the day is coming when I shall have to surrender to it." At last I think she has. Lotte is a very brave and wonderful spirit; a woman of wide culture, who has written some fine poetry. She is, as much now as in her younger days, in every way an artist. Toscanini, who was not in the habit of praising singers, once interrupted a rehearsal of *Fidelio*. From the conductor's rostrum he called out to Lotte: "You are an *artist*." She almost fainted.

RD: You once wrote an open letter in the *Guardian* to that other great actress-singer—of rather different temperament to Lotte Lehmann—Maria Callas.

NC: Maria Callas has always been an enigma to me. Early in her career she was singing in Wagner operas. She sang Isolde and Kundry. Then she became a coloratura soprano, devoting herself to operas such as *Norma* and *La Traviata*. You don't need the degree of insight and dramatic genius that she possesses in order to sing in that *genre* of Italian opera. In the mid-Sixties I wrote that open letter to her, and I suggested that she was wasting her great gifts: "Your career has been the wrong way round. You sang Isolde at a time when you didn't fully understand the part; now, when you could do justice to Isolde, you are singing Bellini. If you shriek or get out of tune you have ruined Bellini; but as Kundry, a high shriek—if you are acting with body, eyes, and temperament, as well as with the voice—can intensify the part." Wagner always said that he wanted Isolde sung as though it were written by Bellini, but he didn't really mean that. He meant that he wanted the part sung in tune—and Callas could always do that—but it is not necessary to be a perfect coloratura soprano in order to sing Isolde and Kundry.

It seemed to me that Callas was wasting her dramatic genius by concentrating on Italian operas that don't require or call for her insight and range of protean imagination. I was not belittling Bellini and Verdi and Donizetti; I was simply saying that Callas had certain gifts, and a range of understanding of dramatic character, that were not being used to the full.

In that open letter I said, "Maria, you should go on the stage." That was not an insult to her voice; it was a great compliment to her abilities as an actress. I am sure that even now she could modulate to the theatre, if she feels that she can no longer sing coloratura in the way that Tetrazzini and Lily Pons, and the other virtuoso singers of the past, sang when they were at their peak. Maria would *stagger* us if she played Lady Macbeth. She has been one of the greatest actresses that we have ever seen on the opera stage—spending 75 per cent of her time in operas that don't demand great acting.

RD: A few weeks ago I heard an old "78" record of Dennis

Noble singing "Passing by". I was very moved by his sense of
pathos and warmth of tone, and I envy your having heard him
in *Belshazzar's Feast*.

NC: I can speak of Dennis Noble from first-hand knowledge
and affection, because I knew him personally. He was a very
fine artist. I am sure that Willie Walton himself would be the
first to say that there has never been a better exponent of
Belshazzar. I particularly remember Dennis Noble's eloquence
in the marvellous six-bar passage when the soloist sings "Praise
ye, praise ye the god of gold."

Dennis belonged to the inter-war period during which we
were still struggling to be recognized as a great musical nation.
In those days there were very few opportunities for British
artists to sing in opera. We had Sadler's Wells, and we had one
or two touring companies, but the Covent Garden season then
lasted for only a few weeks. Foreign singers by the dozen came
over to England to perform at Covent Garden. Dennis never
achieved the acclaim he deserved, and would have received
had he been at his peak in the post-war years.

You mentioned his recording of "Passing by". In the days
when I was young, I used to read the London papers and see
advertisements for Chappell Ballad Concerts on Saturday
afternoons. Some very fine ballads used to be sung, and a lot
of awful stuff too. Kennerley Rumford and Charles Tree used
to sing "Grey days are your grey eyes", "Rolling down to Rio",
and "Trumpeter, what are you sounding now?" These were
drawing-room ballads. I remember a composer, of late
Victorian and early Edwardian times, with the beautiful name
Maude Valérie White. She used to write drawing-room ballads
of a rather *superior* type.

There was no radio in those days, and no television, so
people used to make their own music at home. And they used
to sing these very sentimental ballads. Very little was then
known, in this country, of *Lieder* singing; whereas today the
Festival Hall is a sell-out for Schwarzkopf or Fischer-Dieskau.
Gerhardt was the first to put *Lieder* on the map in this country.
At first she sang in the Wigmore Hall on Saturday afternoons
to audiences of 300 or 400. She was quite right to choose the
Wigmore Hall: *Lieder* suffer from a loss of intimacy if sung in a
vast auditorium.

RD: You once heard a Gigli recital in—of all places—the Albert Hall.

NC: I'm allergic to Italian tenors, but Gigli was a favourite tenor of mine. He could sing quite simply, without any melo-drama, without any shock tactics. His tone and his phrasing were bewitching. On that evening you mentioned, he sang "Plaisir d'amour" and he gave the crowded Albert Hall the atmosphere of a chamber concert. He was entirely relaxed. He seemed to forget he had ever sung in Italian opera. How he got everyone in that vast place to hear every note, I shall never know. Many of today's singers would ask for two or three microphones.

Caruso was another wonderful tenor—I heard him sing in *Butterfly*—and he was also a very good actor. Some Italian tenors of those days used to make a travesty of music. They did what they liked; they held on to notes for as long as they wanted to. They didn't follow the conductor; the conductor had to follow the singer. Caruso could be a law unto himself, but when he sang in opera he could be as obedient to the conductor as any member of the chorus. Klemperer used to tell the story of the season, just before World War One, when he conducted *Rigoletto*. Caruso's manager had warned Klemperer that when Caruso arrived the rehearsal would have to be interrupted so that his part could be concentrated on. But Caruso arrived all smiles and wouldn't allow his manager to interrupt the rehearsal.

I don't want to dwell too much on the past. Today we have several really first-class singers. A few years ago I went so far as to say that Fischer-Dieskau is one of the finest *Lieder* singers that God has ever created. I am a great admirer of Schwarzkopf. She is one of the best singers of Hugo Wolf I have ever heard. In this country today we have a precious singer in Janet Baker. There is a very gifted Australian singer, Yvonne Minton. Joan Sutherland can be mentioned alongside Melba and the other great sopranos of the past. There's Norman Bailey who sings Wotan at Bayreuth as well as many fine singers have sung the part. And so I could go on: there are probably a lot of names I have left out. This is not an age that you can disparage. There is an extraordinary amount of talent—so much, indeed, that not all of it is or can be fully recognized.

Singing is going through a renaissance of technical accomplishment. Some of the great singers of the past, if they came back now, would have to be at their best to keep up with today's standards. In some ways the singers of today are more *musically* educated. Someone such as Melba could sing "Home, sweet home" at a concert. She could sing anything she wanted to. But you can't imagine Joan Sutherland, intent on maintaining the best Italian traditions, singing "Home, sweet home" or "Alice, where art thou?".

I feel I must again mention Marjorie Lawrence, the great Australian artist-singer. She was one of the best Salomes I have ever heard. The last time I heard Marjorie sing was in Sydney. She had to be wheeled on to the platform because she had been crippled by polio. Sitting in her wheel-chair, she sang the *Liebestod* from *Tristan*. It was a performance that has been excelled by only one woman, and that was the finest of all Isoldes—Kirsten Flagstad. *There* was a voice. I remember Ernest Newman, when he was well into his eighties, saying to me: "Thank God I have lived long enough to hear Flagstad."

RD: 1973, the centenary of Chaliapin's birth, was a quietly-celebrated centenary. It wasn't given as much attention as it deserved.

NC: No. I read only one or two articles about him, and I heard a few of his recordings on the radio. Of course it is wonderful to have even one record of a great artist of the past, but you can get no more idea of Chaliapin from a gramophone record than you get of a pterodactyl by looking at a skeleton preserved in a museum—because he was such an enormous, abounding personality on the stage. He dwarfed an ensemble. It was as though he was the only man on the stage; and all the other artists just appeared and disappeared, running round him as though round the legs of a great colossus.

I realized, when I heard him the other day on a long-playing record, that a lot of the things he did would be considered rather ham nowadays: he expressed himself without any inhibitions. The amazing thing about Chaliapin is that he was more a consequence of nature than of art. He was much more than a singer: his physical stature dominated everything. His voice, rich and deep and marvellously inflected by his actor's imagination, filled the largest theatre or concert hall or opera house. His *pianissimi* were like a powerful resonance turned low.

He was, as I've said, more of a natural artist than a cultivated artist. He could never have sung German *Lieder*. His art began from songs of the simplest kind, and it ended in a personal synthesis of music, acting, mimicry, gesture, and rhetoric. He was the Russian peasant in apotheosis. He sang with a natural peasant geniality, and he had the power to present—beyond life-size, and with a regal authority—the Russian peasant's view of the human tragi-comedy. In his simplification of emotion, and in his love of stark contrasts of feeling and of character, he was a true primitive. He is in the company of Mussorgsky and Dostoevsky in being able to express and sum up the Russian character of his period.

Chaliapin never seemed technically or consciously to sing; by that I mean he did not need to make any obvious effort or laryngeal adjustment to modulate from his speaking voice. Fischer-Dieskau is a singer from a different climate, a different civilization, a man who has been made into an artist by art; whereas Chaliapin was made an artist by nature—he might have come straight out of the Russian fields. Chaliapin had an enormous, reverberating voice. He is famous for his perform-ance of the death scene in *Boris*. When you hear it on record it does sound rather ham, with all his deep throaty sounds. But I have watched people in the stalls at Covent Garden, when Chaliapin was in the throes of the death scene, and I could see their hair bristling.

I want to tell you one of the most amusing experiences I have ever had in an opera house. Sir Thomas Beecham was re-hearsing Chaliapin in *Don Quichotte* of Massenet, in the death scene. Don Quichotte is dying in a forest, propped up against a tree. In his delirium he has a vision of his beloved Dulcinée. The voice of Dulcinée is heard from off-stage, the last sound of the earthly world that Don Quichotte ever hears. At this rehearsal the young girl who was singing the part of Dulcinée came in too late on three occasions, so Beecham called her up to the footlights. "My dear Miss Nelis, three times Mr Chaliapin has died with the most affecting realism; three times you have come in too late. Why?" The poor girl was trembling and could hardly speak. She tried to make excuses for herself: "Oh, Sir Thomas, it is n-n-not my f-fault." "And *whose* fault do you think it is?" "It is not your fault, Sir Thomas. I think it is Mr

Chaliapin's fault. He dies too soon." Beecham made this historic reply: "My dear Miss Nelis, no opera singer ever dies too soon!" Chaliapin, knowing only the vestiges of English, couldn't follow the conversation. And remember that Massenet wrote *Don Quichotte* specifically for Chaliapin, who sang the part in the opera's first-ever production. With growing impatience and confusion, Chaliapin roared: "I no soon? No soon I die? Not so soon I die? No soon?"

He was never subtle, never austere, never withdrawn, never enigmatic. As he sang he sometimes used to sun himself in the beauty of his own phrasing, and beam at the audience; within a few moments he would modulate to the grotesque. He used to sing a song of Glinka called "The Midnight Review" in which his voice faded into a ghostly mist, his face tensed, suggesting the grimness of a ghostly procession. Then, just as your hair was beginning to stand on end, he would relax; a big, broad, genial smile would spread across his face as though he was telling a story to the audience and was saying, "Well, children, that's the way it was once upon a time and it all ended happily." He had no sense of tragic poignancy. He was play-acting. He wanted to tell you a story, give you entertainment, and then send you home happy.

As a young man, Chaliapin was brought up under the last Tsars. The paradox about life under the so-called tyranny of the Tsars is that the peasants enjoyed a more democratic way of life than they do now. They may have been serfs on an estate, but they were part of the estate, part of the family. You have only to read the plays of Chekhov and Tolstoy to discover that the serfs on an estate were not looked upon as impersonal pieces of human machinery. Chaliapin expressed that classless way of life. He could sing before princes; he could sing at Covent Garden; and you could imagine him singing round a camp fire in Russia. He had a great all-embracing humanity.

I remember one occasion when Chaliapin had a concert engagement in Manchester. He was staying at the country house of some wealthy friends in a very elegant district on the outskirts of Manchester called Bowdon. He gave instructions to the staff that he never came down for breakfast. Coffee in his room—that is all he would want. In those days wealthy English households used to have marvellous breakfasts: sideboards laden with liver and bacon and kidney and sausages.

The aroma of this plentiful array of food wafted up to Chaliapin's room. A quarter of an hour later he appeared at the doorway in his dressing-gown: "Vat a luffly aroma!" He walked along the sideboard with a plate in his hand, helping himself to liver and kidney, about two pounds of bacon, and nine or ten sausages. He retired into a corner and demolished the whole plateful in no time. He couldn't resist what he called, with a trill on the "r", "this luffly arrr-ohma".

Chaliapin was a man without inhibitions: everything was overdone. He was enormous of stature and enormous in personality. He had a truly wonderful bass voice, as rich as any I have ever heard in my life. I cannot differentiate between Chaliapin the man and Chaliapin the artist. He was always and everywhere the same, expressing the same bigness, the same geniality, the same gusto.

RD: I know of one other singer you would dearly like to recall.

NC: Ah, Kathleen. I'm always in a dilemma about Kathleen: I don't know whether I loved her more as a singer or as a friend. I knew her as one of the most wonderful and beautiful creatures who has ever been born into this world. I met her quite by accident: in 1947 at the first Edinburgh Festival. I had just come back from Australia. I had been told while I was out there that a new singer had emerged from Blackburn, which isn't very far from Manchester where I was born. I thought to myself: "A Lancashire girl singing the *Song of the Earth* in Edinburgh with Bruno Walter—surely not." I couldn't imagine a girl born in Lancashire singing music by the most un-English of all composers. Mahler was a nervous man, tense, cosmopolitan, quite un-English.

I went to the concert and she sang the *Song of the Earth* beautifully. At the end there are several repetitions of the word *Ewig*—"ever". She sang the first three, and then she broke down. She couldn't finish. She was in tears. As soon as the performance was over she scurried off the platform, without waiting to make any bows. She left Bruno Walter and the orchestra to take all the applause. Summoning up my courage, I went straight to the artists' room. And there was Kathleen, alone. I told her that she had given a marvellous performance. I had never met her before in my life, but I felt as though we were meeting for the hundredth time. "Oh dear," she said, "what a fool I've made of myself. What will Dr Walter say?" "I don't think you need worry about what Dr Walter will say," I replied. At that very moment he strode into the room. She rushed up to him, apologizing. Taking both her hands in his, he said, "My dear child,"—he always called her "My dear child"—"if we had all been artists as noble and as sensitive as you are, we too would have wept."

Kathleen's qualities were innate, inborn. The timbre of her voice was the timbre of Kathleen Ferrier: it was part of her, just as her eyes, her mouth, her smile, were part of her. Technically, she wasn't the greatest singer in the world. She hadn't the range of a singer such as Janet Baker. But Kathleen had something that very few singers have: she had the capacity, the poignancy, to get you into tears over the simplest thing. On the radio the other day somebody chose, as one of his *Desert Island Discs*, "Blow the wind southerly". She sang this song unaccompanied. Even though it is almost *Kitsch* music, she sang it with the same fervency and simplicity with which she sang Bach. I felt tears coming to my eyes as I remembered the beauty of her.

Before she became a singer she wanted to be a pianist: she might not have become world-famous, but she could have made a living as a concert pianist. But thank Heaven she chose to express herself through her voice. She was unique among all the great singers I have heard. I have known many great singers, and when I think of them I can detach their technique, their voice, from their personality. You meet a wonderfully gifted singer such as Joan Sutherland. Her voice is something akin to Yehudi's violin. Once she has left the platform, she has, as it were, put away her Stradivarius for the night. When I meet her at a cocktail party I don't think of her as a singer. But whenever Kathleen spoke to you, the Strad was in her throat all the time: she carried her instrument with her. When she was telling the most comic and bawdy Lancashire stories—she had an enormous range of humour—she used to make them sound like poetry—never vulgar. When Kathleen swore, it sounded like Restoration poetry. She had great charm and great simplicity, and at the end—when she was stricken by cancer—a bravery beyond our imagining.

I saw her for the last time a few months before she died. She was rehearsing *Orfeo* at the Garden. I went to the first performance and to the second. She could hardly stand up. These were the last performances she gave. I saw her once or twice in a little pub near the Garden, and to this day I can see the pallor of her face. She was so brave that somehow I felt she was going to win through by sheer will-power and love. But she didn't.

It is both amazing and tragic that this growth, this cancer, should have afflicted such a beautiful young woman. When I first met her in Edinburgh she had the complexion of a rose: she didn't use any make-up, not even lipstick. She was a beautiful flower of a woman. And she was as brave in the face of death as she was happy among her friends and radiant in her art and in her singing.

7

VIOLINISTS

RD: You were remarking the other day on the fact that the great advances in the last 30 or 40 years in piano technique and in the quality of orchestral playing did not seem to have been matched by a comparable advance in the quality of violin playing.

NC: In my lifetime I've witnessed the most striking advances in the all-round excellence and standard of *ensemble* of orchestral playing. One reason for this is that subsidies from many sources —from the Arts Council to big industrial concerns—allow for more rehearsals. I've also witnessed an incredible advance in piano technique. Young players of 15 and 16 are now playing works that at one time only a master-pianist would have attempted: a number of students in the music colleges are not daunted even by the Handel-Brahms Variations. But I have not seen the same advance in violin technique. In the early years of this century, within a period of 15 or 20 years, a number of great violinists were born, including Yehudi, Isaac Stern, David Oistrakh, and Milstein. Where are their equals today? And, come to think of it, when was the last great violin concerto written? Those by Berg, Hindemith, Walton, Britten, and Schoenberg, were all written in the Thirties. And as for the violin sonata, I have no idea who composed the last one of real stature.

It is an extraordinary fact that virtually all the great violinists of the twentieth century were of Jewish descent. After Joachim, who from the descriptions I've read of him was an intellectual player who didn't woo the impressionable senses, we had this great succession: Elman, Milstein, David Oistrakh, Yehudi, and Isaac Stern; and I'm sure I must have missed out one or two famous names. It is an extraordinary fact that four of the five were born in Russia. The exception is Yehudi who was born in New York, but this doesn't disprove my point—because his parents were both born in Russia.

Jews seem to be able to play the violin with an extra intimacy, an extra richness of tone and phrasing. In a way you are more in touch with the violin than you are with the piano. You touch the keyboard but it is the hammers that produce the sound. The violinist, by contrast, touches the living strings; it is almost as though he were kissing his beloved's lips. The Jews have the ideal temperament to become great violinists: they are really passionate players, with a wonderful sense of beauty and a minimum of artistic inhibitions.

I suppose Kreisler must have had the Jew in him. Huberman was a Jew, but he was an exception: he wasn't a sensuous player. Huberman was an exceptionally penetrative player, with a sharp intellect. I used to imagine Huberman as coming from the same stable as Mahler: Huberman could be penetrative and yet he could also give you warmth and humanity. He raised the stature of the Tchaikovsky violin concerto, which isn't in the same class as the Beethoven or the Brahms. Huberman made it sound so absolutely Russian. He gave a wonderful lift and lilt to the music. He always used to say that when he was playing the *finale* he "imagined a drunken peasant in the streets of St Petersburg". He was a very fine violinist whose ability was never fully recognized in this country, probably because he had to compete with the beautiful tone of Elman and of Kreisler. You have to pay a price for everything in this world. If you're going to be a player like Huberman, then you have to pay a price for it; and if you're going to be a player like Kreisler, then you've got to pay the price for that.

Kreisler was not the most profound of violinists, but in terms of pure beauty he had a tone of which I have never heard the equal. His tone came from within the fiddle. It was born within that beautiful wood, and it emerged as though burnished by sunshine. I would even stay for his encores—and critics seldom do. We want to get away and write our notices. I used to stay to hear him play his dances: *Caprice viennois* and *Tambourin chinois*. There was something luscious about them.

If you asked me to name the most penetrating violinist I've ever heard—someone to get to the heart of the Beethoven concerto or the Bach Chaconne for unaccompanied violin— I would say Huberman. His tone went beyond the senses. He went beyond the sensuous into the *inner* world. He was prepared to sacrifice sensuous appeal in order to go deeply into the music.

In the Beethoven concerto, in the higher reaches of the *larghetto*, his tone, his playing, became almost disembodied. It was as though the music was reaching the mind of the listener without passing through the ear. The music reached you from some other channel—the channel of the *spirit*, the *soul*.

I did my best to get Huberman more widely appreciated in this country, and I helped him to obtain engagements in Manchester: he used to pack the Free Trade Hall. I once said to Beecham, "Why don't you invite Huberman to play at a London Philharmonic concert? He is a wonderful artist." "Yes," Beecham replied, in a *blasé* voice bordering on sarcasm, "yes, I agree. He is a most wonderful artist—deep understanding of music, superb penetration of tone—but, you know, Neville, as a violinist he has one rather serious defect." "What's that?" "He can't play the violin!"

Beecham was only interested in the *sound* of music. He often used to say to me: "I'm not interested in the meaning of music. Music has no meaning. You critics try to put meaning into music. No, music is an art of sound: it must sound beautiful." That is why he was so stimulating a conductor of composers who appeal to our sense of the beautiful in sound: Haydn, Delius, Debussy. He seldom conducted the profounder Beethoven; he didn't relish conducting the ninth symphony. I once heard him conduct the ninth in Edinburgh. He soon lost patience with the work, and the performance became almost a shambles.

There's one great violinist I haven't mentioned. I can't think of his name at the moment. Whenever I leave out one or two famous names from an article on great musicians, a lot of readers write to me.

RD: Heifetz?

NC: Oh Lord, yes. Of course. Jascha Heifetz—yet another Russian-born violinist of Jewish descent. Good heavens, to forget Heifetz is as embarrassing as leaving out Toscanini from a list of great conductors. Heifetz had the most amazing technique and beauty of tone. His name is not generally associated with Elgar, but I've got an idea that he recorded the Elgar violin concerto. It was another violinist of Jewish descent who put the Elgar concerto on the map, and that was the wonderful boy, Yehudi.

An Englishman, Albert Sammons, helped to perpetuate the concerto's reputation. He was a very fine violinist who, being an Englishman in an era of so many great foreign violinists, didn't get the recognition he deserved. If Albert Sammons were at the peak of his career now, he would be acclaimed at home and abroad as an outstanding violinist, because London is now regarded by everybody—except perhaps by the Viennese!—as the musical capital of the world. Every great player, from all over the world, wants to come and play in London. I'm old enough to remember the time when this was *"Das Land ohne Musik"*—"the land without music". A truer description would have been "the land without English music".

RD: We still tend to under-value our own musicians, particularly conductors. If you were a young English conductor and I were your agent, I would suggest that you called yourself Nephistopolus Cardissimi. The public would say, "Ah, he must have studied in Rome, in Munich, in Europe's leading *conservatoires*."

NC: Even one of our composers, Edward German, had to emphasize the *German*. His real name was Edward German *Jones*!

But, today, English orchestras, such as the LSO, the BBC, the London Philharmonic, go all over the world—to Japan, America, Vienna. Can you imagine an English orchestra in 1930 playing in Vienna? When I was a boy we used to think that the Hallé was a fine orchestra because it was staffed mainly by Germans: Richter brought many of them to Manchester, particularly string players. The one section of the orchestra we did know about in Lancashire was the brass section, thanks to our brass-band tradition. We knew something about tuba playing and trombone playing.

RD: Perhaps you would say a bit more about Heifetz.

NC: I wouldn't go to Heifetz for a profound performance of the Bach Chaconne. I wouldn't particularly want to hear him play the Beethoven concerto. No, on second thoughts, I would *love* to hear him play this concerto, because we usually overdo the austere side of Beethoven. Heifetz would bring out Beethoven's other side, the Beethoven who could write the most marvellous melodies. People in the nineteenth century tended to think of Beethoven as a high-powered Titan who wrote nothing but the fifth symphony. In fact he wrote a lot of very charming music. I remember one particular Beecham performance of the "Eroica", a symphony he really liked. "Why," I asked, "do you like the 'Eroica'? Because it is one of the most triumphant symphonies?" "Not at all," Beecham replied. "I like the 'Eroica' because it is full of the most delightful tunes."

I once heard Heifetz play the "Kreutzer" sonata; I forget who the pianist was. Personally, I don't regard the "Kreutzer" as the greatest violin sonata Beethoven ever wrote: I think the variations can sound very monotonous. But Heifetz brought such beauty to the music that I thought to myself: "Beethoven was an artist as well as a thinker. We've overdone his rough, turbulent side." The Germans were largely responsible for that. They dominated music in the nineteenth century. Wagner was the great cataclysm of music. When I was a boy nearly all the music we heard at concerts was German. This brought us wonderful fruits, but we had to pay a price for them. Thanks to the radio and the gramophone, the old barriers have been broken down and the boundaries of music have been extended.

RD: For real depth of feeling, I suppose you would choose Menuhin.

NC: If I wanted a violinist who could penetrate right into the core, the inner meaning, of Bach or Beethoven, then I would choose Huberman. As I've said, he was prepared to pay for his gifts of insight: he was prepared to sacrifice sensuous appeal. Yehudi, when he was in his twenties, made a wonderful synthesis of the two. From his childhood onwards he had a marvellous tone, and then as he grew older his grasp and understanding of music deepened. He had a maturity not usually attained by a musician until after the age of 40.

The boy Yehudi was a phenomenon. When he was 17 or 18 he played the Elgar concerto with such a gorgeous tone that nowadays you wonder if it was just a dream. But beauty of tone can become a tyranny. Even when he was playing Bach, Yehudi would produce the same sensuous tone. One of his problems as an artist was that he had to break free: he had to get away from the tyranny of beauty; he had to get away from the tyranny of a standardized tone that was not doing justice to the individuality of each composer. For example, he used to play the second subject of the first movement of the Elgar concerto gorgeously—too gorgeously. He made it sound like Max Bruch.

And so Yehudi had to discipline himself. He had to learn to put his palette, his beautiful range of colours, at the service of his developing mind and musical insights. Then the critics began to say that he was losing his beauty of tone, and that his intonation was less accurate than before. Critics can take a terribly long time to change their opinions. They had labelled Yehudi in the same way that a naturalist labels a butterfly. Many critics are slow to realize that every great artist has to go through metamorphoses, shed skin. Only the second-rate remain static.

8

PIANISTS

RD: What is the difference between a good performer and a great performer?

NC: That is yet another question, Robert, which is going to take me to the depths of the psychology of aesthetics.

A good performer is a performer who plays the right notes. That is something to be thankful for: to hear the notes as written by the composer. But you can go to a performance that is note-perfect and you can forget it an hour later. You've heard an impeccable performance; you've heard all the notes correctly played. But, as Mahler said, "Not all the music is in the notes." The difference between the good and the great performer reflects the difference between the performers themselves—not only as musicians, but as people, as personalities, as experiencers of life.

A performer can only give what is in him. He can of course be taught technique. A lot of young people today can make short work of the Handel-Brahms Variations, but they don't necessarily make *music*. When I was in Australia, I got to know a very gifted girl. She still plays in Sydney. She is a very fine pianist, and she should have got to the top. Her name is Muriel Cohen. She was going to California for a holiday and she asked me if I thought Rubinstein would give her a lesson or two. Artur Rubinstein is not only one of the busiest, he is also one of the kindest and most wonderful of all musicians, and he agreed to hear her. He wanted Muriel to learn a piece by heart and then come and play it to him. She spent the next six months learning the Liszt B minor sonata and then went to play in front of Rubinstein. When she had finished, he said: "Very good, my dear, very good. But—not enough wrong notes."

Muriel told me that this was the best lesson she had ever had in her life. After leaving Rubinstein, she realized she had over-studied the Liszt sonata. She had played all the right notes but she hadn't given them enough *freedom*. In simple passage-work, a good pianist is likely to play routinely, but a great pianist will give something extra to the music; will introduce subtle nuances. This is something to do with a person's mind, imagination, individuality. It can be awakened, but it can't be taught.

You wouldn't have to be told that Schnabel was a man of distinction. His conversation within ten minutes would have made you think to yourself: "Who is he? What does he do? He's either a philosopher, a writer, a painter, or a musician." You knew at once, if you came into contact with a man like Beecham, that this was no ordinary man: he said things and did things in a way that no one else did. If you had met Winston Churchill, even when he was a young man, you would have known that he was going to make an exceptional impact on some aspect of life. There is a French saying, "Style is the man himself." It is so true.

RD: You mentioned Schnabel. You were always a great admirer of him.

NC: He was a very great Beethoven player. Nobody understands why a pianist can play a particular composer's work better than anyone else can. We only know that he does. It is a matter of personal affinity. You can't explain, using technical terms, why Schnabel's Beethoven playing was more memorable than that of, say, Backhaus. But, after trying to analyse Schnabel's special gifts, I came to the conclusion that one of the wonderful things about his playing of Beethoven—especially late Beethoven—was the way he calculated—no, that's the wrong word—the way he *played* silences. You can make a pause in music and the music stops, or you can make a pause in such a way that the music doesn't stop. I remember the way Furtwängler began *Tristan*. There is a pause in the opening bars of the Prelude, and in the silence I could feel every beat of the conductor's baton as if it were a heart-beat. Schnabel had that same extraordinary faculty.

These days I often hear young critics say that, although Schnabel was a wonderful thinker, he didn't have a very good technique. The fact is that Schnabel had an extraordinarily good technique. He had enough technique for his purposes. You were never conscious of his playing until *after* a performance, or years later when you heard him on record. Then you listened to his left hand, finding it truly remarkable. You hadn't particularly noticed it during the performance because his playing was no less than a re-creation of the composer's spirit.

You can only produce from your instrument—whether it is a baton, a pen, or a cricket bat—what is in you. Even if I were given the combined technique of Horowitz, Schnabel, and Rubinstein, I wouldn't be able to play Beethoven as Schnabel could—because he had an insight, an empathy, a communication with Beethoven, that I haven't got.

I often wonder what my repertoire would be if I were a concert pianist. Being a music critic, and hearing and loving so many different kinds of music, I'd probably play them all quite well, without revealing the absolute truth about any of them. I would want to play Chopin and Debussy and Schubert; I'd want to play the Grieg concerto as well as the "Emperor". A great artist can't be a salesman like that. Oscar Wilde said that only the auctioneer must appreciate, equally, all schools of art. You've got to make your decision. You've got to decide which composer is going to be your religion.

I don't mean to suggest that Schnabel couldn't play anything else but Beethoven. He played Mozart wonderfully, and the Schubert sonatas, but he had his limitations, and he would be the first to admit them. He could play the notes of Chopin, but he wasn't quite the natural Chopin player. He couldn't play—how can I put it?—on top of the keyboard, as you must do with some of the nocturnes and some of the waltzes. He wasn't that kind of player. Once, when he played some Chopin pieces in Vienna, he played them as though they had been composed by Beethoven or Bach. Moriz Rosenthal, who was a perfect Chopin player, went round to the artists' room after the recital. Schnabel, who had rather attractive little vanities, said, "Well, Rosenthal, what do you think of my Chopin?" "You play Chopin differently from *my* school and tradition." And Schnabel retorted, "I'm trying to bring out the *thinking* in Chopin, perhaps you could even say *the philosophy*." So Rosenthal, who had a great wit, sometimes a very cruel wit, said, "I see. Chopinhauer."

Of course there is more to Chopin's music than the romantic, the aristocratic, the delicate. Some pianists play Chopin as though he wrote just for the right hand, and Wagner once said as much. Many pianists used to play Chopin as though he were the sentimental product of a French *salon*. But there is power and strength and depth in much of Chopin's music: he admitted that he admired Bach.

Chopin's writing for the left hand is very rich and original. Take the *études*, for example. Anybody who can play the *études* of Chopin, and play them well, can play just about anything. Almost every problem of piano playing, so far as technique is concerned, is concealed somewhere in the *études*. Busoni—there was a great pianist for you—once said that whenever he travelled he always took the *études* with him, for practice; I don't think he often played them in public. They contain a whole literature of piano technique.

Rosenthal—he had played with Liszt at Weimar—was at the other extreme to Schnabel. The nearest approach we have today to Rosenthal is Artur Rubinstein. These two are the sort of pianists whose playing I would take with me to my desert island, but I wouldn't expect a great performance of Op. 111 from either of them.

I wouldn't expect to hear a great performance by Rubinstein of the "Emperor" concerto. I'd expect a good technical performance, a very musical performance, but not the Beethoven "thing in itself". Artur Rubinstein would be the first to tell you that—like Rosenthal—he belongs to a different school from Schnabel. Rubinstein is the artist, first; the musician, second; and third, the thinker. This doesn't mean that Rubinstein doesn't need to think about the works he chooses to play. You can't play a mazurka of Chopin without having an extremely fine and concentrated musical-thinking-apparatus.

In fact, if I were a pianist, I would tremble less before playing the "Emperor" than I would before playing a Chopin or a Mozart concerto. In Chopin and Mozart there's nothing to conceal me; no curtain of metaphysics to hide behind. In Mozart especially, no note can be allowed to have pre-eminence: they must all be related like a string of pearls. But if I were playing Beethoven, a wrong note wouldn't seem to matter quite as much; because Beethoven, especially in his late music, in Op. 109 and Op. 111, is searching *beyond* music. If I played a wrong note in his presence, I think he'd be charitable enough to say, bearing in mind the state of his sketch-books, "Perhaps *that* was the note I was looking for!"

In the Thirties, Schnabel was a great revelation to me. He

used to come to Manchester and he played Beethoven and
Brahms in a way I'd never heard before and have never heard
since. I was very fond of the man himself, with his wit and his
philosophy. I became an out-and-out Schnabelite. Then a new
pianist was announced in London: Vladimir Horowitz. I was
based in Manchester in those days but I used to come down to
London nearly every week to review a concert or an opera
production.

Horowitz was announced as "the greatest living pianist".
This rather annoyed me because I was all for Schnabel—the
*un*romantic, superbly honest pianist. And so I went to the
Queen's Hall with my critical antennae outstretched: I was
going to be on my guard against this Horowitz. He played
Scarlatti to begin with, and this interested me. Then he played
Funérailles of Liszt, and that made my hair stand on end.
Finally he played the Handel-Brahms Variations, which
totally enchanted me.

I wrote a notice in which I said: "Horowitz is not only the
greatest living pianist. I am quite ready to believe that he is
the greatest of all pianists, alive *or* dead." By enlarging the
publicity blurb, I was intending to be rather satirical, because
at heart I was still a Schnabelite. But those two sentences were
extracted from my notice and quoted all over the world, and
were printed on gramophone-record sleeves, in several
languages. And I received a letter from a very aged musician,
whose name I can't mention, who also had missed the irony
of my remarks. He wanted to know if I had ever heard Liszt,
which was rather much to expect of a man in his early forties,
in 1931. Liszt died in 1886.

After a later recital I wrote: "It was once said of Horowitz
that he is the greatest pianist alive or dead. That seems now to
have been an understatement—it was perhaps not positive
enough about the pianists still unborn." Horowitz had extraordinary magnetism of touch. Every sound from the piano
came so lightly and yet with great strength in the left hand:
his playing was harmonically very beautifully blended. He
could make a piano sound as if it had no hammers in it. He
could make a piano sound like a rather lush Aeolian harp.

Horowitz played the mazurkas of Chopin in a very aristocratic way, with great poise; but he couldn't always get to the
heart of the mazurkas in the parts where they relate to the

peasant side of Poland. The mazurkas are almost a biological and sociological history of Poland. I've only heard one pianist play the mazurkas better than Horowitz. For me, the greatest player of them was undoubtedly Ignaz Friedman.

Friedman came from Poland. I heard him once in England, not at a Hallé concert. He was appearing at a Saturday night concert, in a rather popular programme, and I wasn't too enthusiastic about his playing. The curious fact about Friedman is that he was famous in Europe. In Vienna, in Berlin, he was considered to be in the class of Rosenthal and Lhévinne and all the great pianists of the period. For some reason he was never fully recognized in England. Even Rubinstein had some difficulty in establishing himself in this country.

Friedman came over here in the late Twenties when we were very much under the influence of the anti-romantic movement. Schnabel and Backhaus were dominating the musical scene; Friedman was considered by some of the critics to be too romantic. Amazing as it may seem now, many of the younger critics were reacting against Wagner. One very famous critic, then in his mid-thirties, assured me one night in Pagani's that Wagner was finished; that in ten or fifteen years no young people would go to *The Ring*. And yet these days you can't get a seat for a performance of *The Ring* unless you book six months in advance, and there are always a great many young people in the audience.

Friedman, who was a Jew, went to Australia to escape from the Nazis. He settled in Sydney and I came to know him well. He played the B minor sonata of Liszt as I've never heard anybody play it. He presented not only the boudoir side of Liszt, the room with all its embellishments and decorations, the bevy of mistresses, curled up on their couches, listening to him; Friedman also played with impressive power. This was the complete Liszt, warts and all, long hair and a touch of astrakhan, the faint odour of cigar, and the presence of alluring women.

To hear Friedman play the Chopin mazurkas was an enchantment. He had a touch and a lilt that I hear from only one pianist nowadays—Artur Rubinstein. Rubinstein has that same gift; he knows that secret. And I know for a fact that Rubinstein when he was young was a great admirer of Friedman. I feel very sad that I know of no recordings by Friedman,

and I find it incredible to meet musicians of the age of 35 who
have never heard of him.

He was a man of enormous wit and he could tell the best
Jewish stories. When he was a small boy in Poland, his father
died. His mother, who was old, came to him and said: "Ignaz,
you are very young but one day you vill be grown up. I shall
be gone and you vill be alone in the vorlt. And it is a very
vicked vorlt, my son, so listen to vat I say to you. Ven anyone
vants to gif to you—take, my son. Vatever it is, take. Old bits
of string, old tin cans, or small moneys—take, my son. But if
anybody vants to take anything from you—call for the po-lice."

Then he had the delightful story of when he was a young
student. An old Polish tenor, who had been out of work for
some time, decided to make a come-back. He went to young
Friedman, then about 18 or 19, and said, "I'm going to make a
come-back and I want an accompanist. I hear you are very
good." Friedman said, "I hope so." "Well now, listen. I come
back. Next week I sing in public for the first time for six or
seven years, and I am not quite sure of my voice." This tenor
did not have absolute pitch, so he said to young Friedman,
"When we begin the recital and I sing my first song, perhaps I
am not good, perhaps a bit flat. If I don't like what I sing, I
tap on the piano—then you transpose one third down. Can
you transpose?" "Yes, sir." "Good. I give you extra moneys
for being so clever." They went on tour and the tenor was in
very good form. "I had no need to transpose, so I was not
getting any extra moneys. One night I had an inspiration.
This tenor did not have absolute pitch. So at the next recital
I began the accompaniment a third too high!"

As a piano teacher, Friedman was extremely influential. He
used to insist that his pupils should master the left hand. In
Brahms, in Chopin, the left hand is not just providing basic
harmonies. I know someone who studied with him in Australia,
and that is Muriel Cohen, one of the finest of women pianists.
Friedman made her practise Chopin's "Funeral March" sonata
for a month, with nothing but the left hand. It may sound
drastic, but he had a lot of success as a teacher.

He was a very great pianist and I cannot understand why he
is not known today. He is fit to be mentioned with the other
great romantic pianists: Rubinstein, Moriz Rosenthal, Josef
Lhévinne. They were not the greatest of Beethoven players.

They were Liszt players, Chopin players. I define piano music as the sort of music the piano would compose if it were a composer: it would compose like Chopin, like Liszt, like Debussy. I don't think a piano would compose like late Beethoven. Some of the late Beethoven sonatas go beyond music. In the same way, the late quartets go beyond chamber music: their material is suitable for the vast canvas of an orchestra.

The technique of piano playing, and of all aspects of the performance of music, has made incredible advances. If you go, for example, to the Leeds Competition, you hear youngsters of 17 or 18 playing music that, a generation or two ago, only the masters dared to play.

When I used to live in Manchester I came to know Adolf Brodsky, who was Principal of the Royal Manchester College of Music. Brodsky had been a close friend of Grieg, Brahms, and Tchaikovsky. Brodsky was one of the first violinists to play the Brahms concerto, and he was soloist in the first performance of the Tchaikovsky concerto. He used to ring me up: "Come round to the College, Neville. One of our young students is going to play the Paganini Variations of Brahms." In those days that was something of an event. Today there are students in every music college in London who can play the Paganini Variations. Whether or not they are all making music, I'm not sure.

Oscar Wilde, making one of his famous paradoxical statements, said, "Nature copies the arts." And the arts copy nature, life, society. The arts always represent the age. This is the age of technology, the age of machines—from washing-machines to computers. The housekeeper of 50 years ago wouldn't know what to do in today's all-purpose home. You can get on a plane and be in Sydney in next to no time. Man can even go to the moon. This wonderful technology is being represented in music by the astounding technique of young musicians and by the bewildering productions—here I don't feel able to use the word "compositions"—of some present-day composers. Where is the imagination? Are imagination and feeling keeping pace with the technical advances?

RD: We still have Clifford Curzon.

NC: He is the kind of pianist that I would like to be. And if I had my life over again, I think I would want to be a pianist,

because the piano is the complete instrument. If I were a singer,
I'd have to have an accompanist. If I were a violinist, I'd have
to have an accompanist or an orchestra, or be a member of a
quartet. But, as a pianist, I can play all kinds of music, from
all periods. I can even amuse myself by playing a piano arrangement of *Tristan*. What music would I feel happy to play in the
presence of the composer himself? And I wouldn't want to
play for any composer unless I could play his music to *his* own
pleasure. First of all I would want to play in front of Mozart—
and of course I would at the same time be terrified!

To me, Clifford Curzon is the perfect Mozart player of today.
I'll try and tell you why, even if I have to call upon the terminology of musical analysis. First of all, like Horowitz, Curzon
has the facility, the genius, of being able to play on top of the
keyboard in such a way that we are not always conscious of
the piano being a percussive instrument with hammers. There
is gentleness of touch in his playing of Mozart, but he doesn't
make the notes sound light-weight; he makes them sound clear
and gem-like. Secondly, he has the ability to illuminate the
left hand in Mozart, which sometimes does not *seem* interesting
in the way that the left hand is in Debussy, for example, with
richer harmonic shades and colours to reveal. Sometimes the
left hand in Mozart is just a tonic and dominant accompaniment, but it is never mechanical writing; it is all part of the
star-like firmament he creates.

Clifford can play with great power—his technique is equal
to the Brahms concertos—and he can also play an eighteenth-
century sonata. He puts his technique at the service of the
composer. He is a virtuoso who doesn't need to display or prove
his virtuosity. Another thing about Clifford is that he is never
routine. He is sensible enough to space his public appearances
in such a way that his piano playing always has something fresh
to say. If I were the Almighty and I wanted to create the
perfect interpreter, I would give life to a pianist who combined,
in equal proportions, the amateur and the professional: the
amateur mind, the amateur outlook and freshness; and the
professional technique and thoroughness.

Clifford has these qualities in ideal balance. He has enough
technique to take your breath away. He could sit down and
play *La Campanella* of Liszt, and make Rubinstein envious. But
he doesn't do that. He faces up to the problems of playing

Mozart, with all Mozart's *fineness*: there is no superfluity anywhere in his music. But he must never be treated as merely eighteenth-century, and Clifford has the God-given gift of being able to understand the comprehensiveness of Mozart. When Clifford plays what is seemingly the simplest piano piece of Mozart, he can produce overtones to make you remember that Mozart also wrote the second-act *finale* of *Don Giovanni*, with the Commandant—that terrific orchestral energy that makes even Beethoven sound meek and unassertive. Clifford Curzon is a Mozart player and a Schubert player *par excellence*. And what could be better than to have the special gifts to be able to play—and do justice to—the music of those two composers?

Next I want to talk about one of the other great pianists of our time: I have a great admiration for Claudio Arrau. If I want to hear either the D minor or the B flat concerto of Brahms, if I want to hear Beethoven in all his stature—intellectual and philosophical—I go to Arrau. Having been able to scale those summits, he comes down to the lowlands and plays Debussy or *Waldesrauschen* of Liszt, and he brings with him some of the ether, some of the refined air, from the high peaks. He can't divest himself of austerity. The curious fact is that, as a friend, Claudio Arrau is one of the most joyous and young and amusing of men; and I do sometimes wish he could smile a bit more in his playing. But you can't have the power and dimensions of an elephant and the grace of a gazelle. You can't have everything. Whoever and whatever you are, you've got to pay your price.

RD: What a terrible and tragic price Solomon had to pay.

NC: Solomon had to pay his price, physically. He also had to pay a price for the period he lived in. He not only had to compete with Schnabel, Horowitz, and Backhaus; in those days it was very difficult for a British musician to achieve an international reputation. Even Beecham was virtually unknown in cities such as Vienna and Warsaw. Since the Thirties, the world has become much smaller because of air travel. If Solomon were now 35 or 40, he would be playing in Berlin, Vienna, and Tokyo—because he was such a complete, all-round pianist. He wasn't a Schnabel and he wasn't a Horowitz, but he had some of the elements of greatness and he wove them into the marvellous Solomon synthesis. Nobody of his period played the "Moonlight" sonata so beautifully. And he played Chopin with a rare skill and sensitivity.

There are some pianists who speak to you as Schnabel did, as though with the voice of God. There are some pianists who speak to you in the colours of a painter: the paint has been transmuted into music with a perfect blend of light and shade. When Gieseking played Debussy, you would think you were looking at a Monet, a Cézanne, or a Degas. And then there have been pianists, such as Solomon, whom I have liked not only for their artistry but also as lovable human beings.

There were many legendary pianists who retired before I was old enough to hear them. I've heard so much about Josef Lhévinne. I imagine that technically he was a marvel. When I was quite young I heard Godowsky. In fact, he played at the first Hallé concert I wrote about, as music critic of the *Manchester Guardian*. Sammy Langford, my predecessor, died in 1927, and at that first Hallé concert I had to cope with the C minor symphony of Brahms; and Godowsky played, I think, the fourth piano concerto of Beethoven. James Huneker, a brilliant American music critic who is quite forgotten now, used to write about "Godowsky's bedevilments". Godowsky used to add all sorts of intervals to Chopin: tenths, ninths, and God knows what. I can remember writing my notice of that Hallé concert. Godowsky played the Beethoven with great brilliance of finger-work, but some of his own—what shall we say?—"inspirations" strayed into the music. He was a marvellous technician, a wonderful performer of the keyboard, but not a pianist of great profundity.

Paderewski I heard, but only when he was a very old man. He played the *Etudes symphoniques* of Schumann and Op. 111. I was very much moved by his playing of Op. 111, because Paderewski was then in his old age, and his technique was no longer quite equal to late Beethoven; but there was something of great pathos and dignity about this old man trying to find his way back into the labyrinth of Op. 111, occasionally taking wrong turnings. There was also something very sublime about Paderewski's playing, something that almost certainly would have appealed to Beethoven, more so than a note-perfect performance, because Beethoven himself was always *searching*.

I didn't hear Paderewski when he was the golden-haired

virtuoso. What has always mystified me about him is that, when I was a boy, living in a far-from-cultured environment, everybody—cab drivers, bricklayers, people who clean the sewers—everybody had heard of Paderewski. How did he become so well known to all levels of society? He had international fame before the days of television, before the age of PR-men.

Pachmann was his own publicity agent. He was an eccentric. He used to play heaven knows how many encores at the end of a recital. There is a very good story about Pachmann which indirectly describes the sort of player he was. Another pianist went round to see him after he had given a recital, and there was Pachmann, in the artists' room, kissing his own fingers—making a tribute of love to his fingers. He had an extraordinary felicity of touch. He could play the nocturnes and the waltzes of Chopin, but he could not always do full justice to the bigger-scale works. When he played the ballades of Chopin, something went wrong: it was like too many lovely roses overwhelming the trellis, and the trellis fell down.

I first heard Cortot at a Hallé concert, just after World War One, when he played Schumann's piano concerto. So far as I can recall, Cortot actually came on to the platform dressed in uniform. He was not decoratively dressed; he was wearing the uniform of a corporal or a sergeant. His face was pale and clean-shaven, with deep-set eyes: it was a face worthy of being drawn by one of the French Impressionists.

Cortot wasn't a big player in the mould of an Arrau or a Serkin; he was a perfectly French pianist and a beautiful Chopin player. Few have played the ballades, the waltzes, and the nocturnes, with such style and elegance. Some people used to complain about his wrong notes—just as people today talk about Rubinstein's wrong notes—but these lapses were proof of his humanity: they didn't seriously detract from what was a wonderfully flexible and effortless technique. Cortot's playing was as natural as speech.

Cortot was a musician in the widest sense. It is not generally remembered that at about the turn of the century he was assistant conductor to Richter at Bayreuth, and Cortot conducted the first performance in Paris of *Götterdämmerung*. By contrast, I cherish the memory of hearing on 78s his accompaniment of Maggie Teyte in Debussy's *Chansons de Bilitis*. It is amazing that the French and German sides of Cortot's artistic personality were both so highly developed.

Rachmaninov—in my estimation—ranks as one of the great masters of the keyboard, but he was not just a lover of the keyboard with a wonderful technique: he didn't just kiss or blandish or rape the keyboard. When Rachmaninov played the solo part of his own concertos, he gave them something that nobody else could. They are not the greatest of all concertos, but they contain very fine and comprehensive piano music. When he was playing his concertos, you were hearing a piano in full bloom. Some pianists can make the piano sound like springtime; some make it sound like summer. Rachmaninov made the piano sound as though it was enjoying a golden autumn. All the notes were mature and mellow.

When Rachmaninov played another composer's music, he played with a fellow-composer's insight. He played *from within*, as though he was inspecting the other composer's workshop: "What did his sketch-books look like? What sort of colours was he using?" You felt that Rachmaninov was working from within *out*, not—as most pianists have to do—from without *in*.

Rachmaninov was a creative pianist and a creative composer. I won't let anyone belittle Rachmaninov as a composer. Of course he wasn't a Chopin; of course he wasn't a Beethoven. I don't know why some people have to keep measuring composers alongside the Gods. We don't do that in literature. We don't expect every novelist to be a Tolstoy or a Balzac; we find room for P. G. Wodehouse. Like the *études* of Chopin, Rachmaninov's *Rhapsody on a theme of Paganini* represents just about the whole technique of piano playing. And Rachmaninov wrote some of the most beautiful piano music I know. The preludes, for example, should be played more often. They sit so well on the keyboard; they could have been born there.

RD: Do any of the younger school of pianists impress you?

NC: Today we have an extraordinary school of young pianists. I can't keep pace with them. Every week I hear a gifted new player. Sometimes I turn on the radio in the middle of a recital, and I say to myself, "My God, I wonder who is playing. This is not Horowitz. This is not Arrau. This is not Rubinstein. Not quite of their stature, but it is certainly a pianist of great ability." Then at the end I'm told I've been listening to a performance by a Mr George Washington or some other pianist I have never heard of in my life. There are a lot of extraordinarily able young people playing the piano today.

RD: Barenboim is one of the most brilliant of them.

NC: Barenboim to me is an enigma. A year or two ago I saw him in a hotel in Scotland. I went over to him, touched him on the forehead, and said, "Danny, you've got something very dangerous behind there." He was intrigued. "What is it?" he asked. "Genius," I replied, "and it can be very dangerous. It can make you or it can ruin you." As Goethe said, "In limitations he first shows himself the master".

Barenboim probably has more talent than any young musician since Busoni. My question now is: "What is Barenboim going to be?" I only hope he doesn't begin to compose. Busoni played and conducted and composed. As a pianist he was outstanding—the best and most convincing player of the "Emperor" concerto I've ever heard. He played that *diminuendo* octave passage in the first movement with such a ravishing tone that it took your breath away.

Busoni accumulated all the materials for composition—the firewood, the coal—but he could not apply the spark: his music never quite ignited. And as a conductor he failed to some extent, because I don't believe it is psychologically possible to to play, say, the D minor concerto of Brahms on Tuesday and conduct it on Saturday. Playing and conducting are two such different dimensions.

Even if I had omniscience I couldn't be sure in which direction Barenboim is going, or should go. If I were asked which he should concentrate on—being a pianist or a conductor—I wouldn't be able to answer. But of two things I am certain: if he does not waste his talents or wear himself out, he will fulfil the genius that is in him; and he has gifts that have not been given so abundantly to any young man since Ferrucio Busoni.

In my lifetime, which has been quite a long one, I have seen the development of many artists in many different fields: painting, theatre, sport, writing, piano playing, violin playing. I've seen the development of Yehudi: from the young phenomenon —who played the Elgar concerto—to the mature Menuhin. Yehudi at 16 played the violin as well as he has ever done in

Left: Cardus aged seven
Above: Cardus in his seventies

427

154, Moseley Road,
Fallowfield,
Manchester.

Jan 13, 1917.

Dear Sir,

I am writing to ask if you would
be so very kind as to let me know whether
there are at present any vacancies on the
staff of the 'Manchester Guardian', amongst
the proof-readers, or in the general offices.
I am a young student intent upon
devoting his life to politics and art. In these
times, however, I am finding it hard to keep
alive. My particular fear is that necessity
will drive me to at least suspending my
studies, which happen to be at a critical and
fascinating stage. I have had to educate
myself, and my culture, such as it is, has
been got by scorning delights and living
laborious days for some eight years. Immediate employment would enable me to
find the means whereby to continue my
education, and I would gladly accept any
position, however modest, that you might
possibly be able to offer me.
I enclose some specimens of

A letter to C. P. Scott

C. P. Scott

Samuel Langford

Ernest Newman

Hamilton Harty

Above: Artur Schnabel with Joseph Szigeti, William Primrose, and Pierre Fournier   *Below:* Lotte Lehmann with Grace Bumbry

Kathleen Ferrier

Mahler in 1898

Above: With Sir Thomas Beecham and Norman Collins   *Below:* Sir John Barbirolli looks on, as Cardus speaks at the Hallé concert in 1966, given in celebration of his 50th anniversary with the *Guardian*

Above: Reading *his* paper   *Below:* With Robin Daniels

Cardus at 85, the last-ever photograph

his life. When, in terms of years, he was still only a boy, his tone came fully-fledged. I couldn't believe that he had to study or practise the violin. His technique was mature, seemingly from the beginning. What made him into a great musician was his growth as a person, his accumulated experience of life. There were no sudden advances: his maturity was simply and splendidly an enlargement of what he was as a boy.

I remember Denis Compton at the age of 20, facing Australian bowling in a Test March for the first time, and scoring a century. The Australian attack included E. L. McCormick, a fearsomely fast bowler, and W. J. ("Bill") O'Reilly, known to his colleagues as "The Tiger". Denis Compton's maturing art, like Yehudi's, was a development of experience, not a development of technique. As Denis got older, he learned which stroke *not* to perform: he learned the art of selection. There was no text-book development of his batsmanship: his style was born, fully-fledged and fully-realized, from whatever it is that produces genius.

With Bradman on the other hand—and I'm not belittling "The Don"—his run-machine simply got bigger and more formidable as he grew older: he added new cogs and wheels and drive-belts, and he increased the voltage. With Bradman I didn't get—as I did with Menuhin and Compton, and as I do now with Barenboim—the feeling of spontaneous combustion.

E

9

CONDUCTORS

RD: Why is it that British orchestras never seem able to match the subtle beauty of string tone achieved by the Germans and the Viennese?

NC: That is a question I've asked many orchestral players, and it is still a mystery to me. Few orchestras in the world today can compare with ours in quality of brass and woodwind tone, and we have accurate and very musical string playing, but we don't produce the deep gutty tone that is needed, for example, in Bruckner. To hear an English orchestra play Bruckner—if I can put it in terms of the seasons—is to hear a Bruckner of springtime. But his music should sound autumnal. Is this a question of the technique of violin playing or is it perhaps something to do with the conducting?

I remember a week at the Edinburgh Festival when this subject of difference of tone-colour was exemplified for me, within the space of three nights, in a most astonishing and dramatic way. The New York Philharmonic played on the Monday under Mitropoulos, who conducted the fourth symphony of Vaughan Williams. The tone was what you would expect from an American orchestra: bright and brilliant, steely, streamlined. On the Wednesday, Bruno Walter conducted this same orchestra in the C major symphony of Schubert, and the tone was different: it was brown; it was deeper, richer. I asked one or two of the players of the New York Philharmonic what the reason was. They said they didn't know. One suggested that perhaps Bruno Walter had given more emphasis to the lower-pitched instruments: he might have attended more to the cellos, the violas. But that didn't seem to me to be the complete answer. I asked this same question only the other week to a player in the BBC Orchestra. He thought it was to do with teaching, but he didn't go into detail. He didn't want to commit himself; he didn't want to criticize our teaching methods.

I am sure the conductor has a lot to do with the tone, the personality, of an orchestra, and the texture of a performance. Beecham always used to inspire brilliant, springy, elastic, performances. That's why he was so wonderful in Mozart and Haydn; but he wasn't a memorable *Tristan* conductor, because he used to give seemingly exclusive attention to the melody. I sometimes used to criticize him for this, and he once staggered me by saying that I was going entirely against Wagner's own instructions to conductors. This is how our argument would develop.

Beecham: "Wagner didn't say, of his own works, 'Attend to the melody and attend to the bass.' Wagner said, 'Find out where the melody is and phrase it.' "

Cardus: "Yes, but in Wagner there are a lot of contrapuntal melodies. You just concentrate on the top line."

Beecham: "Because the top line is always the most important!"

RD: You once annoyed Beecham with a comment you made on the string tone of his orchestra.

NC: That was in the early Thirties when he had just formed the London Philharmonic. The Orchestra's first appearance was at a concert in the beautiful old Queen's Hall. Paul Beard was the leader; Beecham had brought him down from Birmingham. They began with the *Carnaval Romain* overture of Berlioz and also played the "Prague" symphony of Mozart. In my notice I said that the orchestra was brilliant but that the string tone was light. The Berlin Philharmonic had recently visited London under Furtwängler, and I said that the LPO couldn't match the depth and richness of the Germans' string tone. This annoyed Beecham. I had lunch with him shortly afterwards. As soon as we sat down, he asked abruptly, "What's the matter with my orchestra?" I said, "Your strings are brilliant, resilient, responsive, but they are not sensuous enough, not warm enough." "Well what do you think I should do?" "You should employ more Jews," I replied. And Beecham—for probably the first and last time in our long friendship—agreed with me.

RD: Who are the greatest conductors of your lifetime?

NC: That depends to some extent on which works I want to hear. If I wanted to hear *Tristan*, I would have no hesitation in nominating Furtwängler: he had the rare gift of being able to take a phrase at a slow tempo and yet maintain intensity. If I wanted to hear the Requiem of Verdi then I'd be in a dilemma. I would want either Toscanini or—and you may well be astonished that I mention him alongside Toscanini—de Sabata. Some years ago I heard de Sabata conduct the Verdi Requiem in London and then I heard Toscanini conduct it in Salzburg. I can't say which performance was the better. They were both marvellous.

If I wanted to hear *Così fan tutte*, I would choose Beecham. Furtwängler was a great conductor of certain parts of the repertory, but I wouldn't want to hear him conduct *Così*, and I doubt if he had ever *heard* of—let alone conducted—Delius. I am always staggered when I recall the range of Beecham. He ranged from Mozart to his own favourite "lollipops": these were not encores, but musical sweets, if you like, that Beecham would conduct at the end of the concert programme. A Beecham "lollipop" would usually be a short piece of music with an engaging tune, such as an extract from the *Peer Gynt* suite or from the *Casse-noisette*.

Beecham wasn't a great conductor in profound works such as the ninth symphony of Beethoven. He never had the aura of a Klemperer: the Germans always like their conductors to have a certain austerity. But Beecham was an almost perfect Haydn conductor. He was the conductor of one's dreams in *The Magic Flute*. He could conduct Delius as no one else has ever done. He could give a very good performance of the fourth symphony of Beethoven, a first-class performance of *Meistersinger*, and a beautiful performance of the *Enigma Variations*, even though Elgar was a composer he was not particularly enamoured of.

I remember one night when he was conducting at a Hallé concert. He gave an encore—this was long before he began conducting "lollipops". Of course critics never wait for encores. I wanted to get out of the hall but I couldn't because the doors were still closed. Beecham was conducting *Valse Triste* of Sibelius which we had all heard often enough, in cinemas and on seaside piers. The *Valse* came to me as a revelation. He had transformed a melodrama into a little masterpiece. That was the work of a creative conductor.

At rehearsal Beecham was incorrigible. One day there was

a new face in the woodwind section. "Mr, ah . . .?" "Ball," came the reply. "I beg your pardon?" "Ball, Sir Thomas." "Ball? Oh, *Ball*. How very singular!"

One evening, at a rehearsal of *Messiah*, the soprano soloist was mis-reading the score. Beecham called her to him, and told her she must improve before the public performance. "I-I-I'll be all right to-to-tomorrow, Sir T-Thomas. I've been studying the score for w-weeks, and I've been t-t-taking it to b-bed with me every night." "In that case," said Sir Thomas with a smirk, "I'm sure we shall have an immaculate conception."

RD: Brilliant. That's one of the best Beecham stories I've ever heard. Now let's get back to your list of leading conductors.

NC: My eight conductors for my desert island—if I were allowed to take a portable gramophone—would be: Toscanini, Furtwängler, Beecham, Bruno Walter, Klemperer, Hamilton Harty, and Franz Schalk, a Viennese conductor who never won a big reputation in England, although he conducted the best *Fidelio* I've ever heard. I must have left somebody out.

RD: Who will you choose as your No. 8? Weingartner, perhaps?

NC: Yes, Weingartner for Beethoven. But what I really would like to hear this very afternoon is a performance of the fourth symphony of Brahms, as conducted by Harty in about 1932. I'll never forget his treatment of the second theme of the slow movement. He took it very slowly, with most devout and beautiful phrasing; and I can still remember the wonder of his *pianissimi* in this movement. Harty was very much under-rated. If he were alive today, I am sure he would be considered one of the world's leading conductors.

Harty conducted most of the Hallé concerts after only one rehearsal. For instance, if on Thursday night they were going to play the fourth symphony of Brahms or the second symphony of Beethoven, or even the seventh symphony of Beethoven or the "Pathétique" of Tchaikovsky, the rehearsal would be on Thursday morning. He would be given only slightly more time for a new work. He conducted one of the first performances in England of the ninth symphony of Mahler, after only three rehearsals. He was a man of great gifts and I feel very sad that now he is almost forgotten.

He conducted the finest performance of the *Mass of Life* that I have ever heard; and that is saying a lot, since I have to take into account Beecham's interpretation. Delius wrote a letter to me from Grez-sur-Loing in France where he was living, paralysed and blind. He had been listening to the radio broadcast from Manchester of Hamilton Harty conducting the *Mass of Life*. Delius said, "I have just written to Hamilton Harty and I have decided to write to you as well. I have not heard a finer or more beautiful performance of the *Mass of Life* by any conductor. P.S. For God's sake, don't convey this opinion to Sir Thomas."

RD: What are your memories of Toscanini?

NC: I remember two Toscaninis: the post-war Toscanini, ageing and losing his vitality, who conducted in the Festival Hall when it was first opened; and Toscanini in the Twenties and Thirties, when he was at his best. I remember him when he came over from America in 1930 with the New York Philharmonic, and in the late Thirties when he conducted the BBC Symphony Orchestra in the Queen's Hall. On that first visit to London I heard him conduct the second symphony of Brahms. His performance combined the German solidity of Brahms with an Italian lyricism and a most lovely *legato*.

When Toscanini came to England just before the war, he was getting on in years—he was about 70—and he was always very intense, unsparing of himself. He conducted one or two performances that I didn't much like—including a rigid ninth symphony of Beethoven—and one or two that were unforgettable. He conducted a performance of the "Pastoral" that was of heavenly beauty, and all simplicity in the smiles and calm of the ending. The hymn of thanksgiving brought tears to my eye. To think that after a thunderstorm, when the thunder and lightning had ceased, there should be a *thanksgiving*: "Thank God that the sun shines again. Thank God for the rainbow."

RD: Toscanini's mood at rehearsal was thunderstorm rather than thanksgiving.

NC: I've spoken to people who played in orchestras conducted by Toscanini, and I used to know one or two players in the New York Philharmonic who knew him very well. He would not permit any laziness, any slackness. He would not allow orchestral players at rehearsal to be smoking pipes or reading newspapers when they didn't have to be playing. They had to listen. But he used to lose his temper most severely with himself. He was a perfectionist. When he did something wrong he would go into the artists' room and smite himself. He was *ruthless* with himself.

One night at a concert the New York Philharmonic was playing a piece by Debussy, and something went wrong in the woodwind section. Toscanini ordered all the woodwind players to be brought to him in the artists' room. He said: "You have been playing this marvellous music disgracefully out of tune. I suppose you now will go home. *You* will go to bed and sleep —either with your wives or your mistresses. Will I sleep? No. *I* won't sleep." That is the sort of conductor he was: utterly dedicated to the composer. He did get ruthless with his players; every conductor does, now and then. Beecham occasionally used to show his temper, but in a joking way. He would rave at the orchestra, and then give a good-humoured wink. All orchestras loved Beecham, but I doubt if many orchestral players loved Toscanini. I think they feared him.

I respected Toscanini because, like Klemperer, he was absolutely dedicated. Toscanini wasn't considering the effect he was making on the audience; he was considering how he could penetrate to the heart of the music and find the truth. I met Toscanini once or twice and he never talked about music at all. I remember a story told to me by Bill Primrose, who used to play Willie Walton's viola concerto and was principal viola player under Toscanini in New York. One day after rehearsal the *maestro* said: "Primrose, you will come to dinner with me tonight. My wife is away and so we shall be alone." Primrose nearly fainted. To think that he was going to have an evening with the *maestro*! He would hear all about how Toscanini began his career, how he played, as a second-desk cellist, in the first performance of Verdi's *Otello*. He was going to have a wonderful evening.

He goes to Toscanini's house. They're alone, with the butler in attendance. Toscanini gobbles up his spaghetti, swallows his Chianti without a word, and then rushes into the television room. He turns to the station that features wrestling and watches with a non-stop verbal accompaniment: "Hit 'im in ze stomm-ahk. Get 'im by ze leg. Jomp on 'im." Poor Primrose. Music was never discussed.

RD: How would you contrast Toscanini with the more easy-going Bruno Walter?

NC: They were poles apart: Toscanini, the Dionysian; Walter, the Apollonian. Toscanini was daemonic. Sometimes it would have been appropriate to call him "the Ares among conductors". Bruno Walter was altogether more gentle.

RD: I can still see and hear Walter at a rehearsal of a Mozart symphony. "Let the music *sing*," he kept pleading.

NC: Mozart, yes. And he did wonderful things for Mahler. But, using quite a lot of *rubato*, he rather over-emphasized what is supposedly the softer side of Mahler: what in this country is called his schmaltzy side. Klemperer complemented that aspect of Walter's conducting by bringing out Mahler's other side: the harder core, the fine thinker. There was a tremendous dichotomy in Mahler, a striking case of split personality. He had a soft Viennese Jewish side; and he also had a tough side —as revealed in the sixth symphony—that anticipated Webern and Schoenberg. Bruno Walter was never particularly effective as a conductor of the sixth symphony; he was more at home in the fourth symphony and in *Das Lied von der Erde*.

I once asked Klemperer, "What do you think of Bruno Walter as a conductor of Mahler?" "Quite good, but not altogether satisfactory." "Why?" I asked. Klemperer thought for a moment. Then, with a typical grunting out-of-the-corner-of-his-mouth chuckle, he said: "Too Jewish." I can see what Klemperer meant by describing Walter as "too Jewish" in Mahler. And there is great irony in his remark, because Mahler was a Jew, Bruno Walter was a Jew, and Klemperer himself was a Jew.

Klemperer's qualities can be summed up in one word— integrity. He never presumed to get in the way of the music. It may sound like a paradox, but he was great *because* of his anonymity. You've got to be great to have a strong and individual personality expressing itself through music and yet be anonymous. By "anonymous" I mean that Klemperer produced the authentic sound and wavelength and bloodstream and mental current of, for example, Beethoven; and, at the end of a concert, the public didn't say, "My God, isn't Klemperer marvellous?" They said, "What marvellous *music*."

RD: His performances of Mozart could be heavy going.

NC: He was not the ideal Mozart conductor. And yet I remember hearing him many years ago conduct *Eine kleine Nachtmusik* with the utmost simplicity. He set the tempo at the beginning and he *released* the music. If he had then taken a seat in the back stalls, the orchestra would have gone on playing with grace and felicity.

I couldn't imagine Beecham ever getting on to the wavelength of Klemperer. Beecham used to regard him as a rather heavy-handed conductor. Beecham was anti-German in his approach to music. He was a *flâneur*, an artist who above all wanted to find enjoyment in his music-making. He would rather have written a few Johann Strauss waltzes or *Manon* of Massenet than all of Bach's preludes and fugues, and he would have admitted it without any sense of shame. He had even less sympathy for Bach than I have. At least I do know Bach was a great composer. I used to say: "Don't be so stupid. You may not *like* Bach—I'm not particularly enraptured by his music, but I know he was a great master." And Beecham would reply: "He was only a provincial German. And he wrote too much counterpoint. And, what is worse, Protestant counterpoint."

RD: But there are some deeply moving movements in Bach. The opening of the slow movement of the double violin concerto brings me to my knees in gratitude for music.

NC: Yes, you're right. It is just a silly blind-spot. As a matter of fact, at the Edinburgh Festival about five years ago, I heard the B minor Mass conducted by Giulini, and Janet Baker was one of the soloists that night. They are two artists for whom I have the utmost admiration. I thought to myself, "It will be a change to hear an Italian conduct the B minor Mass. I wonder how he gets on." I was very much moved by the performance, and I came away converted to the Mass. About a year later I heard it conducted by someone else, and it sounded like the same old piece of Protestant counterpoint. So I suggest we hand it over to the Catholics.

RD: There is a conductor and an orchestra—both of great stature—that we haven't yet mentioned. I have in mind George

Szell and the Cleveland Orchestra, which he led to such heights
of technical and tonal brilliance.

NC: George Szell, if I remember rightly, was in Scotland at
one time. He conducted the Vienna Symphony Orchestra when
he was only 16, and just before World War Two he was appointed
conductor of the Scottish Orchestra. Before that, in the early
Thirties, when Harty left the Hallé, we had an interregnum in
Manchester: various guest conductors came, including Szell.
I was very keen that Szell should succeed Harty. That was long
before John Barbirolli was appointed. John was the salvation
of the Hallé: he re-created the orchestra after the war.

If Szell had taken charge of the Hallé, he might never have
gone to Cleveland; he moulded the Cleveland Orchestra into
a most beautiful instrument. He wasn't a conductor who at
first hearing touched your senses, your emotional responses.
His was a strictly musical approach and a lot of people thought
he was rather cold. I didn't think so. I remember he conducted
the Cleveland Orchestra some years ago at the Edinburgh
Festival, and the concert began with the *Oberon* overture. Music
critics don't usually listen to the *Oberon* overture. I suppose they
may listen to it, but they are not going to write about it. It is a
marvellous overture, but often played, especially at the beginning of a concert, and so you sit back in your seat and read the
programme, the advertisements. This is what I was doing that
evening in Edinburgh. But when I heard the opening horn-
call, answered by muted strings, I suddenly pricked up my
ears. The overture was wonderfully re-created: it was as though
I had never heard it before.

In that same season, Szell conducted a superb performance
of Strauss's *Don Juan*. I wouldn't particularly want to hear Szell
conduct Debussy, and he wouldn't be my ideal conductor if I
wanted to hear *Bohème* . . . and yet his interpretation would be
good, because he was such a very fine and thorough musician.
When he was young, he was a pianist, a child-prodigy. He must
have realized that he had to make up his mind what he was
going to be. You can't be both a great pianist and a great
conductor—not even in those bygone days of comparative
leisure when a musician would get on a train in Vienna, have
a comfortable journey on the Orient Express, and have time to
contemplate. Now a conductor or a pianist or a singer is in

London on Thursday night and in Sydney or Vladivostok on Friday.

You would think, in this period when musicians have so little time between engagements, that they would be more likely to concentrate on one aspect of their talent. But no, they are launching out in all directions. Szell, on the other hand, knew just what he wanted to do. There was single-mindedness and integrity in everything he did. He was a man I greatly respected.

RD: Szell had a quiet authority, which his orchestra felt and responded to as soon as he came on to the rostrum. I remember he would often whistle quietly to himself as he conducted. His arms, hands, and fingers, expressed so much meaning and were so graceful and economical of movement. He was the very opposite of today's school of semaphore signallers.

NC: As you say, Szell was not a showman. He didn't conduct to the audience, and I'm sorry to say that there are a lot of conductors today who do conduct to the audience.

There was an orchestra in Russia that tried to play without a conductor. They were extremely good technically, but when you have 80 players, you have 80 different ideas on phrasing, balance, and overall interpretation. They needed a conductor to bring unity and cohesion. The paradox is that, although orchestras are so much better than they used to be, there are not many conductors whom I would call individual interpreters. 25 or 30 years ago I could have given you a substantial list of twenty individual interpreters: Toscanini, Bruno Walter, Schalk in Vienna, Mengelberg, Ormandy, Clemens Krauss, Szell, Monteux, Furtwängler—I could go on and on. Today there is more time for rehearsal because of subsidies—from the Arts Council and from private industry—and instrumental technique has improved in every section, but I don't think I could name five conductors who could re-create and revivify a work that I have known all my life, as Szell did with the *Oberon* overture.

RD: You have already described the contrasts between Toscanini and Bruno Walter. How do you see the contrasts— in personality and style—between Barbirolli and Boult?

NC: In Barbirolli and Boult you have two extremes, both excellent in their different ways. They represent the difference

between the romantic temperament (Barbirolli)—and I don't
use the word romantic in a belittling sense; I'm only trying in
a shorthand way to describe a man who receives, feels, music
through the medium of his senses—and the classical temperament; Boult, an older man, with a quite different mental
texture. Even though their birth dates were only ten years
apart, Boult seems to belong to another period.

John Barbirolli, who had a romantic, a Latin, temperament,
would reveal the music via his own feelings and his first-class
musical mind. He would give you performances that were
Barbirollian. But if I wanted a performance of, say, a Brahms
symphony, I would go to Adrian for it. He is a man of a
different tradition, of quite different stock, from Barbirolli.
Adrian is absolutely English. From him you could get, you can
still get—it is amazing how he keeps his freshness—a faithful
representation of the score, with no exaggerations, no indul-
gence in temperament or in tempi. There are some conductors
whose virtue is that you remember them, and there are others
whose virtue is that you don't remember them.

In a curious way, one of the highest compliments you can
pay a conductor, a pianist, or a violinist, is to say that you
didn't think of *him* while he was playing; you thought, instead,
of the composer and of the *music*. Which takes me back to my
first meeting with Artur Schnabel. He was giving a recital in
Manchester and it included Op. 111. As a Beethoven player,
Schnabel was like a spiritual medium: it was as though
Beethoven were speaking through him. In those days we
critics weren't forced to cramp our ideas and comments into
short little 400-word bulletins. I wrote almost a whole column
—1,200 words—about Op. 111, because to hear it had been
such a profoundly moving experience. Suddenly I realized I
was coming to the end of my allotted space, and I hadn't even
mentioned Schnabel. So, in the last paragraph, I had only 20
words with which to say that he had played with extreme
insight. When I saw my notice the next morning in the *Manchester Guardian*—an enormous column about Op. 111, and a
little paragraph, a six-line footnote, stitched on at the end
about Schnabel—I thought to myself, "Good God, what will
Schnabel think of this?"

A few hours later, Schnabel rang me from the Midland Hotel
and asked me to have lunch with him. He said that my having

written so much about Beethoven and so little about himself
was the greatest compliment any critic had ever paid him. He
said, "This is just what I always wanted to achieve. I want the
audience to listen to Beethoven, and go home thinking about
Beethoven—not about Schnabel."

Imagine the reaction there would be if I wrote a column
about a Bruckner symphony and added at the end: "The
symphony was admirably conducted by Herbert von Karajan."

RD: Let's modulate to two more English conductors. The first
is Sir Henry Wood.

NC: We've come now not only to a conductor but to a pioneer.
The conditions under which he worked were entirely different
from today. In 1895 he started a series known as the Queen's
Hall Promenade Concerts, later of course re-named the Henry
Wood Promenade Concerts. For half a century—until his death
during World War Two—he was the senior conductor at these
concerts. The Promenade season in the old Queen's Hall used
to last for eight to ten weeks: he conducted six concerts every
week, and there was time for only three rehearsals a week. He
showed genius in coping with this seemingly improvised way
of orchestral conducting on so relentless a scale. I said "*seemingly* improvised" because the secret of his success was the work
he did in his study: he used to spend many, many hours pre-
paring scores and parts. And before every concert he used to
go to the artists' room: all the string players had to come in
and tune to the "fork".

RD: Did he conduct every concert for the whole eight weeks?

NC: Yes, as far as I can remember. I can't recall going to a
Prom when Henry Wood wasn't conducting, except when he
invited a composer to conduct one of his own works. The
orchestra was always the New Queen's Hall Orchestra; this
was before the BBC Symphony Orchestra was formed. There
wasn't a choice of 15 or 20 orchestras and an array of dozens
of conductors during the season, as there are today.

In those appalling conditions, with inadequate rehearsal
time, his amazing achievement was to produce performances
that, if not as streamlined as we have now come to expect,
were nevertheless very genuine. He unearthed and introduced

to English audiences an astonishing amount of new music. He was conducting Mahler in about 1905: I think he gave the first performance in England of the eighth symphony; I know he gave the first performance in England of the seventh. He was also one of the first conductors to reveal to this country the major works of Sibelius, Bruckner, and Scriabin. Henry Wood was a fine and imaginative conductor, with immense ability and terrific energy.

I remember talking to Ernest Newman after one of his trips to Monte Carlo. Newman went to Monte Carlo every winter —not to listen to music, but to break the bank! He was a genius with money and he always used to come away from Monte Carlo with quite a few pounds' profit. He happened to be there when Henry Wood was conducting a permanent and well-established orchestra. Newman said to me: "If only the critics could hear Henry Wood conduct the Berlin Philharmonic or the Vienna Philharmonic. Then they would realize that he is more than just 'a good workman'." Henry Wood used to be looked down on by many of the critics, and at that time they also used to look down on the Proms. In those days the pro-grammes were only semi-classical. The first part would contain, say, a Beethoven or a Schubert symphony, but the second part often degenerated into a sort of ballad concert; the reasoning being that the Promenade public had been submitted to a severe intellectual strain in listening to the "Unfinished" symphony, so they must now hear "Oh dry those tears".

Henry Wood eventually revised the whole concept of the programmes, and then the BBC took charge. Sir William Glock, as the BBC's Controller of Music, made the Promenade season the most comprehensive musical festival in the world. Anybody going to two or three concerts every week can now box the musical compass, from the Middle Ages up to Messiaen and Stockhausen.

RD: He was known as "Timber". Presumably this was a pun on *Wood*.

NC: Yes, orchestral players always gave nicknames to con-ductors, and probably still do. Henry Wood had a warm and natural way of speaking, with perhaps a trace of Cockney, certainly not at all highbrow. At rehearsal he used to say, "What are you violins doing, sawing away regardless of?" Or

"What are you trumpeters doing, regardless of?" One day a friend took him on one side and said, "Look here, Wood, you mustn't say 'regardless of' at the end of a sentence. It is not good English." At the next rehearsal Henry Wood stopped the orchestra and said, "What do you violins think you're doing?" Pause. Then every member of the orchestra shouted "regardless of".

Henry Wood was looked upon with tremendous affection. It would be belittling to remember him just as a conductor: to do this would be as shortsighted as remembering Shakespeare because he was an actor. Henry Wood is part of what you might call the national portrait gallery of great English characters. He is there alongside W. G. Grace and Winston Churchill.

Wood represented middlebrow taste. He opened many a window for people like myself, who could go at reasonable cost to a Wagner night or a Beethoven night: these were rare events in those days. He sometimes used to come up to Manchester. After a performance of the B minor Mass of Bach, a member of the chorus told me that Wood arrived with the parts annotated by himself, in a most detailed way.

He had a very long baton and you could always hear it swish on a down-beat. His theory was that a long baton saved arm movement and was more easily visible to a large chorus or orchestra. He knew what he was doing. His book *About Conducting* is still, 30 years after publication, a text-book of great value. And he was an authority on the voice. He wrote *The Gentle Art of Singing*. Its four volumes contain well over a thousand vocal exercises. At one time he used to teach singing, and he often gave 50 lessons a week in addition to his conducting and church-organist commitments.

He was not only a most comprehensive musician, he was also a man of foresight. I remember once when he was rehearsing the Hallé in a work which in those days was regarded as modern. At that time even *Petrushka* of Stravinsky was considered modern. Somebody in the woodwind section made a mistake, and Henry Wood called him to order, "regardless of". The instrumentalist protested, "This modern music, Sir Henry, is very difficult to play." And Wood replied, "Just you wait and see what you'll be asked to play twenty years from now. Then you'll know what modern music is." A most prophetic remark.

RD: He did a lot for English as well as for foreign music.

NC: Oh yes, he did an enormous amount for English music. But I can't remember him often conducting opera, at least not in his later years. The Covent Garden season used to last only two or three months. Then in the Thirties we saw the beginning of Sadler's Wells, giving London an all-year centre for opera. Henry Wood started his career as the conductor and musical director of a touring opera company. His pay was £2 a week.

RD: Henry Wood helped Malcolm Sargent early on in his career.

NC: Yes, in 1921 Malcolm conducted his own *Impressions of a Windy Day* at a Queen's Hall Prom. He was then only in his mid-twenties, and he was still keen on composition and organ-playing. He hadn't yet decided to devote most of his time to conducting.

It was Beecham who gave Malcolm his first major post as a conductor. When Beecham formed the London Philharmonic Orchestra in the Thirties, he appointed Malcolm as his assistant. Beecham had been inclined not to belittle him but to make jokes about him, always calling him "Flash". I saw Beecham soon after the appointment and said, "Have you such a high opinion of Malcolm?" "Malcolm is an extremely accomplished musician and an incredibly accomplished conductor. I appointed him as my deputy, knowing that my orchestra would be in safe hands when I was not present. I appointed him on the basis of a principle that I recommend also to you. If ever you appoint a deputy, appoint one whom you can trust technically; but his calibre must be such that the public will always be glad to see *you* back again."

RD: Sargent is probably best remembered for his choral work.

NC: I don't think he has been equalled in this country as a choral conductor, but every conductor has his blind-spots. Malcolm knew his limitations. He didn't want to conduct Mahler; he didn't want to conduct Bruckner. There were certain works that Malcolm could handle well; there were also certain musical realms which he could not enter. You could say that about every conductor. I once heard Toscanini conduct *Meistersinger*, but I didn't want to go a second time: his approach to the music seemed uncongenial. Mind you, this was in Toscanini's later years, when his musical arteries were beginning to harden.

Malcolm was the conductor at the first performance of *Belshazzar's Feast*: at a Leeds Festival in the early Thirties. I am sure Willie Walton would agree with me that no first performance has been given with more voltage. The soloist was Dennis Noble. I've never heard *Belshazzar* played or sung better.

Malcolm was the best-ever conductor of *Gerontius*. There was something about the work that touched him. Malcolm was a devout *believer* in *Gerontius*, probably even more than Elgar, who had religious doubts before he finished it. Malcolm was gifted with a certain religious radar, enabling him to get *inside* *Gerontius*. He conducted a performance in the Albert Hall just before the Second War. Toscanini, who had been in the audience, went round afterwards to the artists' room. He embraced Malcolm, kissed him, and wanted to know why he had not heard of this masterpiece long before.

I often wonder why eminent foreign conductors, such as Klemperer and Toscanini, had scarcely heard of *Gerontius*. After all, it was successfully launched as long ago as 1902, at the Lower Rhine Festival in Düsseldorf, two years after it had failed in Birmingham, where Hans Richter conducted the first performance. At Düsseldorf it was none other than Richard Strauss who said of Elgar "Hats off to a genius", echoing the words of Schumann. I've often asked myself why Strauss paid that compliment to Elgar. I don't suppose Strauss ever made another reference to him. Was Strauss trying to get an engagement with the Hallé through Richter? I wonder.

RD: Sargent did a lot for various works and various composers, but I always felt that, like Henry Wood, he was more than a conductor; he was also an ambassador of music.

NC: Malcolm had the sort of personality that transcended his immediate rôle or undertaking. We didn't think of Dan Leno as just a music-hall comedian; we thought of him as a part of our way of life. Dickens was not just a novelist; he was part of the Victorian ethos. During the Proms, Malcolm became a part of the panorama of London life. On the last night he was the idol of all the young people. In my mind's eye I can still see the young maidens gazing upon him through the golden rail that separates the platform from the arena. For them it was "the gold bar of Heaven". And Malcolm gloried in it.

Many of the critics used to belittle him. But why? He was the first to tell you that he was a showman. He would say, "What is a conductor but a man who has to put over a work to the public?" And he did. It mustn't be forgotten that Malcolm served an apprenticeship with the British National Opera Company. I remember Malcolm conducting Vaughan Williams's folk opera *Hugh the Drover*; he was obviously going to be a very good conductor. If in those days there had been as much scope for opera as there is now—we have opera in Cardiff, opera in Glasgow, opera in London at the Coliseum and at the Garden—then Malcolm would undoubtedly have made his name as an opera conductor.

Malcolm was very conscious of his looks, his turnout. When Schnabel first beheld the carnation adorning Malcolm's evening dress, he asked, "Am I also expected to have a flower in my button-hole when I play Brahms?" Beecham called Malcolm "Flash", but this was just a touch of Beecham wit; he didn't use the nickname in a derogatory sense. Beecham used to make jokes about Malcolm the glamour boy, but if anybody had taken them seriously and said, "Oh I agree, he's a second-rate conductor", Beecham would have replied strongly: "What are you talking about? Can't I be amusing and witty without being taken seriously? Do you imagine I would have appointed Malcolm as my co-conductor for a new orchestra if I didn't have faith in him?" Beecham did not under-rate Malcolm.

Beecham made jokes about *everybody*, and some of his best ones were about Malcolm. I once went to see Beecham and I said, "Have you read in the paper about Malcolm in Tokyo?" "Good God," he replied, "Malcolm in Tokyo! What is he doing there?" I said, "Conducting. He's having the most amazing success." "I see," said Beecham, "a Flash in Ja-pan."

RD: Have you, in the past year or so, come across any really promising young conductors?

NC: I don't want to name names, but I often hear performances, which are technically very good, given by young conductors who have not yet matured aesthetically; the next day, I read in the press the sort of language that I would hesitate to use even of Toscanini or Furtwängler. I'm all in favour of encouraging young artists, but you should encourage them in proportion to their age and development, and leave them in no doubt that they still have a lot to learn.

Some young conductors are attempting works which members of the older school look at with awe. Bruno Walter once told me that he didn't *dare* to conduct the G minor symphony until he was 40. And Klemperer said that nowadays the ripening of the gifts of a lot of young conductors is being spoiled: they are doing too much too soon. Music is in danger of becoming more of a commercial than an artistic affair. There are festivals and concerts everywhere. In London alone there seem to be more concerts in one week than we used to have in six months. The demand is overstretching the supply of talent.

Today there is only a handful of really great conductors. Before the war you could have rattled off the names of a dozen or two, from Monteux and Kleiber to Beecham and Hamilton Harty; but all of them were 40 or 50 before they reached the top. They were all men of maturity. In those days, men of 25 or 30 seldom, if ever, conducted the great orchestras. They couldn't. You couldn't stand on the rostrum and face the Vienna Philharmonic until you knew the work-to-be-played as a living experience. The Vienna Philharmonic would play the G minor symphony quite well even if you or I conducted it— because they wouldn't take any notice of our beat. They will only respond to a conductor who has something to say which is in line with what the composer has to say; they will only respond to a conductor who can act as a medium, receiving and communicating the composer's message.

Even a great conductor can't be a medium for all music. For example, I would go anywhere to hear Furtwängler conduct *Tristan*, but I wouldn't want to hear him conduct *Meistersinger*. In the same way, I would go anywhere to hear Klemperer at his best conduct the "Eroica", but I wouldn't go a long way to hear him conduct the *Song of the Earth*, even though he was a Mahlerian. I would rather hear him conduct, say, the third symphony of Mahler. Versatility can be dangerous.

You must know what you can do and what you cannot do, and this applies not only to music; it applies to every aspect of life. An apt example of someone who knew his limitations was

Herbert Sutcliffe. He had nowhere near as good a technique as Walter Hammond or Len Hutton, but he knew what he could not do; and so he did not attempt strokes at which he was not a master. That is the beginning of mastery: realizing that you can't do everything equally well. But these days musicians try to begin the other way round: "I've got to conduct a Mozart concert tomorrow night. A couple of days later, I'm going to conduct the B minor Mass. Next week I'm going to play the D minor concerto of Brahms." Will this sort of versatility allow genius to develop along its natural course?

I like the confidence of youth. It was Goethe who said that to be young means to be drunk, without wine; on the other hand, it was Wilde who said that youth is wasted on the young. Young people have made a tremendous contribution to professional music-making in the last 20 or 30 years, but I do wish they would not be in such a hurry. The aeroplane is flying artists all over the world, east and west. They have no time for leisure. In days past, a conductor such as Weingartner would come for a concert in London. He would get on a train in Vienna, travel on the Orient Express, calmly and comfortably, and study his scores. And Mozart came to London by stagecoach, and wrote one or two sonatas on the way!

10

WOMEN IN MUSIC

RD: Why have women made so small a contribution to the composing of music? This is one of the perennial questions. Is it because music is the most abstract of the arts, and because men seem on the whole to be better at abstract thinking than women?

NC: I wish I knew the answer to this. We've had a few women composers: from Ethel Smyth to Elisabeth Lutyens and Thea Musgrave. No doubt they are very annoyed to be called *women* composers; the main thing is that they are *composers*. Miss Lutyens and Miss Musgrave both show such tenacity and power of thought in their compositions, that nobody hearing their works, without having been told the composer's name, would say, "This was obviously written by a woman."

The usual explanation for the comparatively small contribution made by women to composing is that until recently women have been tied to the home, the nursery, the kitchen. But I can remember the time when, in the English upper classes, every girl was given piano lessons and an education in music. When they went to parties, they were often heard to say, "Oh, I am so sorry. I've forgotten to bring my music." And yet this period didn't produce many women pianists, and very few women composers.

In Britain we've had Jane Austen, George Eliot, Virginia Woolf, Daphne du Maurier. And I could name a score of other women writers. Women have achieved greatness in literature. Why not in music? Music—as Delius used to say—is an expression of feeling and emotion—probably more so than any other art. So you would think that women would find a more natural creative outlet in music than in any other art-form. After all, there are great women singers. There are women orchestral players, women timpani players, even women horn players. But, to this day, a number of orchestras on the Continent don't have women players, and Beecham didn't like to have women players in his orchestras. He didn't object to women on musical grounds. He used to say, "If I had women in my orchestra who were not good-looking, they would be distracting. And women who *were* good-looking would be even more distracting!"

It has always been a mystery to me why there have been so few really great women pianists. If we go back through the last 80 years, there was Sophie Menter, whom Shaw wrote about; there was Myra Hess; and a few others. Myra was that rarity: a woman who could play Brahms. Ernest Newman once wrote that no women under the age of 40, and very few over the age of 40, can do justice to Brahms. Perhaps more than any woman pianist I have known, Myra had the gift of blending the whole of the keyboard; and, for a woman, she had an extraordinary range of tone. I once heard her play a Beethoven concerto, with Furtwängler conducting. It was a great tribute to a woman artist to be invited to collaborate with Furtwängler. Believe me, the combination of Furtwängler and Beethoven was no laughing matter.

In spite of the fact that Women's Lib—God bless them—are trying to make the sexes equal, it is a fact of nature that they are not equal. There is a tendency for women to have less muscular strength and a shorter finger-span than men. Annie Fischer is the only other woman pianist, in my experience, who could play Brahms with depth and strength. But some of the best players of Debussy and Chopin, and even of Liszt, have been women. And if I were pushed into a corner and challenged to say who is the best living player of the Schumann C major *Phantasie*, I would say, "I can't tell you who is the best, but one of the best is Muriel Cohen." If you heard her on a gramophone record, you wouldn't know you were listening to a woman player. If I played a recording of Horowitz immediately afterwards, you would notice his greater fluency of technique, but you would find it difficult to say which is the better interpretation.

We have in this country someone whom I consider to be one of the finest women pianists I have ever heard, a first-class artist. Most concert-goers know her name, but I find that the critics don't write about her in the way I think she should be written about. And I seldom hear her playing with the great foreign conductors. She sometimes plays at a Prom or at a

Festival Hall concert, usually under an English conductor; I don't think she has ever played with Klemperer or Böhm, for example. The pianist I have in mind is Moura Lympany. A year or so ago I heard her play the one-hand concerto of Ravel. She gave an incredibly good performance, but the notices said no more than "quite accomplished" or "technically good".

If Miss Lympany were 25 or 30, no doubt the critics would be raving about her. We have come full circle. When I was young, nobody would take any notice of you until you were 40; now, they don't take any notice of anybody over 40. Youth is winning everywhere. World-class swimmers are retiring at 17 or 18; cricketers are giving up the game at the age of 30. Jack Hobbs was making more runs in his forties than he had ever made in his life, and "Patsy" Hendren played in first-class cricket until he was nearly 50.

RD: Have you ever heard Maria Donska? She studied with Schnabel in Berlin.

NC: After the war I was writing a lot of music notices; I even used to go to the Wigmore Hall. One evening—I think it was in the Fifties—I went to a recital there, just as a matter of duty. I heard Maria Donska and I thought she had exceptional talent, an extraordinarily profound understanding of the keyboard. She made the music sound alive, and her playing expressed something of the deep meaning, the atmosphere, the inwardness, that we learned to expect from Schnabel. I don't remember ever going to another recital or concert of hers. I have often wondered why she didn't go right to the top.

Why is it that a lot of women pianists get so far and no further? When I was in Sydney, I knew five or six young girls, concert pianists, and I thought they all had the potential to reach the top. Then, one by one, they each got married. Now it seems to me that a singer can get married and still have a successful career. You have only to think of Flagstad, Lotte Lehmann, Elisabeth Schumann, Elisabeth Schwarzkopf, and of course Joan Sutherland. I knew Joan when she was first beginning to make a name for herself. I used to hear her sing in Sydney. She was intelligent enough to marry a fellow-musician.

On the other hand, very few women pianists seem to be able

to combine a career and marriage. I once spoke about this to one of the Australian girls—then no longer a girl. "Why did you get married when you were on the way to becoming a great artist?" "Because I wanted a family." Then I said, "Singers get married, and still go to the top; pianists get married, and very few of them go to the top. Why?" "A pianist has got to practise four or five hours a day, and no husband would put up with it. A singer has only got to practise for an hour a day!"

When I was in Australia the Boyd Neel Orchestra came over on tour. Their playing was a revelation to everyone. At one concert they played *Les Illuminations* of Benjamin Britten; the songs were sung by a girl of about 25, with the unpromising name of Peggy Knibb. She gave a wonderful performance. In my notice about her for the *Sydney Morning Herald* I really went off the deep end. *Les Illuminations* can also be sung by a tenor, and when I came back to England I heard the work sung by Peter Pears. He sang well but I did not feel he entered as deeply into the world of the songs as Peggy Knibb had done. The next thing I heard was that she had married a wealthy doctor in Melbourne. She is now the mother of five or six children.

There was another gifted pianist, then a girl of about 22, who played the Schumann concerto under Beecham during his visit to Australia. Beecham said to me afterwards, "I haven't heard a better performance of the Schumann since . . ."—and he went back into the remote past. "This girl," he said, "will go to the top." Her name was Eunice Gardner. She married and soon had four or five children.

I can name a handful of pianists—especially from my years in Australia—who I'm certain could have eventually played in Vienna, in Berlin: Muriel Cohen, Joyce Greer, Eunice Gardner, and Maureen Jones, who played recently at the Proms. And I mustn't forget another gifted pianist, Eileen Ralfph. She married Thomas Matthews, who was once leader of the Liverpool Philharmonic, the London Philharmonic, and the Covent Garden Orchestra, and later became a conductor in Tasmania and in South Australia. Eileen was a fine artist and I'm sure she still is. But men seem to be more purposeful. Women's Lib is probably going to do a lot of good for women in music.

One of the reasons why these Australian girls never reached the top is that they had little or no opportunity to make records in Australia. If I had been a wealthy man, I would have paid for recordings to be made of these girls, and I know their records would have sold well. Some recording companies are not very imaginative. They only want big-name artists.

RD: Artists such as Jacqueline du Pré.

NC: I first heard Jackie in the early Sixties. She was only a girl then. Even in those early days, she played the Elgar concerto as beautifully as anybody I have heard; and I do not exclude one or two very great cellists. I wrote in the *Guardian* that English interpretative music had not been so richly endowed by any young artist since Kathleen Ferrier.

Jackie shares Kathleen's rare quality of communication. Through this not-very-ladylike instrument, the cello, Jackie communicates warmth—with raptness and intensity; with her whole heart—but she does not force or thrash the cello, which is a most intractable instrument: even the best players sometimes produce sounds, during rapid passages, that resemble the noise of a bee trying to get out of a window.

Nine cellists out of ten play *on* the strings, and the sound seems to go *into* the wood. But Jackie achieves clear definition and richness of tone by playing, as it were, from within the wood. Like Casals—and I am paying Jackie the highest possible compliment when I say she can do the same thing—she produces tone as though not from the strings. She releases from the beautiful and richly-stained wood all the music that is stored like a treasure trove within it.

LANCASHIRE AND THE ARTS

RD: You must be very proud of the number of people that Lancashire has given to the world of music.

NC: Not only to the world of music, but to every branch of the arts; and we must remember not only the artists who have been born in Lancashire, but also the artists who have been brought up in Lancashire. If you want me to consider the whole range of artistic and musical life—from the music-hall to pop music —I'm bound to miss out one or two important names. Lancashire has produced Gracie Fields, Kathleen Ferrier, Beecham, Willie Walton, Ernest Newman who came from Liverpool, James Agate who came from Manchester, and George Formby senior, who was a Lancashire comedian, an original for L. S. Lowry. I have always imagined that Lowry got from the music-hall his inspiration for the lean, gawky, spiky Lancastrians he draws.

Formby was a great actor. He used to come on to the platform, cloth cap, his face very pale, looking as if he had walked straight out of a Lowry picture. He would go up to the conductor and say, "Eh, Alf, ah'm feelin' a bit tight on t'chest tonight, but ah'll do me best." There was something very *moving* about Formby. Like Chaplin, like every great comedian, he came very near to pathos. It is only the second-rate comedian who laughs at his own jokes.

RD: What are the special characteristics of the Lancastrian?

NC: The characteristics of the Lancastrian are downright honesty, few or no inhibitions, extraordinary warmth, a down-to-earth nature, a realism that comes from a history of hard times, troubles, famines. The difference between the Lancastrian and the Yorkshireman is the same as the difference between cotton and wool; in Yorkshire you tend to find a more broad, more comfortable, type of person.

I knew Lancashire in the days of the Depression, and I want

to tell you about one of the most moving experiences I have ever had. During that period, I was asked to give a lecture—in Nelson, or somewhere—in the middle of winter. I went into the hall. There were 50 or 60 men and women, all looking as though they needed something to eat, protected against the cold by coats and shawls, waiting for a lecture—on Hugo Wolf! I spoke to the secretary and said I wondered if there was a mistake—I thought I was going to give a lecture to an amateur musical society. "Yes, this is our musical society." "Don't you think I'd better give a talk on cricket?" "No, no," he said, "the gramophone and the records are all here."

I chose the less difficult songs of Wolf, such as "Geh', Geliebter", and told the audience the meaning of the words; and I sang "Kennst du das Land". Afterwards, some of the members came into the artists' room and said, "Eh, luv, that were great music." This moved me very much indeed. These people showed the same qualities that the great artists from Lancashire express. If you take Willie Walton and Kathleen, Lowry and Formby and Gracie Fields, you get a picture of Lancastrians, from their thinking and feeling to their warmth and fun and humour.

In the great Heaven of all Artists, they will all have been deprived of class distinction. Mozart won't want to be introduced to a musicologist, someone who has written a book on atonalism. Mozart will ask, "Who is that over there?" "Bobby Charlton, the footballer," someone will reply. Mozart will say with enthusiasm: "I used to play billiards. Let me try to play football. I want to meet Bobby Charlton." And Franz Lehár will be embraced by Bach; Johann Strauss by Brahms. Nothing is more certain than this. What I have tried to do, all through my life, is to gather the full range of human character into an artistic, humorous, and spiritual, synthesis.

MANCHESTER GUARDIAN

RD: What is your opinion of schools of journalism?

NC: They are a mystery to me. I'm sure they can teach you a lot about the technical side: how to sub-edit; how to use the symbols for correcting proofs. Even now, I don't know all of the symbols, and I don't know how to set up a page. I wonder if schools of journalism teach students how to cut? If they want a professor in the art of cutting, I could teach them a good deal! In my *Manchester Guardian* days, I used to send my copy upstairs after returning from a Hallé concert: not 500 words, which is the maximum length now for a notice, but 1,400. The next morning I would find that, according to the space available, perhaps 200 words—no more—had been eliminated. I sometimes didn't know if any words had been eliminated, because they were taken out *with great care*: the sub-editor would say, "*That* can come out of the first paragraph; *that* can come out of the third paragraph." But today sub-editors sometimes lop off the whole of the last paragraph. They make you feel that your prose is—to quote from *The Mikado*—

Awaiting the sensation of a short, sharp shock
From a cheap and chippy chopper on a big, black block!

No journalist objects to being cut—he knows that there are other contributors to the paper in addition to himself—but my protest against journalism today is that many sub-editors are butchers. They just chop off "copy". The sub-editors' room has become an *abattoir*. I went to a concert once at which Moura Lympany was playing. When I came to write my notice, I first had to deal with a symphony that had been performed. Then I said to myself, "I'm determined to give a verbal bouquet to this very fine pianist"—and I did, in a last paragraph of 150 words. The next day—and I won't disclose the name of the paper; it wasn't the *Guardian*—there was no mention of her name, no evidence that she had been anywhere near the concert.

RC: Have you ever found a way to defeat sub-editors?

NC: There is *no* way of defeating the modern sub-editor. He is fully armed!

I remember when I first started as a music critic in Manchester, on a paper called the *Daily Citizen*, the first Labour newspaper in England. The tragedy of the *Daily Citizen* was that its circulation eventually outpaced its advertisement revenue, and it went bankrupt. The cost of printing the paper must have been more than its sale price of a ha'penny.

The editor of the northern edition was a man I liked very much, Frank Dilnot, and I asked him if I could cover the Hallé concerts. He agreed, but warned me that the *Daily Citizen* didn't receive complimentary tickets: the Committee of the Hallé concerts must have said, "We won't send tickets to illiterate Socialists."

The conductor of the Hallé at that time was Michael Balling, who came after Richter. I wrote to Balling and he sent me tickets for the whole season; I also applied to the various musical societies for tickets. My fee for reviewing concerts was a penny a line. The first notice I wrote would work out at 80 lines, 6/8d.; not bad, I thought, for a week's wages. I was only 24. In those days, people in offices were earning about 10/– a week.

When I saw my notice in the paper, I found they had cut my "copy" to 22 lines. So, instead of getting 6/8d. for 80 lines, I only got 1/10d. I thought to myself, "If the sub-editors are going to cut my 'copy', how can I defeat them?" I decided to join all my sentences together, by using such phrases as "it follows that" and words like "consequently", "therefore", "but". This didn't make the slightest difference. They cut my "copy" just the same.

But we mustn't be too hard on sub-editors. I am sure that every writer for a newspaper must often go down on his knees and thank God for a sub-editor who has the sense to take out some of the nonsense you think is very funny when you are writing late at night. I've often said, "Thank God they didn't allow *that* to go into the paper." On the other hand, I've sometimes needed the patience of Job to see why they have cut out something I felt was worth leaving in. They have a perfect genius for sometimes cutting out the best things, just as they have a perfect genius for saving you from yourself.

RD: In your *Manchester Guardian* days, there was a list of words that could not be used.

NC: It was a long list and I've forgotten most of the words. One of them was "commence". At one stage, I was in charge of Ernest Newman's column. He was then in London and he used to send a fortnightly article to Manchester. Newman's style was above correction, so I could safely send his "copy" upstairs without reading it. One night Scott called me in; he was looking at the proof of a Newman article. He said, "I *presume* you read this piece by Newman before it went up?" "Well," I replied, "Newman is Newman." But Scott was unyielding: "I can't have Mr Newman telling *Manchester Guardian* readers 'The concert commenced . . .' I won't have this word 'commence' in my paper. There's a perfectly good Anglo-Saxon word—'begin'. John's Gospel doesn't say 'In the *commencement* was the Word'." I hadn't the courage to tell Newman by letter. I managed to tell him, in a roundabout way, the next time we met, but he went on using "commence". No doubt he had his reasons. To me, "commence" is a rather middle-class word; I can't remember ever using it.

There were other taboo words and phrases. Scott wouldn't allow "under the auspices of". I once had to go to a flower show in Manchester, and I wrote that it had been given "under the auspices of Lady So-and-so". Scott—who used to read everything in the paper: from the tiniest report to the leading articles—called me in. "Cardus, this phrase 'under the auspices of'—I won't have it." "Well, sir, what should I say instead?" "Can't you say the show was 'under the patronage of'?" "No," I replied, "that wouldn't be quite accurate." "Can't you say it was 'under . . . under the . . .'? Good heavens, we'll have to use it. There's no other phrase." Scott thought for a moment; he didn't want to give way over one of his instructions. So, in the end, he told me to say "The show took place at . . .", without mentioning Lady So-and-so at all. Today, I suppose we'd say "under the sponsorship of". Scott certainly wouldn't have allowed that phrase into his paper, not at any price.

It took a long time to convince Scott that the cinema deserved to be treated in the *Manchester Guardian* as seriously as the theatre and music, and, when at last he did relent, he relented on one condition: that the word must be spelt with a "k"! It is not generally known—and I should like to put it on record—that one of the first film critics was a Manchester girl named Madeline Linford. Then there was C. A. Lejeune: she started her career on the *Manchester Guardian* and later became film critic of the *Observer*. Her book of memoirs *Thank You For Having Me* is well worth reading. She was followed—as queen of film critics—by Dilys Powell of the *Sunday Times*. But it was Madeline Linford who was one of the pioneers of cinema criticism; you could turn naturally from the criticism of Montague and Langford, and read Linford. Her writing was in harmony with those great critics; I can pay her no greater compliment.

RD: Some of the finest writers of the century were allowed to sign their articles in the *Manchester Guardian* only with their initials.

NC: During that period, under Scott, there was a feature called the "Saturday article", about 1,800 words, on an inside page now occupied by the arts page. These articles were signed "B.R." or "J.C." or "A.B."—Bertrand Russell, Joseph Conrad, Arnold Bennett. The only initials that were then widely recognized were G.B.S. (everybody knew Shaw) and G.K.C. (most people knew Chesterton). The fee for the "Saturday article" was three guineas.

At that time, no journalist or contributor to the *Manchester Guardian* had a by-line. One of the most sought-after perquisites of the reporters' room was to be sent to a music-hall. You were allowed to write about 400 words, to be type-set in leaded Minion, which gave the text more prominence; most of the text, in newspapers of this period, was set in solid type. And you were allowed to sign the notice with your initials. It was one of the proudest moments of your life when you saw your initials in the *Manchester Guardian* for the first time.

Scott once said to me, "You are very lucky, you young men, to have your initials in the paper. Mine have never appeared." I said, "Excuse me, Mr Scott, they have." "Never!" he protested. "Never." "Yes, I was in Sheffield one day and I saw your initials in the 'First North'." The "First North" was the first edition. There was little or no time for it to go to the proof readers, and, if you think there are a lot of misprints in the *Guardian* these days, you should have seen the number that appeared in the "First North". I told Scott that at the top of the first leader—which he had written—were the words "proof to C.P.S.". My insistence—that his initials had once appeared —amused him very much. "They appeared only accidentally," he said.

A lot of people have said that Scott had no sense of humour at all, but that is not true. He had a subtle, wry sense of humour and a strong sense of irony. I remember when he was persuaded, only after a great deal of argument, to have an illuminated sign—MANCHESTER GUARDIAN—in neon lights, outside our offices on Cross Street. He didn't like the idea at all, but our advertising people said that we must have an illuminated sign; all the other papers had one. "Very well," Scott said, "but only on the condition that it does not twinkle." I suppose there are some people who thought that even Bernard Shaw or Mark Twain had no sense of humour; sometimes the person on the receiving end is the one who hasn't got a sense of humour.

RD: Did Scott encourage you personally, as a writer?

NC: He was seldom in a position to encourage me directly. He had the gift of delegation, and he had under him men of the calibre of Montague and Haslam Mills—they were the ones who gave appointments to me and the other reporters. Scott gave final approval to all "copy", but on the whole he left the arts side to the specialists. He did not presume to be a judge of the writing of a critic, though he once told me he preferred Newman's writing to Langford's. Scott found Newman's prose clearer and more concrete; he couldn't fully appreciate the poetic imagery of Langford. Scott—for all his greatness—was not a poet. That is the *last* thing you could ever say of him.

RD: At one time you were editor of the Miscellany column.

NC: People from all over the country sent in contributions; they were paid 2/6d. a paragraph. Some days I didn't get any contributions, so I had to write the column myself. One evening, when I was short of "copy", the last paragraph arrived, as if by magic. At 6.30 p.m. the sight of *any* contribution was a blessing. I thought to myself, "Thank God. This has saved the column." Hardly having read it, I sent the paragraph up to the composing-room. At about half-past nine, I was called in to Scott's room; the proofs were on his desk. "You've allowed a contributor to Miscellany to use the phrase 'from thence'. That's not English, Cardus, and it is therefore banned from the *Manchester Guardian*. 'From thence' is as nonsensical as 'to thither'." If he were alive today, I would never dream of challenging Scott: I'd just say, "I'm awfully sorry, sir," and disappear. But I was young then and, being bolder than I am now, I brazened it out. I said, "Mr Scott, there are precedents in the English language for the use of the phrase 'from thence'." "Where?" he asked. I was not going to quote from the Scriptures, so I said, "In *Tom Jones* by Henry Fielding—he often uses the phrase 'from thence'." "Oh does he?" said Scott. "Then all I can say, Cardus, is that Mr Fielding would not use the phrase 'from thence' twice on my newspaper. Goodnight." I said to myself, "If he'd be prepared to sack the father of the English novel, the sooner I get out of this room the better."

Scott was a Puritan on matters of language. He wouldn't allow the word "sex" in his paper. What he would say about some of the words that are allowed in nowadays, I can't imagine. He wouldn't even let us use the word "basically". I often used to wonder on what principle he rejected certain words and accepted others.

Scott came from the nineteenth-century rationalistic school. He was well-read in politics, but I am not sure if he had read widely: I don't suppose he had read Baudelaire or Balzac. In his library there were some beautifully-bound volumes. One day, when he was away in London, I was doing some work in his study, and I saw in a bookcase the collected works of Racine. The pages were uncut.

Scott was extremely courteous to all his staff. If you hadn't done a job well, he didn't curse you or bully you; he would simply tell you that you hadn't done it well, and you always learned something from him. He would tell you what you had done badly; where you had gone wrong. Scott had a nineteenth-century austerity, but some people went so far as to say that he lacked humanity. What do they mean? Humanity takes many different shapes and forms. I often saw him when he was away

F

from his desk—in his house and in social company—and he
was always warm and charming. But there were limits beyond
which you didn't go. You couldn't talk to him about music-
hall. You couldn't tell him a dirty story—but, if you had dared
to, I have no doubt he would have appreciated it to the full!

We all respected Scott. He was more to us than a mandarin;
he was the All-Father. I remember when H. W. Massingham,
who was then editor of the *Nation* and made it one of the great
weeklies of the world, wrote to me. Those who wrote for the
Nation included Bertrand Russell, Shaw, and Bennett. I was
then quite young and I was staggered to get a letter from
Massingham, asking me if I would write an article on cricket.
I thought, "My God, I'm going to have my name in the
Nation."

In those days, you couldn't write for any other paper unless
you had Scott's permission. So I went to Scott and he said, "No,
certainly not." I then wrote to Massingham, telling him that
Scott would not allow me to send him an article, and I expressed
the hope that some day I might have the honour of contributing
to the *Nation*. Massingham wrote a most charming letter in
reply, saying he was surprised that Scott was so restrictive and
that surely it would be very much to the credit of the *Manchester Guardian* if a young writer's article were to appear in
the *Nation*: "Anyhow," he continued, "leave this to me and
I'll see what I can do to persuade the All-Father."

A week or two later I received a note from Scott giving me
permission. I wrote a piece called *The Cricketer as Artist*; it was
published in the *Nation* under my name and I included it in
A Cricketer's Book, which was my very first book. Although it
was a tremendous honour to write for the *Manchester Guardian*,
an even bigger achievement was my first appearance in the
Nation, which eventually modulated into the *New Statesman* of
today, thanks to the pioneering work of that great editor,
Massingham.

RD: Did Scott ever give praise?

NC: Oh yes, Scott could praise, but not in superlatives. He
wouldn't come along and say, "Marvellous"; he would say,
"That was a fine piece you wrote last night." We were prepared
to work on the *Manchester Guardian* for next to nothing: Scott
had an absolute genius for making a compliment just when you

were thinking of asking for an advance of salary. He disarmed you. And he could also—with one short note—make you wish you had never been born, or at least had never set foot in the offices of the *Manchester Guardian*. His little notes—just a few sarcastic words—could break your heart. I want to tell you a story about a sub-editor named H. D. Nichols.

When the cinema was being threatened by the spread of radio, some cinema managers held a meeting to complain about the threat of immediate ruin. Nichols headed his report: "Tragedy in reel life." A few hours later, the heading was sent back to him, pasted on to a piece of paper, with a note: "C.P.S. to H.D.N. Is this intended as a pun? It looks perilously like one." That note from Scott was enough to drive old Nichols into the Thatched House. He had to drink six or seven pints of beer before he could get over the shock, and he thought very seriously about resigning. I never got a note like that from Scott. Since that day I've always been afraid of puns.

One evening, when Pavlova was in Manchester, I was sent by Montague to write about her. She was past her best, and she was dancing in the Free Trade Hall, on an improvised stage, a wooden platform, with no scenery, just a backcloth. She had with her a troupe, a small *corps de ballet*. There was a loose plank on the platform and when, every now and then, a member of the *corps de ballet* danced on that plank, you heard a plonk; but with Pavlova, never. I went back to Cross Street and wrote about Pavlova. I adapted and elaborated the metaphor from the mediaeval concept of angels dancing on the point of a needle. Montague sent me an appreciative note; and, when I was going through the counting house (today they'd call it the "accounts department"), Allan Monkhouse, a wonderful man, then a drama critic, tapped me on the shoulder and said, "Cardus, I want to compliment you on your image about angels dancing on the point of a needle." That was worth more than a £50 advance of salary.

There was a wonderful comradeship on the *Manchester Guardian*: it was the best university in the world. We used to go into the underground cellars in Manchester—they were for men only. No wine was served; just coffee. If you wanted a meal, you stayed upstairs. In those cellars I was given tutorials, as thorough and as wide-ranging as any that an undergraduate has had at Oxford or Cambridge. My tutors included Langford and a leader writer, a Balliol man, with the very Lancastrian name of Sidebotham.

Sidebotham was a brilliant man, not only a student of politics but also one of the greatest leader writers of all time. He wrote one or two books, but they didn't do justice to his *range*. When *Rosenkavalier* was given its first Manchester performance, Langford was engaged elsewhere that night; this was before I joined the *Manchester Guardian*. The man who wrote the notice, three-quarters of a column, was Sidebotham. The *Manchester Guardian* gave its writers a very catholic education. Scott wouldn't appoint a man to the reporters' room if he were a specialist in only one subject. Scott liked writers who took a comprehensive view of life. He wanted, as his music critic, not someone who had been brought up in an academy, but someone who knew what it was to be amongst the people who pay to listen to music.

RD: Were you ever asked to write leaders?

NC: Occasionally; but not serious leaders. Like *The Times*, we used to have a fourth leader (the "Short") which was intended to be amusing and flippant, nothing to do with politics or world affairs. I remember one night getting a note from Scott. He wanted me to write the "Short" on a very serious matter which he would deal with in a long leader the next day. The subject was coast erosion. Well, to be frank, I didn't know what coast erosion meant. All I had to go on was a paragraph saying that the sea had encroached on the coast at a seaside resort—I can't remember which one; we'll call it Umpton-on-Sea—and had done great damage to the pier and promenade. "What could I say?" I wondered. Then I had an inspiration. I described the encroaching sea and the damaged esplanade, and I described the mayor and the members of the town council looking at the stretch of sand where once there had been a pier. At the end I said, "They wept like anything to see such quantities of sand", which is of course a quotation from Lewis Carroll. I thought this was rather good, and with great pride I sent the leader upstairs. An hour later, Scott called me in: "In this 'Short', Cardus, you use a quotation: 'They wept like anything to see such quantities of sand'." "Yes, Mr Scott, it's a quotation from 'The Walrus and the Carpenter'." "Oh is it? And why did they weep?" I couldn't begin to answer that. "Leave it to me," he said, and I went quickly out of his office. The next day the "Short" appeared in the paper. It was a matter-of-fact statement about the damage done to the pier and esplanade at Umpton-on-Sea, and it ended with the question, "What are our safety engineers going to do about it?" No quotation from Lewis Carroll. That was my last attempt to be funny in a *Manchester Guardian* leader.

RD: Did Scott support your judgement on crucial issues?

NC: Oh yes. For example, I once wrote a long leader attacking some aspect of Hallé concert policy; and the Committee made the occasional protest that I could do more to help the orchestra. One or two protests were also made in Newman's time, but Scott stood by his critic, always.

When I was quite young, thirtyish, I was in charge of the daily back-page column: in those days it was the blue riband of journalism. Joseph Conrad sent in an article and, although at the time I was a great Conrad fan, especially of *Lord Jim* and *Victory*, I didn't think this article was up to standard. I took it to Scott and, without even looking at it, he said, "The column is your responsibility, Cardus, and if you don't think this article is good enough, send it back to Conrad." It was wonderful of Scott to put so much trust in me.

MUSIC CRITICISM

RD: What do you see as the rôle of the music critic?

NC: That is a taxing question, and I suppose every critic would answer it in a different way. I can only answer it in my own way. Except for my period in Australia, I have never considered that my job as critic is to educate the public. In fact, I have never in my life written a music notice with the public in mind. I have been absolutely selfish and egocentric in my writing on music: I have written solely to clarify my own impressions.

In my own way I've tried to be an artist. A composer has some impressions of life, and he expresses them in music; I go to a concert and I get some impressions from music—whether they are right or wrong I don't know; they are subjective—and then I put into writing what I have felt about Beethoven, Mozart, Franz Lehár, or whoever. I try to produce a piece of writing that will satisfy me, and give me pleasure to write. If my writing gives pleasure to my readers then I am grateful, but I must insist that I set out, first and foremost, to please myself.

If I were pushed into a corner and asked, "How many times, on finishing an article, have you smitten the table and said, 'By God, that's good'?" I would reply, "Not more than ten or twenty times in my whole life." Your technique pulls you through; you know you haven't made a fool of yourself. You're like a good cricketer: he knows how to play a good ball and how to play a bad ball; and a writer knows how to avoid a clumsy phrase, a bad sentence. But very seldom, if ever, do you come away from your desk thinking, "What I have written expresses everything I have felt about that experience." I am only consoled by the thought of the number of times I have achieved a half-success and by the fact that no great artist has ever smitten the table and said, "I'm satisfied." I'm perfectly certain that Beethoven never did this: he hammered out his music, note by note, bar by bar. No composer has written with such extreme facility as Mozart did, but there was no conceit in him. He didn't slap himself on the shoulder and say, "My God, Wolfgang, you *have* written well this morning." He once wrote a letter to his father to say that he couldn't write down the notes quickly enough. They came to him like ideas from heaven, and he was grateful to the spirit that was inspiring him. It is only the second-rate composer, the second-rate writer, who is satisfied with his work, and believes that it is *his* work.

If I were the editor of a newspaper, and only musicians read the notices of my music critic, I would sack him; and I would deal equally severely with any cricket writer, if only cricketers read his column. A critic must write from the fullness of his personality, and so you'll be a dull critic if music is your only love. My belief will always be that a critic, like a composer, should *produce* something. A critic's job—if I may use pompous language—is to produce literature. But few critics write prose which is more easily identifiable than the "prose" of the latest White Paper or the Trade Descriptions Act. If a young man wanted to join the reporters' room, Scott didn't say, "Have you got a good news sense?" or "Do you know shorthand?" Those questions might come later on. His first question was, "Can you write? Please let me have some specimens of your *prose*." I doubt if any editor, nowadays, asks a budding music critic, "Can you write?"

Culture, to me, means the development of human consciousness. I look upon the arts not in a formal or a highbrow way. I've gained as much cultural pleasure from Marie Lloyd singing "Our lodger's such a nice young man" as I have from Hamlet's "To be, or not to be", because they are both revelations of life. Marie Lloyd, by playing the part of the daughter of a loose woman, gave in a few lines a picture of Cockney life; just as Hamlet in a few lines gives you a philosophical view of life.

I wouldn't engage on my paper a music critic or a drama critic who doesn't know who Bobby Charlton is. Sport is a part of life. Shakespeare knew Falstaff and Sir Toby Belch; he also knew Lear and Macbeth. The arts are the *eyes* of human awareness, and we must see all of life. We mustn't live in the company of Bach all the time. Bach was the last person in the world who would have spent all his time listening to Bach; he didn't spend all his time in the organ-loft. I would encourage any young man of 18 or 19 who wanted to be a music critic or a conductor or a pianist to involve himself in things outside his art.

People are always asking me, "How can you reconcile writing about cricket with writing about music?" In heaven's name, why not? Nearly all great artists have had some ordinary enjoyment. Nobody objected to Mozart playing billiards. Strauss played that German card-game Skat all day. Toscanini's great passion was to watch wrestling on TV. Why shouldn't a writer be as thrilled by an innings from Denis Compton as by a Toscanini performance of a Beethoven symphony? And why shouldn't he be able to write as interestingly about both? Cricket, like music, is a form of human expression.

My whole philosophy is to see, and respond to, as much of human existence as I can. We're only sent here for a certain period. We're given by God a marvellous receiving-set and we must develop it, which we can only do by practice: by reading, by listening. If a young person asks me, "How can I learn to listen to music?" I say: "*Listen* to it. By all means use a textbook, if you want to find out what a diminished seventh is, or a plagal cadence, but beware of the musicologist." "A musicologist," Beecham said to me one day, "is a man who can read music but cannot hear it." That should be a warning to all who want to learn the art of listening; it also illustrates why I object to formal education that does not include a living experience of the senses, the emotions. And all education, and all life, should be savoured and salted by humour and wit: without them, you're lost.

RD: If you were giving advice to an aspiring young critic, what are the common pitfalls you would warn him against?

NC: First of all, the pitfall of being an adjudicator with a score in front of him. He must be careful not to have a prejudiced idea, before the performance begins, of how the music should sound. There are no widely differing views on conducting second-rate works, but, when you come to a masterpiece, there are many different ways of interpreting it and of dealing with the composer's instructions. The composer may label a movement *andante cantabile*, but no two musicians will interpret that marking in the same way. They will have different ideas of basic tempo, rhythmic emphasis, *rubato*.

I was present once when George Szell was rehearsing with Schnabel, and they had a difference of opinion on tempi in one of Beethoven's concertos—I forget which. Szell got very, very impatient: "Artur, I have seen the manuscript in Vienna, in the museum. I have seen it in the *Handschrift* of Beethoven. I have seen the metronome mark written by the pen of Beethoven." "Yes," Schnabel replied, "and I have seen his metronome. It could never have been very accurate."

One day Hamilton Harty was rehearsing the Hallé in the second symphony of Elgar, with Elgar present. During the *scherzo* Elgar suddenly cried out, "Not so fast." Harty turned round and said, "But, Elgar, you have written here *presto*." And Elgar retorted, "I've changed my mind." He hadn't changed his mind to the extent of making a *presto* movement into an *adagio*, but he had now got—*that day*—a slightly different idea of what the basic tempo should be.

Mahler once said—and this should be printed in letters of gold on every music critic's desk—"Not all the music is in the notes." The notes are symbols; and the great conductor, the great interpretative artist, is the man who can treat these symbols as flexible, never static, so that he can have new insights into the music at each performance.

No one can say that he has understood the whole of Beethoven and expressed it to the public. No one. I'd like to tell you a very moving story about the last weeks of Toscanini's life. A friend of mine went to see him: there he was, at the age of about 90, and his bed was covered with Beethoven scores. Toscanini, with tears in his eyes, said to this friend, "I have been conducting them all wrong, all my life." He didn't mean that he had been conducting the Beethoven symphonies incorrectly or had been giving false interpretations, but that he had found some new clues, some new insights, about phrasing or rhythm or tonal balance. Only those who have *steeped* themselves in music know how music can change and yet not change: it is like the movement of the sea. If you watch the tide come in every day, you might think it comes in, wave upon wave, in exactly the same pattern and motion; but above the main current (equivalent to the basic tempo) there can be fluctuations of the ebb and flow. This is what the great interpretative

artists—the Toscaninis and the Furtwänglers—know. And—
to change the metaphor slightly—when we come to the
flow and movement of a Haydn or a Mozart symphony, no
conductor has surpassed the amazing flight of a Beecham
performance: the music seemed to take wing and move of its
own volition.

Interpretation is a mystery no one can explain. How could
Yehudi Menuhin, at the age of 16, suddenly penetrate to the
very inside, the soul, of the Elgar concerto? In 1932 Yehudi
was invited to record the concerto, with Elgar conducting the
LSO to mark his own 75th birthday. It must be unique in the
history of the gramophone for a teenage soloist to record a major
work without having previously given a public performance
of it.

How could a former telephone operator, a girl born in
Preston, who had scarcely heard of Mahler until, in her mid-
thirties, she was introduced to *Das Lied von der Erde*—how could
she so astonish Bruno Walter? He once said to me: "Kathleen
Ferrier gets closer to the heart of Mahler than many great
German and Austrian singers I have heard, even though they
were born in the land where Mahler's music is as well known
as Lancastrian idioms are to factory girls in Preston and Blackburn. Kathleen, in a year or two, has begun to sing Mahler as
though she had been born and bred in the Mahler tradition."
Interpretation is a gift, and I can only explain its source by
repeating the words of Mozart when he was talking about
inspiration: it is a gift from above.

RD: What would you say to a young critic about the use of
jargon?

NC: Langford never used technical language; Newman, only
when he had to. Scott wanted all his critics to be discreet in
their use of technical language: he sometimes made me take
out one or two phrases. Scott used to say: "Can't we avoid
these phrases? The person of average intelligence will read
them and not understand them." It has always been a mystery
to me why music critics make a parade of technical language:
contrary motion, chromaticism, modulation, and so on. A
musician already knows whether a chord is a dominant ninth
or a diminished seventh; the average layman doesn't know
what it means. If a critic says that the structure of a work is

complex, the texture diaphanous, and the key-sequences pro-
gressive, it will not mean anything to most readers; as for the
musician, he will know it already or he can find it out for himself. So the critic has fallen between two stools.

You don't find a drama critic talking about the inverted
stresses in *Macbeth*; we don't contemplate Virgil only in terms
of spondees and dactyls. Shaw in the 1890s wrote a marvellous
parody of the scientific style of music criticism. He showed
how a drama critic—if he were to write in the same way that
dry-as-a-bone music critics do, with all their supertonics—
would disembowel Hamlet's "To be, or not to be": "Shakespeare, dispensing with the customary exordium, announces the
subject at once in the infinitive, . . . after a short connecting
passage in which, brief as it is, we recognise the alternative and
negative forms on which so much of the significance of the
repetition depends. Here we reach a colon; and a pointed
pository phrase, in which the accent falls decisively on the
relative pronoun, brings us to the first full-stop."

What happens, I suppose, is that late at night the poor critic
lacks ideas, so he conjures up some good old jargon about the
modulation to E flat and the number of suspensions and
inversions. This is merely descriptive. Kant made an important
distinction between description and analysis: anybody with
intelligence can be descriptive, but it takes a bigger mind to be
analytic. By "analytic", he didn't mean dealing just with the
anatomy of a given subject; he meant the making of a synthesis,
so that the subject can be seen in a new and clearer way.

There was a time when most music critics wrote like school-
masters. Then we had a whole school of critics, such as Arthur
Symons, who were not technical writers and had not been
trained in an academy. Shaw was not a professional musician:
he learned music in his home, and from all the operas he went
to as a boy. He had more knowledge of music than many people
imagine, but he didn't write in a narrow, academic way. He
wrote about music as though he were writing about Ibsen;
Shaw saw music as an expression of life. After Shaw, there was a
succession of fine critics, including one or two magnificent
writers on music who, I am sad to say, are all but forgotten:
Richard Capell of the *Telegraph*, for example, who wrote a most
beautiful book about Schubert's songs. He would write about
a concert with feeling and humanity—in much the same way

that he would have written about a Shakespeare play—translating into graceful English prose what the music had meant to him.

It was Stravinsky who announced that music doesn't mean anything except itself and cannot be written about. I cannot describe what Beethoven's fifth symphony means, as an object outside my own mind; but I can at least try to describe what it means to *me*. All criticism is a subjective reaction. The only difference between the professional critic's reactions and the average layman's is that the critic, by the nature of his job, has become a specialist. Most men and women who go to a concert have probably been out at work all day, whereas the critic will have spent X hours with his scores.

The layman will say, "I don't like this work. I don't like it at all," implying that therefore it is no good. If it is in fact a great work, the experienced critic will be able to say, "I don't like it, but it is undoubtedly a masterpiece." The critic's subjective reactions, his nervous-system, his bloodstream, and his adrenalin, don't like this piece of music; but his training, his rational mind, and his standards of comparison, tell him that it is a masterpiece.

I could name one or two very great masterpieces that I don't particularly like: for instance, the St Matthew Passion. I can't tune in to it. There is something lacking in my receiving-set. My sense of comparative values convinces me that it is a great work, but it doesn't—as they say in Lancashire—strike on my box, and the loss is mine. But if a layman came up to me and said, "What a dreadful work it is," I would say to him, "Don't be a fool. It is a masterpiece." That is the difference between the professional critic and the amateur.

RD: Desmond Shawe-Taylor, when reviewing a book by David Cairns, said that his prose had a touch of vintage Cardus, with deeper scholarship. How do you react to that?

NC: I'm quite certain that Cairns does have what Desmond would call "deep scholarship". So did Donald Tovey—he probably knew more about the technical make-up of music than some composers do. I'm sure that a Toveyan analysis of a Beethoven symphony would have astonished Beethoven!

Although the deep scholarship Desmond talks about is something to be admired, it isn't relevant to *my* purpose. I believe in knowing what is necessary for my occupation; but if it comes to a question of scholarship, I should like to have the services of an orchestra for a couple of days. I would then challenge Mr Cairns and Mr Shawe-Taylor—assuming that we all three knew the technique of conducting—to go through the whole of *Tristan* without a score, and make as few mistakes as I would make.

A *Times* literary critic, who no doubt was *full* of scholarship, once said that I wrote round cricket—writing amusing stories about Emmott Robinson and purple passages about the style of Woolley, and calling Charlie Macartney "the Figaro of cricket"—but that I didn't seem to have a great technical knowledge of the game. Having been a professional cricketer, I took my technical knowledge for granted and I assumed that my readers would take it for granted: I therefore never felt the need to display my knowledge. I take the technique of cricket as naturally as I take my own breathing. When I met you this morning, I didn't say, "Good morning, Robert, I'm breathing well today and my circulation seems to be normal." We both took that for granted.

"Deep scholarship" is information which my creative sieve rejects in the process of writing. The critic should not assume the mantle of teacher; people don't want to read about a singer's intonation or his handling of *melismata*. Only a few hundred people, or at most a few thousand, will have been to the concert. The rôle of the critic is to *compensate* all those who couldn't attend.

Very few people have worked harder than I have to know and understand music. I know only one man who did work harder, and that was Newman. And he was the first to laugh at what is called "scholarship". I've met some great Shakespearian scholars who couldn't distinguish good acting from bad acting in a Shakespeare play.

Lord Chesterfield said, "Wear your learning, like your watch, in a private pocket: and do not merely pull it out and strike it; merely to show that you have one." I want the scholar to carry his scholarship as he carries his cloak. I don't want him to be submerged and overweighted and disguised by a *cowl* of scholarship, so that you can't hear his voice or see his face. I would warn every young writer to keep his scholarship to himself. Never let your reader know you've got it.

RD: I'm sure you would advise the young critic to avoid the pitfall of over-seriousness.

NC: Humour is one of the things I miss most nowadays in music criticism. When I was young I used to read Newman, John Runciman of the *Saturday Review*, Gerald Cumberland who was music critic in Manchester for the *Courier*, and Bernard Shaw, whose writings on music were reprinted in book form. All of these critics were witty, in the same way that Max Beerbohm and A. B. Walkley were, when they wrote about the theatre. Today I find no wit, either in drama criticism or in music criticism.

Many notices stick in my mind that made me laugh when I was a boy. The great critics wrote not only with wit, but with distinction; they did much more than a mere reporting job. Of course the poor critic of today has very little space, but surely in 500 words he could say something with charm and wit? Wit is what I miss—and not only in music criticism. We don't hear a lot of wit in the House of Commons nowadays; nor, it seems, at universities. A few years ago, I described Webern's *Six Pieces*, Op. 6 as "orchestral bowel releases (without odour)". Someone from the Faculty of Music at the University of London promptly wrote to the editor of the *Guardian*, protesting at what he called my "offensive solecism". I replied that the reader's "solemnly censorious objection to my description of the Webern encourages me to suggest that the University of London might do well to start a Faculty of Humour, as an adjunct to the University's present Faculty of Music".

RD: Do you know of any amusing or unusual occurrences during concerts?

NC: Sir Compton Mackenzie once told me a delightful story about Elgar. Elgar stopped in at the Athenæum one Saturday and said, "Henry Wood is going to conduct my second symphony in the Queen's Hall tonight. Let's go together, Monty." They reached their front-row seats in the circle just as Henry Wood was about to begin the symphony. The tempo didn't suit Elgar, and he suddenly began singing the opening bars and banging the ledge in front of him in time to the tempo *he* would have preferred. All the people near him were calling out "Sh-Sh-Sh" to this silly, ignorant man who obviously didn't know anything about music. . . . He was only the composer.

There was a riot in Paris in 1913 at the *première* of *Sacre du Printemps* of Stravinsky. There was a ground-swell of protests from the beginning of the performance, and, when the curtain opened on the *Danse des adolescents*, there was an uproar. Stravinsky was enraged by the shouts "*Ta gueule*", "shut up". He left the hall, and backstage he found Diaghilev flicking the house lights in an effort to quell the riotous audience.

I can't remember witnessing any non-musical explosion in a concert hall. I don't remember anybody fainting or anybody misbehaving. I have very seldom heard booing. I hear more booing now than in the old days because in public people tend to be more expressive, more vocal. At one time, disapproval used to be shown by a short silence followed by a round of polite applause—this was much more devastating than booing.

RD: How do you prepare for a concert? Let's suppose that next week you are going to a concert consisting of a Berlioz overture, a Beethoven piano concerto, and the first performance of an orchestral work—shall we say a sinfonietta by Malcolm Arnold?

NC: The Beethoven I would know, and I wouldn't need to look at my score before, or during, the concert; but I would get a score of the new work and if possible attend one or two rehearsals. I would never go to a concert if I didn't know 75 per cent of the music more or less by heart. If the sinfonietta impressed me, I would devote the main part of my *Guardian* notice to it; I would make a short comment about the concerto, and probably not mention the Berlioz overture at all.

Nowadays many critics commit themselves to clear-cut opinions after only one hearing, but I wouldn't dream of being dogmatic about a new work, even if I had been to a rehearsal. I need time to *live* with a new work and allow it to enter my bloodstream. That is why I am against the atrocious and utterly imbecile custom in this country of writing concert notices on the night. In Germany and Austria, notices used to be published —perhaps they still are—two or three days after a concert. Why should "First with the news" apply to the arts? Is it necessary to read a notice the very next morning? After all, it is a concert, not a football match. You don't just want the result: Malcolm Arnold 4—von Karajan 0. You want a considered account of the music, and the critic can't do this on the night, especially if he has to write about a new work. If readers can wait a week for the *Observer* critic's views or the *Sunday Times* critic's views, why can't they wait a couple of days for the views of the critic of the *Guardian*?

In the old days, when I was in Manchester, a Hallé concert used to finish at quarter to ten, and there was no strict deadline for the "copy": you could write till 1 or 2 in the morning if you wished. But today, because of the rush of national-newspaper production, the critic has only three-quarters of an hour to write his notice. This is not fair to the critic; it is not fair to the performers; and it is certainly not fair to the composer, who may have spent one or two years on a major work, only to find it dispatched in half an hour's writing.

I sometimes hear a critic boast that he has written about a new work solely from a reading of the score. This is absolute nonsense, because the composer himself doesn't know what a work sounds like until he has heard it played. Wagner sometimes made alterations after a first rehearsal, and Mahler, who had an unusually fine ear for orchestration, was always altering his scores.

A critic often has to go to four concerts in a week. Criticism has become too much of a business. I remember Ernest Newman's advice years ago to a young man who wanted to be a critic. Newman warned him not to become a critic and said, "Enjoy your music." He then told the story of an old French count who used to spend every evening at the *salon* of a very lovely woman. One day a friend said, "If you get so much happiness from being with Mlle So-and-so, why don't you marry her?" "But," the count protested, "if I married her, who would I go to visit in the evenings?" "And so," Newman concluded, "you must regard music not as your wife but as your mistress."

What I have been saying about critics applies also to performers. The ideal interpreter of music is the person who has a professional technique together with the amateur approach. Performances should be creative. Two things that are spoiling the spontaneity of performances are the routine professional approach and what I call the traffic of music. The pace is too fast. The concert pianist of today probably makes more public appearances in one month than Schnabel or Paderewski did in six.

I once put a question about Furtwängler to the leader of the Berlin Philharmonic, Henry Holst, a magnificent violinist, who later came to Manchester as principal professor of the violin at the Royal Manchester College of Music. Furtwängler had a stuttering kind of beat: he used to begin a work with a cross between an up-beat and a down-beat. I said to Henry Holst, "How do you follow Furtwängler's beat?", and he smilingly replied, "Do we?" But Furtwängler always gave me the impression that he was *exploring* a work, finding new veins in it. He was like every good explorer. If, in a symphony, he came to a nook or a cranny that he hadn't been through before, he knew how to get through it. He didn't get stuck. He knew the art of tunnelling. To be an amateur means to maintain the freshness of love and exploration: whenever you play a work, you mustn't give the impression that you are going over old ground.

Toscanini, in his last years, suffered a hardening of the musical arteries. Just before the war, when he conducted his famous series at the Queen's Hall, I was most disappointed by three or four concerts: the technical presentation of the music was marvellous, but there was a lack of spontaneous combustion. I felt: "The music is being played mechanically. Nothing can stop it. There will be no visitations." I certainly never felt that of Furtwängler's conducting, nor of Beecham's.

Some people used to say that Beecham had no baton technique, but orchestras would have played all night for him. Toscanini once described Beecham as an amateur, which, in one sense of the word, he was. Without ever being irresponsible, he was the least routine of any conductor I have known. He lived in more leisurely times than now and he treated music as an adornment, a witty and enchanting addition to the graces of life. Beecham put music on the same level as a beautiful flower, a beautiful woman, or a beautiful wine. Music for him was not burdened with heavy, German, philosophical or metaphysical implications; music was just lovely sound.

For Furtwängler, on the other hand, music was a way of life. Music was to Furtwängler what religion is to a saint. Music was his path for discovering the meaning of life. Toscanini, when he was young, had the gift of making music sing, but in his later years I felt he became something of a dictator-professional. Klemperer's career was a wonderful evolution. In his old age, he would sit in front of his orchestra and conduct with no arm-waving whatever, just delicate movements of hands and fingers. When he set a Beethoven or a Brahms symphony in motion, it was as though he were saying *Fiat lux*. I used to imagine that, if he then left the rostrum, the music would have continued by its own volition, with the notes going like stars to their destined courses.

Klemperer was a conductor of rare genius. I have asked many orchestral players, "What is the secret of Klemperer's greatness?" or "What is the secret of Bruno Walter's greatness?" They don't really know; they can't put their finger on it. Some players say, "There's *something* about him, about his personality"; some say, "His tempi are free and expressive"; some say, "He doesn't keep us tightly reined. He allows us to play"; some say, "He has a marvellous judgement of dynamics." None of these observations—although all of them are true —get us any nearer to the solution of the mystery of personality.

Why should one person play a scale on the piano and make it sound ordinary, and yet another person can make that same scale sound entrancing? Music to me is one of the most mysterious things in the whole world, but I don't look upon the art of music in a highbrow way. I don't take too austere a view of music: I believe that a Franz Lehár waltz and a Johann Strauss waltz are just as marvellous on their plane as the G minor symphony of Mozart is on its plane.

If we could say why a great man *is* a great man, in any walk of life, then we would have discovered one of the secrets of human life; for centuries, philosophers have been looking for the answer. If Jesus Christ came into the world today, no one would be able to explain His divinity and His humanity. I'm inclined to doubt if people would understand Him or believe in Him any more than they did during His first coming. In a wild moment, at a riotous dinner-party some years ago, I said that if Christ ever came back to the world, He would be crucified again, and, what is more, the television cameras would be there!

RD: For years you have expressed objections to score-following at concerts. I usually take a score to a concert because it helps me to hear the texture of the music, the inner parts. I also find that to use my visual as well as my aural sense increases my involvement, my participation, in the music-making; just as, conversely, background music enhances the predominantly visual appeal of a film.

NC: A music critic is supposed to have the score in his head, not his head in the score. I never saw Langford at a concert with a score, because he *knew* them all. But once, on my night off, I went to a chamber concert in Manchester, and I *paid* to go in. Included in the programme was a work by an English composer—I forget who. It didn't strike me as a very interesting piece of music. Then I caught sight of Langford; his eyes were glued to the score! I'd never seen that in my life. In the interval I said to him, "Good heavens, Langford, did you find this work so difficult that you had to follow it with the score?" "No," he replied, "it was so tedious that I decided to go through Beethoven's Op. 132."

I laugh quietly to myself when I see all my colleagues at a concert, each with his head buried in the score. I could understand it if they were listening to the first performance of an atonal work . . . I was going to add "by Schoenberg", but I suppose that, compared to Stockhausen and John Cage, Schoenberg is now old-hat. The joke is that if critics need a score at the Festival Hall, where they have enough light—and, believe me, I've seen critics with a score of the overture to the *Barber of Seville*—how do they manage without a score in the dark of an opera house at a performance of *The Ring* or *Moses and Aaron*? I have never been able to understand how you can listen to music and read it at the same time. For me, listening and reading are two entirely different functions.

A now almost-forgotten French musicologist, Jules Combarieu, suggested that the musical faculty was a thing in itself and that it was controlled from somewhere behind the third frontal cerebellum—or something like that, *pace* all students of anatomy. He tried to prove his theories by experiments and by observation. For example, he found that some people who had had concussion, or a similar accident, forgot their name and forgot where they lived, but hadn't forgotten their music. I am certain there is something in this, and that there is a part of the brain—I can almost put my finger on it—which controls the memory of music. I spoke to a psychologist about this a few weeks ago. Recent research suggests that there are two basic types of memory, each controlled by a different part of the brain: episodic memory, which has to do with past events; and semantic memory, which includes the memory of language. I gather that musical memory is probably nearer to semantic memory; but further research might show that semantic memory and musical memory are separate. Combarieu's pioneering work was obviously on the right lines.

I find it difficult to listen and to follow with the score, and I find it impossible with a work of any complexity. When I listen to a late quartet of Beethoven, I can't even keep my eyes open. I want to go right into *Das Ding an sich*, the thing in itself. I want to leave the visible world and enter into the secret chamber, the mind, of Beethoven. After all, his mind, his incredible musical brain, had ceased to hear anything from the external world.

If I go to a dramatic or picturesque opera such as *Aida* or *Butterfly*, then I want to watch the spectacle as well as listen. But, as I've got older, if I go to an opera which is subtly composed, such as *Tristan*, then I can't watch the stage action. *Tristan* is such an amazing score: every part is woven into a most intricate orchestral and vocal web. The musical faculty is a thing in itself and I do hope the neuropsychologists will go deeper into what Jules Combarieu postulated 60 or 70 years ago.

I remember years ago hearing Schoenberg's *Five Orchestral Pieces* in the Queen's Hall. I took a score with me and held it under my coat: I was reading it as though it were pornographic literature. Newman happened to pass by and, seeing my furtiveness, he said: "My dear Cardus, got a score with you? Well now, do make sure you've got it the right way up. You would make a very bad impression on any member of the public who passed by." In the old days, critics very seldom took scores to concerts; I never saw Newman with one. Scores were a sort of trade secret. We had the scores in our heads. Or at least we pretended we did.

RD: Are you influenced by your moods? Supposing you felt a desire to hear Beethoven. Might you then over-rate a

Beethoven performance, even if the performance in itself was not especially good?

NC: No, I don't think so. The more you want to hear a particular piece of music, the more critical you are. This is a matter of training, because, in the beginning of your career as a critic, you are so much in love with music that even a bad performance doesn't annoy you. When I was young, I must have written enthusiastically about opera productions that would now be called second-rate. Fashions change. In the days when I was deputy to Langford, there were travelling opera companies. It is a curious fact about music in our time that we have a wealth of opera in London, in Wales, in Scotland, where the Scottish Opera has given wonderful performances under the direction of Alec Gibson, but there must be plenty of young people in their twenties, in Manchester, Birmingham, Leeds, and Sheffield, who have had few opportunities to go to a top-class professional production in their own city.

In Manchester we used to have about twenty weeks of opera every year. The travelling companies included the Carl Rosa Opera Company, Joseph O'Mara's Company, and the Moody, Manners Company. From the point of view of production, I don't suppose that the average opera-goer of today would have gone twice to see one of these companies. The operas were produced on a very simple scale because the scenery had to be taken all over the country, but in those days we weren't too concerned about the production, the sets; we went to *hear* the opera.

Now the pendulum has swung the other way: the production has become the tyrant of the opera house. The other day I was reading a notice of a new opera, *Death in Venice*, and I had to go half-way down the column before seeing any mention of Benjamin Britten's music. I've often thought that many beautifully written operas could be staged with nothing but a backcloth, painted with a few symbols. The Chinese used to produce plays this way. The more realistic the stage setting, the more surrealistic it is!

I want more economy in opera production—not so much lavishness. The production should not come between the composer and the audience. The production staff should know the music so intimately that they give you a visual representation

of the composer's imagination. Some of the productions I have
seen in recent years have contradicted that ideal. I went to
Tristan in Bayreuth ten or fifteen years ago. If I had taken to
this production somebody who knew nothing whatever about
the opera or the libretto, and if I had whispered to him, when
the curtain went up, "Where is the set transporting you to?
What are you looking at?" he would never have guessed it was
a ship, even if he had guessed all night. I'm all for symbolism,
but the set bore no resemblance to a ship; that to me was a
distortion. An opera should be produced through the eyes and
ears of the composer.

RD: How long does a performance stay with you? Supposing
that on Monday night you heard Rubinstein play Chopin with
great charm and fineness of touch, and a few days later you
went to a recital given by a much less gifted pianist. Would the
memory of Rubinstein's playing still be with you? If so, would
it affect your objectivity?

NC: All the performances you hear go into the subconscious
and they give you your standards: that's how you *know* if an
artist is not of the top class; that's how you *know* if Rubinstein
himself is not playing as well as he can do—you have a subconscious memory of a better performance by him. Memory is
a gift that some people have and some haven't. If a critic has
got not only a good musical memory but a good aesthetic
memory—so that he can all but re-create the personality of a
player—then he is very fortunate: this, I think is one of the
few gifts I have.

   I may not be able to analyse a score in the way that Donald
Tovey could, but I can re-create an impression. In an almost
clairvoyant way, I can very vividly *hear* Schnabel playing Op.
111; just as vividly as we can remember people we've known
well. You may not have seen them for years, but, if you have
really loved them, you can re-create them, you can still feel
their presence. And I can do the same with a concert, a recital,
an opera.

RD: Every newspaper editor seems to have a preoccupation
with topicality, and this has infected arts criticism.

NC: A while ago I wrote an article—not for the *Guardian*—
about the neglect of Delius. The editor wouldn't publish it

because he said that the music of Delius isn't played very often nowadays. *That* was the whole point of my article.

Unless a concert includes a new work, critics seldom devote space to aesthetic or technical analysis of the music. If a critic hears a well-known symphony, he will tell you whether or not he approved of the tempi and the tonal balance, but he won't write about the music. There was a time when a critic who went to a performance of the fifth symphony of Beethoven— in the Queen's Hall or at a Hallé concert—would write about the fifth symphony of Beethoven!

How can a critic talk about the merit of a performance if he doesn't tell the reader about the style and characteristics of the work that has been performed? A music critic should relate the performance to his aesthetic conception of the music. I don't mean writing round music: "Fate knocking at the door" and all that nonsense. I don't particularly want a critic to describe a Sibelius symphony in terms of Finnish landscape, but I do want him to tell the reader how a Sibelius symphony differs from, say, a symphony of Mahler, in colour, texture, content, meaning. The idea that music doesn't mean anything, and is just a series of abstract patterns that can't be described, is an absolute falsification of the whole theory of criticism. All any critic can do—whether he is a literary critic, a drama critic, or a music critic—is to write about the impressions a work has made on him.

A critic is not an adjudicator writing a report, giving eight marks out of ten for expression. If a critic writes only about the performance, without describing the work, he is like a cricket correspondent who tells his readers about the batting and the bowling, but omits to describe the state of the wicket. A great critic such as Newman used to give an aesthetic account of the work that had been played; only then would he tell you about the performance. He often said, "You can't describe a performance in a vacuum. You can't tell the public if the tempi were right until you explain to them what kind of a movement it is. An *adagio* in Bruckner is quite different from an *adagio* in Brahms."

Some critics say to me, "I *can't* write about the fourth symphony of Brahms because everybody has heard it." This is not true. Every time a Brahms symphony or the G minor of Mozart is played—in the Festival Hall or at a Hallé concert, or in Bournemouth or Glasgow—some young people in the audience are hearing it for the first time. If anyone tells me that the fifth symphony of Beethoven or the "Unfinished" symphony of Schubert is hackneyed, I reply: "There are no hackneyed masterpieces. There are only hackneyed critics." A music critic should have a sufficiently alive and receptive mind and imagination to find new aspects to write about. If I got to the stage when I had nothing more to say about a work, then I wouldn't go and listen to it. But there are very, very few works about which new ideas don't occur to me, or about which old ideas don't return in a different guise.

It is ages since I read a notice in which a critic had written about the "Eroica" as though he had just heard it for the first time. The development section of the first movement is one of the most amazing passages in all music: if you bear in mind how long ago it was written, it makes Stravinsky and Schoenberg sound like freshmen. I could always find something new to write about the "Eroica", that volcanic disturbance, the chaos that was to be changed into cosmos.

Because of the rapid distribution of newspapers all over the country, it is now more important than ever for a critic who is with a national newspaper to describe the music as Newman did. When I was a boy, the *Manchester Guardian* represented north of England, Lancashire. In those days you couldn't get a copy of *The Times* in Manchester until evening. There might then have been some justification for a critic to devote quite a lot of space to the performance because a number of his readers would have been to the concert. Nowadays, if a London-based critic writes a lot about the performance, it may be very interesting to the few thousand who were at the concert, but it won't be of much interest to the reader in Glasgow.

Why do some critics seem to assume that nothing new can be said about a well-known work? Any great masterpiece—whether of literature, music, or painting—has a different significance in different periods. It is only the second-rate work that says the same thing to different generations. What we think today of Bach is entirely different from what we thought of him sixty years ago. I remember a time when Bach was regarded as a pedantic, technically dry, polyphonic composer —for scholars only. Today I meet many young people who are as eager to hear Bach as I—at their age—was eager to hear

Beethoven. They go to hear Bach because he says something to their hearts as well as to their minds. He is now looked upon almost as a romantic composer!

Music criticism should keep a sense of proportion. Critics have got to write about modern music but they should also write about the established repertoire; because your reactions to composers change according to your developing experience of life and of music. For instance, if this week I had to write an article about Wagner, it would be very different from the chapter I wrote for *Ten Composers* 30 years ago. The more you discuss a composition, or any work of art, the more alive it becomes to the public. Take, for example, the famous description by Walter Pater of the *Mona Lisa*: "The presence that rose thus so strangely beside the waters is expressive of what in the ways of a thousand years men had come to desire. Hers is the head upon which all 'the ends of the world are come', and the eyelids are a little weary." Leonardo would have been astonished by this. He might have said, "I never intended my painting to be seen in this way." But there was a period when that essay by Walter Pater illumined the *Mona Lisa* for thousands of people. I remember going to the *Mona Lisa* and seeing her through the eyes of Walter Pater: his description enriched my imagination. Then, in time, I grew away from Pater's conception of the painting; I developed my own way of experiencing it.

Pater's aesthetic sense should be a lesson to many of today's highly-trained critics. If a critic looks at the *Mona Lisa*, or at any work of art, and sees just the technical ability—sees it only in terms of texture and perspective—then he is not seeing the work as *art*. In the same way, I am not at all interested in reading a criticism of the newest music of Stockhausen if I am only given a description of the technical qualities. What I want to know is whether Stockhausen, through the use of his technique—a technique which would have made Beethoven think that music had gone off its head—is *saying* anything. I am not interested in being told that Stockhausen is using this or that atonal method. I want to know if Stockhausen has produced something which will touch my imagination.

In 1971 I wrote in a *Guardian* notice: "Stockhausen has enjoyed a good innings, but now his sins are finding him out . . . a computer will be fed to compose like Stockhausen. I could compose like him myself, if I gave a year's hard study to his system, his know-how." A few days later, a man who said he was Stockhausen's London agent invited me to Cologne for twelve months' free tuition from the composer. I would be given a £1,000 scholarship; but if, at the end of the year, I couldn't compose like Stockhausen, I would have to return the money. I said I might consider the offer if Stockhausen would agree to teach me to compose like Franz Lehár! A day or so later, someone wrote to the *Guardian* saying that I was very much mistaken if I thought I could compose like Stockhausen after a year's study. He ended his letter by saying I could manage it *in a week*.

RD: No doubt people sometimes ask you why you don't write more about contemporary composers.

NC: I *am* interested in the modern composer but he is using a different language from the one that I—and any other critic of my age—was brought up to understand. The language that composers use today is virtually a foreign language: I haven't learned it and, what is more, most of the composers themselves haven't learned it!

Beecham said, "A beautiful melody enters the mind with facility and leaves it with reluctance." My own view of much modern music is the very reverse of this: it enters the mind with great difficulty and leaves it with alacrity!

All the arts are now in a melting-pot period. This is not the first time. It has happened, throughout the history of art, whenever a great tradition has ended. Politically and sociologically and, to use an old-fashioned word, morally, the world is in a greater state of flux than at any time since the beginning of recorded history. We now give scarcely a second thought to innovations which 20 or 30 years ago would have astonished us. We take for granted that on our TV sets we can see a man walking on the moon. We take for granted that we have a machine called the computer which can add up our bank balances—and get them all wrong! We have children of 14 and 15 knowing all the secrets of life, knowing more about sex than Shakespeare ever did, but not being able to say as many good things about it.

The arts are being stirred up in this terrific melting-pot. Forty or fifty years from now, some composer will sum up this period in a way that the pioneers of today cannot imagine, and are probably not even *trying* to imagine, because they are so absorbed in their experimental work. But there have been times in the history of music—and I could choose similar examples from the other arts—when the *avant-garde* have half-imagined that they were setting a permanent pattern for the future. At the end of the sixteenth century, the Florentines wanted to escape from the tyranny of the elaborate polyphony of the Italian madrigal. They set out to create an operatic form in which music would be the servant of the words. But, later, Bellini and Donizetti took opera in an entirely different direction: a florid musical style and vocal virtuosity once again became all-important.

Nobody can accurately predict the future of any of the arts, but you can get a good idea of the way an art will develop by studying what happened in the past. I don't know of any composer who has turned music upside-down and has been heard of for long; the really lasting artists have grown like a branch from a tree. It may be an original branch, a branch different in shape from any other branch on the tree, but it is still related to the trunk and, ultimately, to the roots.

All the great composers were influenced by their contemporaries or by earlier composers, or both. In early Beethoven, for example, we can see the shadow of Haydn. Or take one of the most revolutionary composers of the nineteenth century—Wagner. His early opera *Rienzi* shows the fingerprints of Meyerbeer; and even in the operas in which Wagner begins to reveal his genius more fully, such as *Tannhäuser* and *The Dutchman*, Weber is in the background.

At one time Philipp Emanuel Bach was *the* modern composer, and Johann Sebastian was considered to be an old square. When I was young, at least five composers were regarded as being as advanced—in their time—as Stockhausen and the latest atonalists are today, but, if I were to mention their names now, not many people would know who I was talking about. These composers are now in the history books. They did valuable work. They ploughed the land and sowed seeds. Art, like everything else in life, has to go through changes. The artistic pioneer turns the land over and thinks, "My God, I'm going to grow a potato here that will be unlike any other potato. It will look different. It will taste different. The old varieties will be thrown on to the compost heap." And when the new potato is produced it turns out to be related to the Majestic or to Kerr's Pink or to Craig's Royal. It is not a completely new potato. It is just a new variety.

RD: Having written about music for more than 60 years, you have witnessed enormous changes in musical taste.

NC: So much music is being unearthed now that was not played in the nineteenth century. When I was a boy, we all thought that music began with Haydn, around 1760. I was reading only the other night no less an authority than Ernest Newman, who suggested that Monteverdi was a primitive, experimental composer. We now regard Monteverdi as much more than a period composer. We are rediscovering the baroque era and the music of the great polyphonic composers such as Palestrina, William Byrd, and Josquin des Prés. Our present concept of harmony emanated from the church and from traditional plainsong. But church music was an other-worldly, an introvert art. Music had to break free from this concentration on polyphony. Now we can return to it, with the respect of distance.

The changes of fashion during my years as a critic have been dramatic. It would surprise the young people of today, who go to listen to Messiaen and Stockhausen—if they do *listen* to them—to know that when I was in my twenties Richard Strauss was regarded as very *avant-garde*. At around the time of the First War, if I had been asked to name the three or four composers who led the renaissance of English music, rescuing it from Victorianism, I would have chosen Elgar and Delius, as well as Joseph—he usually spelled his name "Josef"—Holbrooke. It would surprise a lot of people to learn that Holbrooke was as eminent a composer, when I was 22 or 23, as Tippett is now. Newman once wrote that there was no young composer in Europe writing such fine and original music as Holbrooke.

Granville Bantock—when I was young—was the Benjamin Britten of the period. We used to pack the Free Trade Hall to hear *Omar Khayyam*; Bantock had a wonderful flair for orchestration. Until Elgar and Bantock arrived, you couldn't claim that English music was orchestrated from a very richly coloured palette. The scoring of composers such as Stanford and Parry and Mackenzie was black and white: much of it sounded like second-rate Brahms.

The advance of our cultural standards in music, since the early 1900s, has been more rapid and more comprehensive than in any other country. Some of the opera singers of earlier this century would today be laughed off the stage. Sometimes, instead of staying within the scene of the drama, they actually used to come to the front of the stage and sing an important aria to the audience. I heard Melba in her old age. She was a marvellous singer: her voice had the ease, the sweetness, and the penetration, of an oboe. I remember her as Mimi in *Bohème*: in the last act she rose up from her bed and sang while sitting up, making an incredible recovery from consumption which was supposed to be killing her.

The first Proms had a wonderful influence on the young in the days before the gramophone, but Henry Wood seldom gave a wholly serious programme. The first half might be devoted to Beethoven, but he would finish with what we called Chappell and Boosey ballads, the kind of music which then used to be sold widely in sheet-music form, sentimental rubbish that would never be sung today: "Grey days are your grey eyes" and "Because you come to me". Even a great *Lieder* singer such as Elena Gerhardt wouldn't have filled the Queen's Hall. If she gave a recital, she would give it in the Wigmore Hall or the Grotrian Hall, to an audience of three or four hundred.

Sir Arthur Sullivan, who as a composer of light music, operetta, had a touch of genius, was looked upon rather condescendingly by the Victorians. They wanted to know why he wasn't writing serious music such as that dreary overture *In Memoriam*, which Queen Victoria liked so much, and *The Lost Chord*: "Seated one day at the organ, I was weary and ill at ease." The Victorians wanted the composer of *Mikado* to write oratorios. Every English composer—Parry and all the rest of them—were expected to write oratorios. Even Elgar had to write *Gerontius* before he could convince the English public that he could compose. And Mendelssohn was accepted in England on the strength of *Elijah* and the *Hymn of Praise*, rather than for his best music—the octet, the orchestral works, and his writing for the piano. In those days we were oratorio-*mad*. Delius in his old age once said of Sir Hubert Parry that if he had lived long enough he would have set the whole Bible to music.

RD: Nowadays it is the final test for a young musician to play, and be well received, in London.

NC: In the Thirties I used to cover all the major concerts and opera productions in both London and Manchester: once or twice a week I used to travel down to London and back to Manchester. Then the Covent Garden season lasted only a short while: a German season of four weeks, beginning in May —*The Ring*, *Tristan*, and *Meistersinger*—and then an Italian season, also of four weeks—*Butterfly*, *Tosca*, and *Rigoletto*. Covent Garden was more or less closed for the rest of the year, except perhaps in the winter when the Carl Rosa or some other opera company would come for two or three weeks. And in those days there wasn't a concert in London every night; now there and several—in the Festival Hall, the Queen Elizabeth Hall, the Albert Hall, St John's, Smith Square, and also the Fairfield Hall in Croydon.

One of the most extraordinary cultural evolutions in my lifetime has been the emergence of England—from an almost barbaric provincialism—as the world's centre of music. The world's musical capitals used to be Vienna and Berlin; and if you wanted to be a singer, you went to study in Milan or in Rome. Nowadays every artist—from Russia, France, Italy, America—wants to perform in London. London is now the hub of the musical world. A conductor who can establish himself at Covent Garden, as Solti did, gains a world-wide reputation. The Opera House in Vienna was once the most famous of all: Mahler, Bruno Walter, Weingartner, conducted there; but I couldn't tell you who is now the music director. And where are the great composers in Italy, France, Austria, or even Germany, if you leave out the work of Stockhausen? He has cashed in on the modern craze for experimentation in the concert hall, including the sound of the washing machine and the breaking-up of pianos.

When I went to Vienna in the Twenties and Thirties, I used to see a lot of young people at concerts. I also saw lots of young people at the Proms. They went to the Proms straight from Lord's or The Oval. They went to cheer Sir Henry Wood just as they had cheered Jack Hobbs: both were part of the English summer scene. But I wouldn't see many youngsters in the audience if I went to a concert in the Queen's Hall in 1930, even if Bruno Walter or Toscanini or Koussevitzky was conducting. When I was a boy, someone from my status in life, from a working-class home, was considered rather prissy, a freak, if he went to a classical concert. Today when I go to a serious concert at the Festival Hall, to hear, for example, a Bruckner symphony, I see any number of young boys and girls, from all types of background. The gramophone and the radio have had an enormous influence in educating young people.

There have been other changes in the musical scene. In the nineteenth century, and up to 1910 or 1920, music in this country was very much dominated by German influence. Wealthy German Jews made Manchester the Munich of England. London too had its German influences. It was considered decidedly low-brow to go to hear *Rigoletto* or *Traviata*. I remember Ernest Newman once finished a notice, when the German season at Covent Garden was over, by saying: "Next week is the beginning of the Italian part of Covent Garden's annual season. When we go to Italian opera we must take the advice of Lord Chesterfield to his son: 'When you leave your cloak in the cloakroom you leave your intellect with it.'"

As a boy I used to pay a shilling to go to the Free Trade Hall and I would stand at the back to hear Beethoven conducted by Richter, but if I wanted to go to *Rigoletto* or *Traviata* I never told my pals. I used to go up to the gallery alone, disguised. I would never admit to anyone that I had been to an *Italian* opera. Alfred Noyes, who in his day was as famous as John Betjeman is now, wrote a poem called "The Barrel-Organ":

> And there, as the music changes,
>   The song runs round again.
> Once more it turns and ranges
>   Through all its joy and pain,
> Dissects the common carnival
>   Of passions and regrets; . . .
>
> Once more *La Traviata* sighs
>   Another sadder song.
> Once more *Il Trovatore* cries
>   A tale of deeper wrong.

"The song runs round again . . . the common carnival. . . .
Once more *La Traviata* . . .": the implication is that the music
is *only* Verdi. In those days music meant Wagner, Beethoven,
and Brahms. Franz Werfel in the Twenties wrote *Verdi—A
Novel of the Opera*. This book helped to put Verdi on the map,
but in some circles in Germany and Austria, even today, his
music is still considered rather provincial.

I never thought I would live to see the day when London
would be the capital of music. I was present when the acorns
were being planted; now the oak tree has grown and grown.
All the world-famous artists come here. Even when great
singers can't sing any more, they still want to sing in London!

We must now beware of making music too cheap, too easy.
To hear music now is as easy as smoking a cigarette. You can
listen to the radio while you shave or while you do the washing-
up. You can hear a Beethoven quartet at any time of the day.
This over-exposure contains a curse, a danger: we must never
lose sight of the fact that music is the most *miraculous* of the arts.

When I was young we used to go to hear the ninth symphony
of Beethoven, and we went in a devout frame of mind. We
might have gone the previous night to see a play by Ibsen—a
moving experience, but an experience made out of life, out of
words. We could relate the behaviour of the characters to the
way people behave in life itself. When Nora Helmer in *A
Doll's House* bangs the door as she stalks out of the house, we
can ask ourselves, "Would a girl do that in everyday life?" But
when you hear the ninth symphony, you cannot say where it
came from. Even with programme music, when a composer
translates stories and events from the visual world, when a
Strauss writes a symphonic poem about Till Eulenspiegel or
Don Quixote, he takes the characters into the world of sound.

To me music remains one of the most incredible mysteries in
the world. A composer picks up his pen and puts black dots—
which have no meaning in themselves—on to a page of manuscript paper. One morning a man named Schubert went into
his study and began writing a lot of notes on staves; the result
was the "Unfinished" symphony. It may not be the greatest
symphony of all time and Schubert wasn't the greatest composer who ever lived, but he was the most heavenly-inspired
of composers, and the most lovable. When I hear the haunting
opening bars—unaccompanied cellos and basses *pianissimo*—I

see this as not only the "Unfinished" symphony but also as the "Unbegun" symphony: when the work begins I feel I am overhearing music that has been playing for a long, long time. The sun does not rise and set; the sun is always shining somewhere. The "Unfinished" symphony is like dawn; its sun has been shining all the time.

When young people go to hear music, I would prefer them not to say, "We're going to a Karajan concert tonight" or "We're going to hear Artur Rubinstein." I want them to go, saying, "We want to hear Beethoven . . . we want to hear Schubert."

RD: How often do you have to wrestle with your conscience before putting your comments, about a performer, on to paper?

NC: That happens very seldom. My main concerns are: Am I finding the right language to express my emotions? Am I being relevant?

The most important gift a critic must have or cultivate is absolute identification with the composer. If a player has a brilliant technique, and is imposing it on me, thrusting it between me and the composer, then this player is a salesman. He is not putting his technique at the service of the composer. He is not acting as a medium. He is selling himself. He is trying to tell me that, à propos of Beethoven, he is a damn fine violinist. If he is that sort of player, a technical player, then let him play Paganini and show off his acrobatics.

I always *try* to be fair: I always try to understand a performance from the performer's point of view. If I feel he is sincerely trying to identify himself with the composer, then I'm not going to worry about a few wrong notes—though I think he should try to play the right notes—if possible!

RD: Have you ever regretted, a day or so later, something that you wrote in a concert notice? Have you ever felt, on reflection, that you had been too harsh?

NC: No, but I've often regretted that I'd not been harsh enough! Though I do remember one occasion when my conscience worked overtime. Kathleen was giving a *Lieder* recital in the Festival Hall, with Gerald Moore as her accompanist: I think it was her first major *Lieder* recital in London.

G

Everybody adored this beautiful woman, this sincere artist. She was singing Schumann's *Frauenliebe und Leben* song-cycle, and when she came to the *Lied*, "Du Ring an meinem Finger" she made gestures to suggest she was looking at a ring on her finger.

When you sing *Lieder*, you convey emotions by the voice and tone colour, and occasionally by the expression on your face, but you don't act; you don't enter the realms of opera. After the concert I felt I had to criticize Kathleen for this. I walked up and down the Embankment for half an hour, and I had to "sleep on it" for the night, before I could bring myself to be critical of this marvellous singer. But critical I *had* to be, and I pointed out in my *Manchester Guardian* notice that she mustn't do this sort of thing: in *Lieder* a singer mustn't make distracting gestures—smiles and movements of the hands and swayings of the head. My notice was like a love letter. I talked about her as "our beloved Kathleen Ferrier"; I said that the traffic of contemporary concert-giving must not be allowed to hurt, even slightly, the style of this artist. But I had to point out that her extra-vocal appeals to our sense of the dramatic were at the expense of true song.

When the notice appeared in print the next morning, I thought, "Good heavens, what will Kathleen be thinking as she reads this?" So I wrote to her, to explain why I had felt obliged to make my criticism, and I even sent her some flowers. She wrote to me, almost by return, a charming and understanding letter. She said she realized that an artist must take notice of criticism and in future she would try to control her unconscious gestures when singing *Lieder*. When she wrote to me she usually signed her letters "Yours, with love", but this time—bless her—it was "Yours sincerely".

I don't think I've ever been cruel as a critic, but I've done my best to annihilate charlatans, put them down for the full count. Today there is more integrity in interpretation than there was 30 or 40 years ago, when so many virtuoso players wanted only to show off their technique. And the general climate of opinion and taste, the aesthetic of music and opera, is much in advance of what it was 40 years ago. If I had done a Rip van Winkle in 1920, and gone into a long slumber, and on waking 50 years later went to a Promenade concert, I would have been astonished: I would have seen young people in the arena waiting for hours, not to hear the *Peer Gynt* suite, but to hear a Bruckner symphony or Mahler's eighth.

But there are many things which I deplore, not so much in the arts as in the conduct of life itself. If I woke up this year, after going to sleep in 1920, and I walked down the streets of London, I would think I had been sucked into one of the circles of Dante's *Inferno*. It is incredible to realize how much we have adapted ourselves to noise and pollution and the idiotic over-use of the car. I saw a traffic block this morning—eight enormous cars—and I counted the people in them: there was a total of eight people in those eight cars. One of the great paradoxes of today is the contradiction between the standard of taste and human response in the arts—and I'm not talking about quickly-passing *avant-garde* movements—and the increasing inhumanity in the material aspects of life.

If a young *avant-garde* were to come up to me and say, "Stockhausen is in fashion. John Cage is in fashion", I would refer him to a report that came out only the other day, written by the general secretary of one of our leading orchestras. He had analysed which composers in the last twelve months had attracted the biggest audiences to concerts in London. Beethoven, Brahms, Schubert, and Mozart, were top of the league; the *avant-garde* composers were low down in the second division—they weren't even contending for promotion.

RD: We both admire Shaw's criticism for its wit and humour, but can we forgive him for often being cavalier in his treatment of performers and composers?

NC: Shaw, in everything he did, was a great propagandist. Almost all his plays advance some sociological or ethical view-point. He wrote one play as a work of art—non-polemic—and that was *Saint Joan*. As a music critic, Shaw was one of the first to fight for Wagner; as a drama critic, he attacked Shakespeare. He didn't attack Shakespeare as a poet; he attacked him for his ideas. He said Shakespeare's ideas had no more validity than those of a Tammany boss in the politics of America (a foretaste of Watergate). Shaw said that Shakespeare's plays were like operas with marvellous scores, but when you came to look at the ideas, the philosophy, you found them to be second-rate, lacking in originality. Shaw of course was fighting for Ibsen, who, like Wagner, was widely regarded as the anti-Christ.

The idea that Shaw didn't know much about music is non-sense. He had a most comprehensive knowledge of music, and he knew a good deal more than some of the academicians who disliked him. Even as a music critic, Shaw was a propagandist. England was in the grip of the oratorio, obsessed with Handel. Wagner was objected to by the academicians as a composer who couldn't write a melody and couldn't write for the voice. Brahms was the great classical bulwark against the flood of Wagner, which the academicians thought was going to destroy the whole field of music. Shaw decided to fight for Wagner and he was unmerciful. Shaw was outrageous in the way he attacked Brahms, contending that he was "nothing more than a sentimental voluptuary with a wonderful ear".

Shaw saw music not so much with the eyes of an artist, but as a social reformer, using music as one of the means to achieve a better civilization. As a music critic, Shaw was both entertaining and ruthless. I've never understood the law of libel, but Shaw said things that would never be allowed today. Sir Hubert Parry—or, as he was then, Dr Hubert Parry—was always writing oratorios. One of them, *Job*, was performed at the Gloucester Festival. Shaw was then writing for a fashionable weekly, the *World*—he used to contribute a 2,000-word article each week. He said he didn't go to Gloucester to hear Dr Parry's new oratorio because it was the easiest thing in the world not to go to Gloucester. But, sooner or later, *Job* was performed in London, and Shaw had to go. He wrote a most devastating notice and said that only Job would have the patience to listen to this tedious oratorio. Shaw also said that the best place for it, along with another of Parry's oratorios, *Judith*, was a blazing fire.

I also remember a notice Shaw wrote of a recital at the St James's Hall, which was situated between Piccadilly and Regent Street. I forget who the pianist was—perhaps Sophie Menter, or it may even have been Paderewski. "I arrived in time to see the soloist taking a third encore, receiving a bouquet, and leaving Schumann and Bach for dead on top of the piano."

Irony and wit seem to have gone out of music criticism. I still read Shaw's collected writings on music. It is one of the best bedtime books I know, tremendously entertaining. Newman, too, could produce bright flashes of wit. I remember when he wrote about a new work by an academic composer who is completely forgotten now, Algernon Ashton. I think he was at one time a piano teacher at the Royal College of Music. He wrote any number of string quartets and piano pieces, and many songs. Newman had been to a recital and in his notice was being rather harsh about Ashton's new quartet. Then Newman *seemed* to relent: "But we must not be too severe about this latest quartet of Mr Algernon Ashton because, judging from the opus number—385—, it is obviously an early work."

It was for a turn of wit such as this that we used to read the notices of the leading critics. People who never went near a theatre used to read the drama criticism of James Agate. When I was in Australia I used to get the *Sunday Times* two months after publication; because of the war there was no means of getting air-mail editions to Australia. And I read Agate's column avidly, two or even three months late, not because I wanted to know if a new play was good or bad, but because I wanted to read Agate. If you were to ask me about the critics of today—of music or any of the arts—I couldn't name many, and all of them would be more or less of the old school. For instance, I would never dream of missing a book review in the *Sunday Times* by Raymond Mortimer, who is not only a scholar but a critic who can write with charm and wit. That's what I want in arts criticism—charm and wit.

RD: I find you most sensitive towards young musicians. Instead of saying, "She is raw and inexperienced", you say, "Miss X is very young and has much to learn, but she will improve".

NC: I can recall my own formative periods. When I was young I tried to become a singer, and later, when I went on the *Manchester Guardian*, I wanted to be a writer. We all need encouragement, no matter what age we are. The young sprig needs a gardener: it needs tending and watering. After hearing a young player for about an hour, I know if he is going to be an artist or not. By experience—in the same way that I know the taste of a good wine—I can detect if a young player has an inborn musical sense.

I sincerely hope I have never destroyed any young player's reputation, but I would have no regrets if somebody told me that I had hurt or discouraged an older player—if I felt he was not genuine. People have often said to me, "If you knew that by giving So-and-so a bad notice, it would mean he would never get another engagement, and he and his family would starve—would you still write that notice?" Mind you, this is an absurd supposition because no critic has so much power, but my answer would be, "Yes, if he were a bad artist." My responsibility towards the arts comes first. If a man is a bad artist, he shouldn't be playing at all; he is a fraud. You get fined if you sell bad food, but unfortunately you don't get fined if you sell bad performances.

RD: You have known a number of famous musicians: Beecham, Arrau, Curzon, and many others. Shaw once said, "A critic should not know anyone." Have you been able to maintain your friendships without sacrificing your integrity as a critic?

NC: I would go a long way with Shaw's statement. To this day, I try as hard as I can to keep apart from my colleagues. I don't believe a critic should discuss a concert with another critic. You have to stand or fall by your own reactions.

When I began on the *Manchester Guardian*, there was an unwritten law that a critic did not go out to dinner with—or accept any social invitation from—an artist. Scott, quite rightly, didn't want anything to interfere with the independence of his critics. In time, I arrived at a compromise. I made it a principle never to meet any artist until two conditions were met: firstly, he must be an established artist; secondly, I must already have heard him play. I could therefore go out and have dinner with Schnabel or Horowitz or Rachmaninov, but on principle I wouldn't dine with an artist whose reputation was not yet established. In any case, if I have dinner with Rubinstein before a concert and then write an unfavourable notice, it doesn't matter: he's probably in Moscow before my notice appears the next morning!

As a critic, I have never been put into an embarrassing position by my friendships with artists. I can go to their concerts knowing that they are artists of such stature that they will not do anything musically crude. If I do slate them, I will be slating them at quite a sophisticated level.

I would never dream of going to a publicity lunch. For instance, if a conductor or a pianist had written a book and the publishers were giving a lunch to celebrate the publication day, and I knew I was going to review the book, I wouldn't go. I've never done this in my life; I'm too fond of good wine. A soft Claret might temporarily disarm the critic in me.

I can remember only one occasion when I slightly bent my principle of not going to a meal with an artist before it was clear if he or she would achieve eminence as a performer. An Israeli girl, named Pnina Salzman, came to Australia. When she arrived in Sydney, her agent rang me and asked if I would go to lunch with Miss Salzman. I had never heard of Pnina Salzman, and I said, "I never go to lunch with any artist unless I have heard her play. If Miss Salzman would like to invite me to lunch *after* I have written about her, then I'd be pleased to accept."

I went to her recital, which was given on VJ day. I had the impression that she was the only pianist in the world giving a recital that night. She was a most beautiful young girl, 21 or 22. Her programme included *Variations sérieuses* of Mendelssohn and the "Appassionata". I wrote a very kind notice. I said: "The Mendelssohn and the Fauré were beautifully played, but the 'Appassionata' was beyond her. She should wait. She is too young to play it." When we had lunch together, she said, "You were very hard on my playing of the 'Appassionata'." I said, "Yes, Miss Salzman, but why play it while you are so young? Wait till you are more mature." "Ah," she said, "but you must admit I made it sound like the 'Waldstein'!"

That was one of the wittiest comebacks I had ever heard, and she became one of the most charming of all my friends.

RD: The *Guardian* is world-famous for its misprints. A couple of recent ones have gained a place in my own anthology: two lovers decided to get married "because of their two sins, aged two and four"; and then there was the man who was sent to the Old Bailey "for attempting corruptly to accept a bride". What amusing misprints have occurred in your writings for the *Guardian*?

NC: Oh dear me, innumerable. Many years ago, when the Wells was based in Rosebery Avenue, I went to a performance of Verdi's *Otello*. *Otello* was written when Verdi was an old man, but, at the end of the second act, in a duet between Iago and Otello, Verdi for some extraordinary reason goes right back in style to the days of *Il Trovatore* and *Rigoletto*. I said in my notice, "Verdi brings down the curtain with a curiously atavistic banal duet between Otello and Iago." This appeared the next day as "a canal duel between Otello and Iago". My notice should have been given a sub-title: "Verdi's *Otello* or Dirty Work on the Grand Canal".

One of the most amusing misprints in the history of music criticism occurred not in the *Manchester Guardian*, but in the *Yorkshire Post*. It appeared in a notice by a venerable music critic, Dr Herbert Thompson, whom we all respected. He retired in the mid-Thirties after serving as music critic on the *Post* for exactly 50 years. Writing about Sir Charles Santley, Dr Thompson said, "In response to very spirited applause, Sir Charles sang as an encore an aria from Handel's *Acis and Galatea*: *O ruddier than the cherry*." In print this appeared as *O ruddier than the clergy*. This proves to me that there is always a hidden truth in Freudian slips—because some clergymen do look very ruddy.

I am reminded of a wonderful remark Bernard Shaw made to me as we were coming out of Worcester Cathedral one afternoon. Elgar, white-haired, had conducted *Gerontius*. Shaw was very deeply moved and so was I. As we came out of the porch of the Cathedral into a beautiful autumn afternoon, Shaw tapped me on the shoulder and said, "Cardus, this music seems to have moved the two of us, who are agnostics, a damn sight more than it moved the clergy."

Two most incredible misprints occurred when I was attending the Edinburgh Festival about ten years ago. There was a time when you could simply put a German title to a song; you were not expected to translate it. Scott and A. P. Wadsworth assumed that everybody who read the *Manchester Guardian* knew —or should know—some German. Later a rule was made that you had to give a translation of a German title if the words were not well known. Irmgard Seefried had been singing some songs of Hugo Wolf, including one called "Das verlassene Mägdlein". I translated this as "The Forsaken Little Maiden". It came out in the paper as "The Forsaken Civil Servant".

And then the very next night this same singer, the lovely Irmgard Seefried, had to sing a very difficult concert aria by Alban Berg called *Der Wein*. I said, "In spite of the difficulty of this music, she was quite eloquent." This came out the next day—as a consequence of telephoning—as "she was a white elephant".

14

WRITING

RD: You didn't come from a literary home.

NC: Oh my goodness, no. My grandfather had been a police-man. His only distinction was that he had three permanent lumps upon his head, personally administered with a crowbar by Charles Peace, a very famous criminal of the 1870s. Charles Peace wasn't like the vulgar people who send letter bombs through the post. He did *honest* crimes. He would burgle at night and then play the violin to children in Sunday School, and he got away with it for quite a while. When at last the police caught him, he did not give in without a struggle. My grandfather was present when he was arrested; he was proud of his bumps, proofs of his association with a famous person.

My grandfather used to belong to the Mechanics Institute. This was a kind of night school, locally run for working-class people. Why it was called the *Mechanics* Institute, I don't know. I suppose it was started by machinists from the mills. My grandfather used to pore over a book by Thomas Huxley or the *Sporting Chronicle Handicap Book* or the Holy Bible: it probably took him a year to read the New Testament. I couldn't call him a cultured man, but he had a sort of horse-sense about books.

In those days there was no television and no radio to raise—or to lower?—cultural standards. When people did read, they often read a serious book with an intellectual or even a philosophical content. When I was about 13 I got a book out of the library by none other than Tolstoy, in translation of course. What I was doing at the age of 13 trying to read *Anna Karenina*, I can't imagine; I couldn't understand very much of it. My grandfather saw me with this book and what do you think he said? "What are you reading, Neville? Let me see it. . . . Read a serious, a *proper*, book. Don't waste your time on a novelette." In his view, fiction was only light reading. He wanted me to read a serious book, by which he meant a book that would teach me something. He wanted me to go into the Free Library and read Herbert Spencer.

When I mention the name Herbert Spencer I can imagine a lot of young people asking, "Who was he?" They would be astonished to know that when I was young, at the turn of the century, Herbert Spencer was as influential—as a philosopher and sociologist—as Bertrand Russell ever was. Spencer was world-famous. The other night I was re-reading Arnold Bennett's *Journals*. When Bennett was about 45 he said he had been reading Spencer's *First Principles* and he considered it to be one of the most important books ever written: "*First Principles* . . . has altered my whole view of life . . . you can see *First Principles* in nearly every line I write." Unless you are taking a high-powered university course in the philosophy of Spencer's period, you will seldom hear his name mentioned. I personally haven't seen his name in print for the last twenty years.

John Stuart Mill is having a revival now because of Women's Lib. His *On the Subjection of Women* was published around 1870. He was an early campaigner for women to be recognized as individuals, and not as slaves to any one particular rôle in life, such as the home. Mill is coming back on a topical swing, but I can't imagine what sort of swing would bring back Herbert Spencer.

RD: You have already spoken of the influence of Newman and Langford. Which other writers have influenced you, by virtue of their style, imagination, and power of description?

NC: I suppose that, when you are in the cradle, something makes you want to be a writer. When I consciously began to want to write, at about 17 or 18, I didn't say, "I'm going to write like Shaw" or "I'm going to write like Newman".

You've read a lot by these writers and subconsciously you're using their vocabulary, their phrasing, their lengths of para-graphs. Then in time you have to break the mould. You've got to step out of the plaster-of-Paris cast that the gods have put round you, to make you.

I was very fortunate to be on the *Manchester Guardian* in C. E. Montague's heyday. Montague was a brilliant, sophisti-cated, and self-conscious writer—I'm not belittling him, heaven

knows. We younger writers could see him carefully choosing his
adjectives. He made us *want* to write. His own writings awakened
our half-formed longings to be *Manchester Guardian* men. On the
stairs of our offices in Cross Street, we would often hear one
reporter say to another, "Good stuff of yours today". This
wouldn't refer to a scoop, to clever news-gathering. No, nothing
so mundane as that. It would be a compliment on an article
or an arts notice written in fine, personal, all-knowing English.

These early influences were wonderfully stimulating, but it
took me a long time to get rid of them. It took me a long time
to realize that I could choose an adjective that a bus conductor
might use; that I didn't need to find an esoteric adjective to
describe something ordinary; that I didn't have to say, "a
night of something-or-the-other, something-or-other gloom"—
I could just say it was a "black" or "dirty" or "dark" night.

The first writer who really thrilled me was Dickens. I was
then about 15; I probably read him too soon. He is a great
satirist, with a deep insight into the follies of human nature.
My theory now is that you can't read Dickens with real understanding until you are about 40. After Dickens, I read Hardy: I
soaked myself in Hardy for years. Great writers make an
imprint on your mind and then, in time, you find your own
way, your own style. The people who influence you are like
the colours on a painter's palette: you mix them.

There are no truly original writers. All great artists have
developed from the roots of their predecessors. Only a second-
rate writer, a literary freak, is foolish enough to imagine that
he is completely original. Occasionally you get a writer or a
composer who is what the zoologists and the botanists call a
"sport": a freak of nature that deviates from normal type.
Every artist has to face the test of years. At one time, Philipp
Emanuel Bach was considered a more original composer than
his father, but now his father is regarded with much more awe.
Originality is not enough in itself.

If a young person came to me and said, "How does one
learn to write?" I'd reply: "You can only write if you've got
a vocabulary and something to *say*." But what gives you the
gift of *having* something to say, and what gives you the gift of
being able to say it in a compelling way? I can't account for
that. Perhaps religious people can, but I can't. I only know
that you either have or haven't got the gift. How could Yehudi

Menuhin at the age of 18 or, still more remarkable, at the age of 8, play the violin as though music was his natural form of speech? These are mysteries that we can't resolve.

I am always baffled when I hear of young people who have gone to university to study English. I ask, "What did you study there?" "Well, we read." "What?" "Whatever was in the syllabus for the period: Milton or Shelley or T. S. Eliot." I can understand the need for an education in technology, in in subjects which you can't teach yourself. A young person must go to school or college if he wants to learn mathematics or if he wants to become a chemist, but why you have to go to university to be taught how to read English—this is beyond me.

I meet some of the young men who come down from university, having taken a degree in literature, and they have gone through the whole gamut from Beowulf to the present day. I sometimes ask them, "Have you ever heard of Franz Grillparzer?" "No." "Have you heard of Lermontov?" "No, he wasn't in the syllabus." Then they ask how I, who never went to university, got to know about Grillparzer and Lermontov; they are astounded.

No doubt a great lecturer such as Quiller-Couch could stimulate and guide a young person's reading. When I was young I probably wasted a lot of time reading rubbish: you have to learn by trial and error. But I *enjoyed* the rubbish. You can't fully enjoy the best until you have worked your way through the dregs.

If someone says to me that he can't listen to Bach after listening to Franz Lehár, I reply, "But Bach would have been the first to listen to Franz Lehár, and with great enjoyment. You must go through the whole gamut of musical experience." I am prepared to listen to a folk song or a Cockney song, such as "Knock'd 'em in the old Kent Road", or to a song of Hugo Wolf—so long as each is presented with honesty.

RD: Did you read much of Walter Pater's writings?

NC: Yes, I used to read Walter Pater. Every so often, nature provides purges. English prose had been through a rather stuffy period and there was a need for a Walter Pater. He made his contribution. I can remember some wonderful passages, for example in *The Renaissance* and in *Appreciations*.

On the one hand, I'm not sure if I would advise any young

man to read Pater now: today his writing would seem over-
written and rather precious. But, on the other hand, this might
be a good time for us to go back to Pater. Our language is
being so corrupted that verbs are made into nouns, and I can't
listen to a talk on the radio without hearing "You know . . .
I mean . . . I mean . . . you know."

   If someone on the radio is asked, "What do you think of
So-and-so?" he is certain to begin, "Well, basically . . ." In
the old days if someone was asked, "What do you think of
Lloyd George?", he didn't say, "Basically . . ."; he said,
"Lloyd George is a marvellous Prime Minister" or "He is an
absolute crook"—one of the two. No, on second thoughts we
didn't call politicians "crooks"; we only called criminals
"crooks". We called politicians "rogues". There is a subtle
distinction between a rogue and a crook.

RD: No doubt you read John Ruskin.

NC: Yes. He, like Pater, had an enormous influence at the turn
of the century. He cleared away a lot of Victorian smoke and
ugliness. This present age, which I suspect will go down in
history as the Phoney Age, looks back patronizingly—almost
with superiority—upon the Victorians. No one should turn up
his nose at an age that produced some of the greatest men who
ever lived. I could name, without stopping, twenty people from
Victorian England who are still famous today. Let's take
literature as an example. If the second half of the nineteenth
century had only produced Shaw and Wilde, it would have
been a notable period. But it also produced Churchill, the two
Lawrences, Yeats, T. S. Eliot, Bertrand Russell, Somerset
Maugham, Arnold Bennett, E. M. Forster, James Joyce—and
I could go on adding to this list. It was a great period and I
am very proud to have been born during it.

RD: Now I'm going to bowl a full toss: you can really step
out and hit this for six. What in your opinion are the qualities
to be found in a good English prose style?

NC: Samuel Butler—that is to say, the nineteenth-century
Samuel Butler—said that the man who considered style at all
was probably a very bad writer. Personally I think that Butler
himself could have been a much better writer if he *had* thought
more about style. I'm all against style as a self-conscious thing,

but it is very natural for young writers to go through a period of being conscious stylists. In my early days, many writers took Walter Pater as their model. On the *Manchester Guardian* we modelled ourselves on Montague and we probably over-used his influence: we almost got to the stage of thinking which remote adjectives we were going to use, before we sat down to write. That was a good discipline of its kind while we were learning to write, but it was a habit we had to shed.

The real stylist isn't aware of his style. He has learned his vocabulary and he can now use it instinctively. He has passed through the stage when every word is a precious coin. Adjectives were beautiful things when he was a young man; in those days he didn't want to use simple words. Max Beerbohm —I think it was—once asked a friend who was a connoisseur of words, "Do you think ermine is a beautiful word?" "Oh yes." "Why?" "Because it has such a lovely sound." "Well," continued Beerbohm, "do you think vermin is also a beautiful word?" His friend was rather taken aback.

The whole question of style is a very subtle one. It all comes down to the old French saying that "Style is the man himself". You have words and ideas in your system, and when you are writing you are not conscious of style. I don't know what you *are* conscious of when you are writing. I suppose you are conscious of the fact that you want to *say* something.

I don't know where the right word comes from; it has always been a mystery to me. If you look in a dictionary, you will find five or six synonyms for most words; but when you are writing, some influence—from God knows where—finds the *one* word for that particular context. And when you come to read the passage years later, you say to yourself, "That was the right word. How did I find it?"

A writer must absorb himself in his subject. Unless he is enjoying his subject—*as* he is writing—he won't produce anything which his readers will enjoy. The writer has pleasures in parturition. He can feel the labour pains coming and when he sees the baby he has created he thinks, "Well it's not too bad." Then he sees it in book form: "Not quite as good as I thought it was, but as Mrs Gamp said, 'Thrive it did, though bandy.' " A week or so later, when the reviews are published, you feel rather sorry you wrote the book. Ten years pass. One night you pick up the book and begin reading it, and you say to yourself, "My God, I could write then. I'll never write like that again." The writer's life is full of ironies.

RD: I'm sure that every week you receive appreciative letters from your readers.

NC: Oh yes, one gets touching letters. I remember in parti-cular a letter from Len Hutton. He wrote to me from hospital, saying he was afraid he might never play again, but that my book *Days in the Sun* was giving him a lot of consolation. That letter gave *me* consolation; and of course he did play again.

I don't know if it is an experience personal to me, among writers, but about 70 per cent of letters I get are from women. Is it because women have more time or is it perhaps because—at least in *this* respect!—they are not as conceited as men? Many men probably think, "This is a good book, but if I had been a writer instead of an engineer I could have written just as well as this."

Learning to write is like learning to compose: you've got to learn the technique. A lot of people seem to think that—because literature is made out of the words of everyday speech—every-body can write. Men who spend the whole of their lives flying all over the world—prime ministers and explorers, statesmen and pianists—produce a long book in twelve months. When and where do they write?

I've just been sent a book to review. It is by a world-famous musician and it contains about 450 pages. A book of that length would take me, a professional writer, about three years, working four or five hours a day. It always baffles me how some people manage to write a book in their leisure time. And the assumption is that *everybody* can write. The famous musician who wrote that book would be very astonished if I said, "In a year or two I'm going to give a piano recital." He would say, "But have you ever played in public before?" "No, but I do a bit of practising at home in my spare time. I'm going to become a virtuoso." "To be a virtuoso you have to have a masterly technique." "Yes," I'd reply, "and in order to write a book you have to have a masterly technique. And, what is more, it is much more difficult to master the English language than to master the keyboard." That would be sure to provoke him.

Many girls and boys of 16 or 17 could go to my piano and

play a Beethoven sonata, but I have never seen a piece of fine English prose by a youngster of that age unless he was a genius. Writing is among the most difficult of all the arts; you never master it. Instead of musical notation—which is unique to music—the writer has to use the words of everyday speech. He has to try to give new life, new meaning, new nuance, to the same words that are written and spoken thousands of times every day.

A writer deals with ideas, and they come from within himself. Rubinstein has a Beethoven concerto waiting for him to play tonight; Karajan is rehearsing Bruckner. They don't have to go on to the platform and create material. But the writer—even if he has written millions of words—has to start with a blank piece of paper. Even Shakespeare, if he were reincarnate today, would have to sit down in front of a blank piece of paper.

The great tragedy of a writer's life is *extreme* loneliness. And writing is the most uninteresting of all the arts, in the activity of production. If I were a painter, I would have the joy of splashing colours on a canvas. Whether or not you produce a masterpiece, there is physical enjoyment in the act of painting. The sculptor, the violinist, the ballet dancer—for them the activity of art is bracing and inspiring. But to sit alone in your room—with a pen and paper or the click-click click-click of a typewriter—is a lonely life, and you seldom see the results of your labour. You may get a letter now and then, and one or two good reviews, but, unlike other artists, a writer can't share in the public's enjoyment of his work. You don't see people in the buses and trains reading your books: you don't know who is reading them. But if I were a painter, I could go to an exhibition and see the public either liking or disliking my work. If I were a composer, I could go and hear my music being performed in the concert hall. And if I wrote a play, I could sit in a box at the theatre and hear the audience applaud.

I remember once seeing a dramatist, a man who gave me and a lot of other people a great deal of pleasure. In the Thirties there was a play at the Haymarket by Frederick Lonsdale—I forget the name of the play but it was a very amusing one and the theatre was packed. In those days the audience at the Haymarket was very distinguished, all in evening dress. At about 9 o'clock, through the door came the author, Frederick Lonsdale, in a white muffler. He leaned over the parapet of the circle, contemplated the audience, heard the laughter, and then went out of the theatre and back to his club.

Here was a famous dramatist who used to be a page boy on an ocean liner. Now he could justifiably sing *Nunc Dimittis*. He had seen the enchantment of his audience; and he had seen their amusement. He had seen his creation on the stage, beautifully acted by beautiful people; and, what is more, he could look round the crowded theatre and say to himself, "10 per cent!"

RD: One of your essays was reprinted in a school textbook, alongside the writings of D. H. Lawrence, Lytton Strachey, and Aldous Huxley.

NC: Yes, many years ago A. J. J. Ratcliff reprinted an essay of mine called *Cricket and Cricketers*. At the end of the book there were a lot of questions about style and grammar: "Discuss and give examples of Mr Cardus's habit of treating the game and its conditions symbolically. . . . What use is made of anecdote and illustration? . . . Give examples of allusion." I would have failed completely in that examination, even though it was based on my own writing. I couldn't have answered a single question!

There is probably no man who has been a writer for as long as I have who knows so little about grammar. I know what a noun is; mind you, it's easier for me to spot a noun in German because the first letter is always a capital. I know what a preposition is because when I was about 13 I read in a grammar book that "Prepositions should not be used to end sentences with." I know what a verb is, and I know what an adjective is: so I should, because I'm sure I've used more adjectives than any writer since Shakespeare.

I wouldn't be able to pass an elementary-school test in grammar; I'd be out of my depth in no time. To this day, I could not guarantee to detect an adverb, and what the gerundial infinitive is—I haven't the faintest idea. Only in German can I spot the accusative because German nouns are inflected according to the case.

As regards other forms of education, I don't suppose there is any man in the world who is as ignorant as I am about science. Geography? I know roughly where Asia and Africa are, but what the capitals of countries are or what the world's longest river is, I don't know. There's talk about our going over to the metric system: is this to do with measurement in hundreds or in millions? I don't know.

So I've always described myself as an extremely well-educated uneducated man. My last words on earth will probably be: "No man I have ever met has had to work as hard as I have to learn music." I've never had any serious teaching, so I've had to work damned hard to learn music. Writing, on the other hand, came to me easily.

These days there are so many more means of coming to know music. This afternoon, if I wished, I could put on a record of a Mahler symphony. If I played it several times I would have heard it more often than the composer himself ever did. Or I could listen to *Das Lied von der Erde* which Mahler never heard even once.

You can turn on the radio in the morning and hear a string quartet of Beethoven. You can hear music of all periods. Radio and the gramophone are marvellous inventions, and yet I'm not sure if people who listen to them really come to *know* and *learn* the music they hear.

RD: What outward conditions do you need for writing?

NC: I don't think they matter very much to me. Sixty to seventy per cent of the essays in my early books on cricket—*Days in the Sun* and *Good Days*—were written in press boxes, amid all the clatter and rattle. If I am writing and I have something to say, and an electric drill is at work outside, I won't hear it.

What is disturbing is an interruption that is not expected. If the telephone rings, I say to myself, "Oh damn it!" and I go and answer it, but an interruption doesn't break the thread of my conception. If I'm writing and you drop in—somebody I want to see—I can put away my writing for an hour and come back to it. In order to write I don't have to go to an ivory tower and have absolute silence.

It all depends on what I'm writing. If I'm writing a chapter for a book, and I want to produce some sustained work, then obviously I need conditions of comfort. But if I've got a column to write after a concert, I could write it in a post office—in fact all my concert notices in Australia were written in the General Post Office, Martin Place, Sydney. I never went to the offices of the *Sydney Morning Herald* after a concert because I knew what the very hospitable Australian journalists would offer me. Since the pubs closed early, bottles of beer and champagne were taken upstairs to the reporters' room. If I had joined my colleagues, I would never have got beyond the first couple of lines of my notice.

The very first time I went into the GPO to write, it was 10.30 in the evening, and there were only a few people about. I was standing up at a counter, and in the middle of a long notice, when the man in charge came up to me and said "Yer roitin a very long cable, ar-en't yer?" The staff soon came to know that I was a music critic and they were always friendly to me.

RD: You used to take pleasure in writing on board ship, on your way to Australia.

NC: I don't think I ever made the journey to Australia—with the England cricket team—without producing a book. A ship is a very good place for writing; the conditions are perfect, and there is something about the rhythm of the motion of the ship that helps you. All you need is a well-stocked mind. There is usually a library, but not a specialized library, and so you have to go prepared.

I am a great believer in the value of a period of meditation before I write. Supposing I did want to continue with my work on Mahler and analyse the last five symphonies, I would study hard for about three months, going through the symphonies, and then I would copy out the musical examples I wanted for the text.

All this thinking goes down into the subconscious and—especially if you go away to do your writing—it is *amazing* how all the material comes out, full-blown. Sometimes you don't even have to think about what you're doing: you can't get the words down quickly enough.

You might well say, "But in the old days when you used to slap off a column after a concert—you didn't have much time to meditate." The fact is that the notices I used to write for the *Manchester Guardian* were 1,200 to 1,500 words in length. We always used to write about the *music* in those days, and so, apart from the details devoted to the performance, the substance of the notice had been in my subconscious for a long time; a marvellous concert conducted by Harty or by Beecham would conjure out the material. It is always somebody else who does the writing for you.

A writer is a kind of medium. If I write a dull concert notice, the fault is not mine; it is the fault of the performer. And if I ever went to a cricket match and wrote a dull article, it was not my fault; it was the batsmen or the bowlers who caused the dullness. Out of nothing, nothing can come. Somebody once asked Rossini, "What are the essential qualities of a good singer?" and he replied, "Voice, voice, and voice." I would adapt that—for operas other than those by Rossini!—to "Voice, some brains, and a good temperament." Rossini went one better by saying that opera would be wonderful if there were *no* voices.

Writing can become a technique as natural as speech. To anybody who wants to be a writer, I say, "You must practise writing just as a pianist practises the piano." When I was 17 or 18 I used to sit down and write. I probably wrote a lot of rubbish, and usually I'd tear up what I had done, but I was acquiring the habit of writing. If you can't write something original, if words won't come to you of their own accord, then copy something. Get words into your system. Find a page of Bernard Shaw or Max Beerbohm and copy it with the same dedication as a young pianist who has to practise five-finger exercises. You then get *acquainted* with vocabulary. You won't learn how to write by reading a dictionary. You must meet words in context, put into a sentence by a fine writer in such a way that every word becomes like a note in music: the words are related to each other to make a harmony.

Learn how great writers put a sentence together. If you copy a beautiful sentence or a witty phrase, it becomes a part of you—you'll never forget it. I shall always remember, when I was quite young, discovering the word "porphyry". I first saw it in a strikingly original context. Oscar Wilde, talking to his friend Robert Ross, said, "When we are lying in our eternal porphyries, Robbie, and the last trump is sounded, let's pretend we didn't hear it." When I was young, the last trump was always associated in my mind with Wilde saying, "let's pretend we didn't hear it". The meaning of porphyry, and the meaning of wit and death, were all orchestrated for me in that one sentence.

You may have to look up words in a dictionary when you

are starting to write, but by the time you are about 25 you should have a wide enough vocabulary with which to experiment. Once you have a good basic vocabulary, you can always go on adding to it, but if you haven't got an instinctive vocabulary by the time you are 25 or 30, you never will. The next stage usually comes when a writer is in his mid-thirties—now he has to prune his garden. He has too many adjectives, too many blooms. There are too many gorgeous colours on his palette and he has to refine them down to the essentials, and that is hard work. He has to take stock of his vocabulary and say: "Out with this word; and that one has been over the counter too often. Too many times have the shadows 'fallen over the greensward at 6 o'clock'. Too many times has the ball been 'square-cut like the pounding of a hammer-blow'." The writer now has to find words that have been neglected and bring them to life again; so many words are lingering in the dictionary, waiting to be reborn.

RD: You have spoken about the need—before writing—to let the inner processes do their preparatory work. Do these same processes help you to overcome a sterile period?

NC: Sterile periods can come at any time, but probably they come more often as you get older. The older you get, the more critical you become: you put your material through a much finer sieve than when you were young. And, what is more, when you are 25 or 30 or 40 you've got a lot to say. Now, after being a writer for 65 years, I have to think very hard before I write, trying to find something I haven't already said.

RD: How do you cope with the pressure of time?

NC: Sometimes this pressure is a spur. A lot of my pieces on cricket and music wouldn't have been half as well written if I hadn't had a deadline to meet. But writing a book is different. I wouldn't like to be told that I had to produce a book by this time next year. I like to begin a book and leave it to the process of gestation: it is like having a baby, and sometimes writing one book is like having a succession of babies. Some books take nine months to write; some take three or four times longer.

Today the job of the music critic and the drama critic is such a scramble that it is difficult for them to produce a really good piece of writing. If a concert finishes at 10 o'clock and your "copy" has to be in at 11, the most you can write is 500 words, and you can't *say* much in that space. In the old days when I used to go to Covent Garden, *Parsifal*, for example, finished at 11 or half past, and the *Manchester Guardian* didn't want my notice until the next morning.

Nowadays newspapers want to publish the very next day, as though a concert or a new play were a sporting event. It is as if Harold Pinter, instead of completing a new play, had made a century before lunch—which I'm sure he would like to do because he is a very keen cricketer.

RD: Yehudi Menuhin said recently: "An artist's instrument— be it a violin or a painter's brush—must fuse with his anatomy." Does this apply to a writer's pen?

NC: Until ten years ago I was never conscious that I was using a pen. The older you get, the more conscious you are of the physical act of writing, which I now find rather tedious. But I must be in touch with the living word. I must shape it, form it, and when it is in itself a lovely word, or the right word in the right place, I want to put it on to paper with my own hand. I don't want to communicate through a typewriter, a machine.

I get great pleasure when the right word comes, but that doesn't mean—as many reviewers seem to think—that I'm only interested in beautiful words. One of the best inspirations I ever had has now become common language. When I first began writing about cricket I saw "Patsy" Hendren, who was one of the most genial of batsmen and a wonderful hooker. I described a stroke he made one day as a *"vicious* hook". I thought it was rather an overstatement at the time, but every week during the season I see the phrase "vicious hook" in match reports.

The idea that the writings of young Cardus were all romantic is nonsense. You will find a lot of ironic comments in my early writings. I used to raise hell if Lancashire scored only 300 runs in a day, and this caused me to be criticized by members of my beloved team.

I got into trouble with Harty many times, and the Hallé Orchestra once made a deputation to the *Manchester Guardian*, demanding that I should be removed. Sir Thomas Beecham kept me out of Covent Garden for a while. Not because I was writing romantically, using beautiful adjectives, but because I was saying some cruel and ruthless things.

I really must correct the notion that Neville Cardus will go down in history as "the last of the romantic writers". It would be more accurate to call me "one of the first of the realists".

RD: When you lived in Sydney you had to modulate from writing a newspaper column to writing a book.

NC: Yes, that was a curious experience because, except for a short book, *Cricket*, which was published in 1930, I had never attempted a book as a book. All the other books I had written before the early Forties were based on selected pieces from the *Manchester Guardian*. I had got into the habit of writing a column of 1,500 words, and subconsciously I thought in terms of that form and that length. When I began writing *Ten Composers* I used to find that, as soon as I had done 1,500 words, I was out of breath as a writer; just as Chopin, who was happier composing nocturnes and *études*, was rather baffled when he came to write a piano concerto.

A chapter of 1,500 words is too short. All of a sudden I realized that I was like a racehorse who will pant hard over the last few furlongs if it was used to one-mile courses and was then forced to compete in a $1\frac{1}{2}$-mile race. It took me about three months to adjust to the idea of a chapter of 5, to 6,000 words. I don't know if this experience has happened to any other writer; I've never read about it. Nowadays critics are confined to 500-word notices; I wonder if this will make it even more difficult for *them* to write books?

I am often asked by beginners, "Do you have any particular form in mind when you are writing?" I suppose I must have, subconsciously. For instance, when I was writing *Ten Composers*, I found that each composer subconsciously conditioned my way of writing. In those days César Franck's music was considered richly chromatic, with a whiff of Catholic incense about it, and when I finished the chapter I saw that I had used adjectives which I would never have dreamed of including if I had been writing about Sibelius. By contrast, I found myself writing in a lighter—modesty prevents me from saying "lyrical"—way about Schubert. When I came to re-read the whole manuscript I found that, from composer to composer, there were differences: not only in the vocabulary I used, not only in the content, the conception, but in the texture of the writing. A writer is very much affected by the subject. If I were writing a music notice late at night, and I had been to a Kathleen Ferrier recital, my pen would go into a different key, take on a different rhythm, than if I were writing about Maria Callas.

People sometimes ask me why I use a pen and not a type-writer. As I've said, I like to *feel* each word as I write. And I must be in touch with the paper as well as with the pen. If I used a typewriter, I would feel a long way off. Some people don't agree with me. In fact, a writer whom I respect tremend-ously, J. B. Priestley, called me to task at a dinner party the other week. I had written in the *Guardian* about getting inspira-tion from the feel of the pen on the paper, just as a pianist gets inspiration from the feel of his fingers on the keyboard. "But," Priestley argued, "*my* inspiration comes from the typewriter keyboard." I could only reply that I was speaking generally and that a genius is an exception. "You always have a bloody clever reply, don't you?" Priestley grunted.

I am always telling young writers: "You must develop an extensive *instinctive* vocabulary." When you have experience with words, they are not dead things as they are in a dictionary. Just as colours on a palette, ready to be mixed, are vivid and alive, so also do words come alive when they float onto the palette of your mind. They are then ready to be picked out by your paintbrush—which is your pen—and mixed with the blues and reds and golds. That is, if you are a *writer*.

I'm sorry to say that good writing is out of fashion. In news-paper offices "good writing" has almost become a term of abuse, of sarcasm. When a young reporter applies for a job, the editor asks him if he has good news-sense. But the first function of a journalist—whether he is writing about an art exhibition or a football match—is to *communicate*. And he can only communicate if he writes interestingly. I am always very pleased if somebody says that, even though he knows little or nothing about cricket, he has read with interest one of my cricket books.

I used to read, with great enjoyment, Bernard Darwin's writings on golf in *The Times*. I didn't know what he was talking about as regards the technique of golf, but I could apprehend the scene he created, and the landscape and the human beings he put into it. Bernard Darwin gave you a living picture; it didn't matter if you didn't know the difference between a tee and a mashie.

It is very rare today to come across writing that depicts a scene and makes you wish to God you had been there. Brian Glanville and one or two others can do this. And you, Robert, did it in your book *Blackpool Football*: you made football come alive. In just the same way, the music critic must try to re-create the aesthetic—the scene as it was for the people in the audience—and the effect that the music made, on the ear and on the imagination.

RD: Are you able to evaluate your own writings?

NC: This to me is a baffling subject. There are writers who are confident that everything they write is good—I've met one or two in my life. I always used to admire and envy Howard Spring, who was one of my colleagues in the reporters' room of the *Manchester Guardian*. He later became a famous novelist and wrote what I now consider to be one of the finest novels in the English language, *Fame is the Spur*. Three or four years before "Bobby" Spring died, I wrote to him, saying that I had re-read *Fame is the Spur* for the fifth or sixth time. "It may be a masterpiece," I said, "but I can't quite make up my mind." He wrote back to me from his home in Cornwall: "Why are you dithering about *Fame is the Spur*? Of *course* it is a masterpiece."

I've met very few writers who are sure about the value of their work. As I've said, you sometimes think a book is better ten years after you've written it. If I were forced into a corner and asked which is my favourite book, of the ones I've written, I wouldn't know. I have never sent a manuscript with any alacrity to a publisher: normally the deadline has arrived and the publisher has had to ask me for the manuscript. If I had complete control over the publishing process, I would probably *still* be looking at the manuscript of *Full Score*, my most recent book.

When I had finished the major part of my autobiography I obeyed Somerset Maugham's injunction: "When you've finished a book, put it away in a drawer, and don't look at it for six months." I can still see that afternoon six months later. I tremble, to this day, when I think of it. I was in my top-floor

flat in the Chelsea of Sydney, 35 Crick Avenue, the sun stream-
ing into the room. I took my manuscript out of the drawer and
an hour later I found myself still reading, standing in front of
my desk. I thought that what I had written was a complete
flop, a miscarriage. Almost every writer probably hesitates
after completing a manuscript—he thinks, "I could have done
this better; I could have done *that* better"—but I can't imagine
why I felt such a revulsion towards my book. I wasn't conscious
of the reason at the time. Perhaps I was afraid of launching an
autobiography on the world when I was only in my fifties.

I left my room and went down the corridor to the incinerator
and, believe me, I was about to burn as much of my autobiography as I had then written, about three-quarters of it.
Then a voice spoke to me: "If anybody is going to reject this
manuscript, don't you reject it. Let a publisher see it." So I
took the manuscript back to my room and I decided to send it
to Freddie Smith, Collins's agent in Sydney. Six weeks later,
I had a phone call one morning, at dawn. "Why on earth
should anybody ring me at 7 o'clock?" I wondered. It was
Freddie Smith. He said, "I've been up all night finishing your
manuscript. This book is going to be a winner." And thank
the Lord it was. Otherwise I would be in today's equivalent
of the workhouse.

When I look at my autobiography now—30 years after
writing it—I come across parts that I like very much, but there
is a lot that I would knock out if I had to produce a revised
edition. This is a natural reaction for a writer because—apart
from someone with the divine gifts of a Mozart—the geniuses,
the really creative writers and composers, were forever altering
and altering. We have the sketch-books of Beethoven as proofs
of his struggles to create. We have Mahler who never heard a
performance of his music without going back to his desk and
altering the scoring. And we have Balzac who corrected and
re-corrected his proofs so often that in the end they were almost
impossible to decipher.

Writing is hard work. The man who sits in an office, from
half-past nine until half-past five, is not all the time creating.
The writer works for four hours and is exhausted. The next
morning he doesn't wake up to find a lot of invoices to author-
ize, a lot of investments to attend to; he has a blank piece of
paper on his desk. And he has no immediate confirmation that

what he has done is good. He hears no universal applause. In fact, if a writer took any notice of book reviews, he wouldn't write at all. In my experience, reviewers praise the obvious things, the professional things, but they often miss the little inspirations, the things that give the writer great delight because, in a way, he didn't think of them himself: they just came to him.

Take an example from my own career. When I was young I began writing about cricket in a manner and style similar to every other cricket reporter. Then one day, at a Lancashire and Yorkshire match, I looked at the cricketers on the field and I suddenly got the idea that I would write about them as though they were characters in a play. People say I invented Emmott Robinson. I didn't. I attributed to him the words I thought God intended him to say.

I got tremendous pleasure from writing about cricket: for me the game was a subject for dramatization. I seldom used to take any notice of the scoreboard, but I had to tame that romantic way of looking at cricket because a writer has to comment on technique and tactics, and the progress of a game. Eventually I achieved a balance. In the Thirties, in my middle period, when I was writing *Good Days* and *Australian Summer*, which I think were my best cricket books, I was dealing with individual technique—and at the same time cutting out a lot of my favourite adjectives!—but I was still relating the technique to the *man*, showing, for example, that Hammond wasn't only a technician—he was also an artist, a great personality expressing himself through cricket.

I tried hard to keep my eye on the ball and on the scoreboard, but the book reviewers didn't notice this change until ten or fifteen years later. They went on saying that I was writing beautifully, gracefully, adjectivally. The same thing happened to me when I brought out a book in 1965: *Gustav Mahler—His Mind and his Music*. Detailed musical analysis was an entirely new venture for me. I examined the first five Mahler symphonies *bar by bar*, and yet the reviewers—not in Germany, not in America, but in this country—seemed to suggest that I had been writing round Mahler: they talked about my book in terms of my nostalgia for Mahler's music and the heartbreaks in his life. The thorough-going Germans, on the other hand, immediately examined the technical analysis. They didn't always agree with me, but they did at least recognize that I was seeing the music *qua* music.

Arnold Bennett once said that if a painter produced a splendidly realistic picture of a policeman, and it was then exhibited in the National Gallery, the critics would praise it and then expect him to go on painting policemen for the rest of his life; and if he didn't paint policemen, the critics would no doubt find evidence in his pictures to suggest that he had.

RD: Was your Mahler book translated into German?

NC: No, but *Ten Composers* was translated into Swedish; and *A Composers Eleven* was translated into German—and, curiously enough, into Japanese, by Hajime Shinoda. I have a copy of the Japanese edition. The calligraphy is beautiful—the book is like a work of art—but of course it is quite incomprehensible to me. You start reading at the back of the book and work towards the front. The type is set vertically. You start at the right of each page and read across to the left, beginning at the top of each column.

RD: For many years you reviewed an average of three concerts a week. Did you ever find you needed to take a holiday from music and from writing?

NC: No, I never felt that need; even though my three notices a week would amount to about 4,000 words. In one week on the *Manchester Guardian* I probably wrote more than most *Guardian* journalists now write in a month.

In the Thirties I was enjoying a fruitful period. The gods give you this rich soil. Those people who have it mustn't be vain, because they haven't given it to themselves; they've inherited it. No particular credit is due to you for having sensibility. Sensibility is like good eyesight: some people have good eyesight and some people haven't.

If anyone comes to me and says, "You must have worked hard; you had no education," my reply is, "I had the best education in the world." If I'd gone to school for any length of time I would have been expected to pass examinations: I would have been asked to answer questions of no value to me whatsoever. I've never taken an examination in my life, and if I'd gone to university I would probably never have known half as much as I do now.

I went to a school where I was taught reading, handwriting, and adding-up. Later I educated myself by reading books in the library and by going to concerts. No artist can justly say, "I did this all by myself." Beethoven wouldn't say, "I have just completed this work. Aren't I a great composer?" Beethoven would struggle with his sketch-books and beat his fists on the desk, and when he finished a composition he would no doubt say, "This was presented to me by life itself. I was a vessel."

It is only the second-rate artist who thinks he does everything himself. As a fact, it is *only* the second-rate stuff that you do yourself. If you're a journalist you have to write late at night, and often you get by thanks to your technique. Your article is published in the paper the next day: it reads fairly well but you know it is not first-rate. The paradox is that it is for your second-rate work—the hack work you've done, on an unpromising subject, under the pressure and strain of time—that people ought to come up to you and say "Bravo", because you've been on a sticky wicket. You've kept at it when the ball was turning and you couldn't strike the ball with the middle of the bat. Your pen couldn't find the right words and when you finished your article you were nearly fainting with exhaustion. The next day people say, "It wasn't up to standard." But I had *slaved*.

When I've heard Janet Baker sing, my *Guardian* notice writes itself. People say, "You wrote a most beautiful notice last night," and I reply, "No, I didn't write it. Janet Baker wrote it. You ought to congratulate *her*."

In 1938, England lost three cheap wickets at Lord's against the furious bowling of McCormick. Wally Hammond came in and made 200. It was the easiest thing in the world to write about that great innings; it was as easy as making love to a beautiful woman. We writers don't get credit for our *hard* work; we only get credit for the work that has given us pleasure: the passages we couldn't write down quickly enough, the prose that comes from the grace of God.

It doesn't often happen, but there have been a few times in my life when I have written as though taking down dictation. I remember in particular one occasion when I was in Sydney. I was walking down William Street when suddenly a feeling came into my mind—without any words at that stage—of the incubation, the early stirrings, and gradual growth, of the second act of *Tristan*.

Tristan was a personal manifestation of Wagner, an ectoplasm. *Tristan* contains the *essence* of Wagner's life at that time, his romantic conception of love. The very texture of his emotions and mind was incorporated into the music. *Tristan* is not just an opera; it is a musical incarnation. At that moment I was participating. I was re-living the music's creation. It was as though I had become a demisemiquaver, a part of the score. I felt drawn into the conception of *Tristan* in such a way that all my thinking about life and love became illuminated.

I ran back to my flat and wrote a long stretch of the Wagner essay for *Ten Composers* as though Wagner himself were dictating it. I'm not exaggerating. All I had to do the next day was alter one or two words.

RD: Neville, who do you write for?

NC: I've never consciously written for a public or even for an editor. I write for my own enjoyment and self-enlightenment. A writer has to struggle with himself: you write to satisfy the critic who stares at you from the back of your mind. This critic is watching every line, every word, saying, "No, that won't do. Take that out." In a way, I envy the writers who seem to be without this critical spectator; such as "Bobby" Spring, who was certain that virtually everything he wrote was a masterpiece.

In the Thirties, when I was fully launched as music critic of the *Manchester Guardian*, in its heyday, having until midnight, or later if I wished, to write a 1,500-word concert notice—in those days I probably used to think, while I was writing, "Bernard Shaw or Newman or Elgar or Delius might read this tomorrow." I wasn't writing for them, and yet subconsciously I may have said to myself, "Newman will think this is damn silly. I'd better take it out." But I wasn't writing for anybody; it is difficult enough to please yourself.

When I *have* written something that I've liked myself—which is very seldom—it has been absolutely unimportant to me what anybody else has thought. I've been writing for 60 years and, to be honest, I couldn't name ten instances in all that time when I felt I could say *Nunc Dimittis*; when I thought, "Well, I can now finish writing for ever. It doesn't matter if I die tomorrow."

One or two pieces I treasure, such as one I wrote years ago about Kathleen Ferrier, and the portrait-in-words of my Aunt Beatrice in my autobiography. There she is, for all time; and it is all done in about 1,500 words. I envy the Cardus who could write that. In Australia I had a vision based on the reality of this beautiful and wonderful person in my life when I was a boy. I've got a very good memory—in fact I can remember my boyhood days much more vividly than I can remember what happened last week. I thought about my Aunt Beatrice and then she spoke, came into my being. She contributed the material; I was the medium.

One of the best pieces I ever wrote in my life was of Op. 111 of Beethoven. That day, for the first time, I had heard Artur Schnabel play this sonata. Schnabel revealed it to me anew and I wrote three-quarters of a column as though taking down dictation. That experience almost made me believe in some spiritual influence.

It is easy to write about a marvellous performance; and it is quite easy to write about a very bad one—you can be satirical. But it is difficult to write about mediocrity. When you write about mediocrity, you have to write the piece yourself, you have to sweat blood—and nobody else, except another writer, realizes how much.

The life of a writer is arduous. I wouldn't advise anybody to become a writer unless he had to; unless it was an absolute necessity. I write a book not because it will be published, not because a lot of copies will be sold. Naturally I want the book to sell well, because I have to live on the royalties, but I'm not *writing* for that reason. Never in my life have I written to make money. I've never written to add to education. I've never written to increase culture. I've never wanted to improve the world. I've only wanted to get the words onto paper. I've had an affair—a *literary* affair—with an artist (that is to say, my subject) and all I've wanted to do was to help our baby be born.

RD: In one of our previous conversations, you spoke about Strauss's ten commandments for conductors. What are Cardus's ten commandments for writers?

NC: I'll do my best to find ten. You'll have to give me plenty of time for reflection.

1. *Don't use a typewriter.* This is an outrageous commandment and I shall probably be laughed out of court by every writer of today, but I don't think you can produce good English prose on a typewriter. Sometimes the *right* word comes and sometimes it doesn't, but when it does come I like to shape it with a pen.

2. *Good writing depends on good reading.*

3. *Don't write about anything you haven't experienced.* I'm not saying to a young writer that he has to go out into life and get drunk or fornicate. By "experience" I mean "experience actually or imaginatively". When I was about 16 I read Thomas Hardy's *Tess of the D'Urbervilles*. I really went into the book. I went into the poor girl's mind and I suffered with her. That was an experience.

You cannot be a creative writer unless your imagination goes hand-in-hand with your observation. For example, if you write about a tree, it is no good producing a verbal photograph. You must see this tree—which thousands of people have seen before —from a new aspect. You must bring something from your imagination to your observing and to your writing.

Whether or not you have imagination—or can make use of your imagination—depends on destiny. I think that everything is settled by the time we are in the cradle; but I'm not excluding the part played by the environment. If Mozart had been brought up in Iceland, the chances of his becoming a world-famous composer would have been remote. But he could never have been a clod-hopping commonplace fellow. He probably would have become the world's most artistic fisherman!

4. *When you have done your research, and given a good deal of thought to your subject, allow time for your subconscious to work for you.*

5. *Don't be afraid of adjectives.* Although I would advise young writers not to be afraid of adjectives—and these days so many writers seem to be—I would also warn them to be on their guard against adjectives.

I had an adjectival period—I blush when I re-read some of my early cricket books—and yet to this day I get letters from people who want me to write like that again. They like the imagery I used: Woolley's bat "like a wand in his hands"; "A. W. Carr smiting the ball as though he were wielding a scimitar".

Metaphorical writing has gone out of fashion. In my *Manchester Guardian* days we couldn't even describe a wet day without using a metaphor. I think it was Aristotle who said that all good writing is metaphorical. It wouldn't satisfy me just to write: "Denis Compton came to the wicket when the score was 84 for 2. He completed his 50 in 65 minutes, including four accomplished leg-glances." That wouldn't interest me at all. I want to get to the quiddity. I want to get to the essence of this man. I want to find out why Denis Compton scores his runs in a different manner and style from Bill Edrich. They are two different personalities, as different as Kreisler was from Heifetz. What is it that makes two cricketers different? I want to relate the game to the man himself, and that's what I've done all my life.

But the game of cricket has changed. The public don't seem to want to go to County Championship matches; instead they pack the grounds on Saturdays and Sundays for the highly competitive one-day matches. In limited-over cricket, it doesn't matter how you make your strokes: you or I could go out and flash our bats, swipe at the ball, even play cross-bat—and it wouldn't matter. Everyone would cheer.

What used to interest the public was the match *within* the match—Larwood bowling at Bradman; Tate bowling at Hobbs. Then your imagination could take flight, and cricket writers such as Robertson-Glasgow, Beau Vincent and A. C. M. Croome of *The Times*, and myself, in my own modest way in Manchester—we lured people to Old Trafford and Lord's, just as music critics helped to lure people to a Toscanini concert.

Emmott Robinson never played for England, but the crowds packed Old Trafford to see him play—partly because I had given them a vivid picture of him, not only as a cricketer but also as a *character*. I got to know these players and in time I came to see them in apotheosis. If people say to me, "You invented Emmott Robinson", I reply, "No, I didn't invent Emmott Robinson. I *enlarged* him."

6. *Humour must not be imposed; it must be allowed to arise naturally.* I don't any longer read books for instruction. Nowadays I'm not prepared to read any book if there's no wit or humour in it. I can't imagine living without humour. I can't imagine writing without humour—about any subject. But you mustn't

H

be *deliberately* funny. You mustn't say to yourself, "Now I'm going to make a joke."

What I deplore today is the revival of the pun. I see in several newspapers the headline: WILSON PUTS HIS BEST FOOT* FORWARD. I agree with John Dennis who said, "A man who could make so vile a pun would not scruple to pick a pocket." Punning *is* a way of robbing—changing the meaning of a word, in order to be facetious. No, I don't believe in that sort of humour.

For me the great humorist in the English language is Dickens. He was humorous without trying to be humorous. He created life-like characters such as Mrs Gamp and Mr Pecksniff who are humorous without realizing it. Cricketers such as Emmott Robinson and Wilfred Rhodes never dreamed that they were saying funny things, but, with your perception of humour, you *knew* they were saying funny things. Once when I remarked to Wilfred that the square-cut was going out of the game, he said, "Eh, it were never a business stroke." I laughed inwardly, but he wasn't laughing; he was being very serious. The square-cut is not a business stroke because it is a risky stroke. Humour must not be imposed; it must arise naturally out of the character of the person you are writing about.

7. *Don't be dilettante.* Sooner or later you've got to specialize in one subject or, for preference, two. If you have only one subject you will eventually find yourself in a *cul-de-sac*. Having two related or complementary subjects is therapeutic: you can refresh yourself by going from one to the other. After a heavy winter of music criticism I would then go to Lord's, and I felt like a new man, cleansed and renewed. I used to be asked—and I am still being asked—"How can you reconcile cricket with music?" Why shouldn't someone write about cricket in the summer and music in the winter? Why shouldn't one write about any two subjects if one has an affinity for them? Which leads me to my next commandment.

8. *You must love writing as passionately as a man loves his mistress.*

9. *Don't write anything unless you are inwardly compelled to write.* You may be writing for a newspaper, or a publisher may want to commission a book, but don't write unless you want to write, *have* to write.

Never mind how much money is offered to you. There is

* i.e. Michael Foot.

nothing worse than hack work. Don't write anything unless you feel a child kicking inside you, impatient to be born.

10. *You must go before the Muse every morning.* Go to your desk every morning and write. The Muse may not come; she has other writers to attend to. But you must go before the Muse *every* day, as an expression of faith; and one day she will come. Even if she doesn't come for a fortnight, you must continue to write. I have written and written for days and thrown everything in the wastepaper basket. But still, I've made my obeisance; I've made my genuflexion before the Muse. Eventually she will come, and when she comes she dictates, and that is when grace descends upon you.

15

AESTHETICS

RD: Is listening to music an art?

NC: Ideally, there is a collaboration between the composer, the performer, and the listener.

When I was young, opera had for me as much visual as aural appeal. I would go to see *Aida* and was thrilled at the spectacle. In my twenties I would go to *Tristan* and I was interested in what I *saw*: the ship, the garden, the love-potion, the appearance—the costumes, gestures, and facial expressions—of the principals. And I would ask myself: "Does the Isolde fit my conception of Isolde?" Nine times out of ten the answer was "No", because in those days the Isoldes were usually *enormous*. The Isoldes of today come much closer to my ideal.

Later on, as I became a more accomplished listener, an opera or a concert became an entirely aural experience. Nowadays when I go to a concert, I close my eyes. I don't just listen to the themes and the harmony. I don't do what most of my colleagues seem to do—follow the music with a score, to find out if the conductor's phrasing and tempi are authentic. I leave the visual world and go into the world of sound. I try to enter into the mind of the composer.

I do the same thing when I go to opera. I know what is happening in *Carmen*, in *Meistersinger*, in *Tristan*—I've seen them so many times. I now find myself concentrating totally on the music; and I've gone beyond the sensuous approach. When I go to *Tristan*, I watch the stage for a minute or two, and then the music absorbs me and I go into the brain cells of the composer. I listen, amazed at what Wagner is doing. He is using a tonal language which is so far from everyday life, so abstract, and yet, with his marvellous weaving of musical ideas, of motifs, he makes that language so logical. Just like a sentence, a sonnet of Shakespeare, a poem—everything is balanced.

The ebb and flow of the music follows the natural course of the drama. A lot of critics used to object to the great scene in the second act of *Tristan* when King Marke finds the lovers and begins a long lament at Tristan's disloyalty. These critics said that this expostulation—in the context of the passion and romantic stress of the Act—is boring. My view is that it was necessary at that moment for Wagner to introduce a sort of slow movement: his operas are as closely woven as any symphony. I know *Tristan* so well that, seated in this chair, I could close my eyes and conduct the whole opera—and *hear* it.

Wagner wrote his own music-dramas: he wrote his own libretti and integrated them with his musical conception. In the ideal opera, the libretto *should* be written by the composer. Today we've gone to the other extreme. Novels are adapted and made into operas, and I don't find enough continuity between the libretto and the music. After all, the novels were written as novels.

Listening is definitely an art, but I've been speaking from the point of view of the musician and the music critic; I don't think it is necessary for the average member of a concert audience to listen with the intensity I've been speaking of. I've often wondered when I've looked round an audience, during the performance of a great symphony such as the "Eroica", which has cost a composer of genius tremendous metaphysical as well as musical struggles—I've often wondered how many people really know what is going on.

Beecham used to argue with me about the meaning of music. He used to say: "Music should sound beautiful. That's all it was intended to do. No time should be wasted wondering about metaphysics or philosophy or criticism of life or what the composer is saying. Music is just sound." "In which case," I once asked him, "how do you differentiate between the music of a lyrically beautiful composer such as Schubert and the Beethoven of the last quartets? Are they both to be evaluated only in terms of sound?" Beecham tried to wriggle out of the argument by saying that Beethoven's last quartets were written by a deaf man and should be listened to only by deaf men! Which was quite preposterous.

There is a difference between sound *qua* sound and sound that has extra-musical significance. I was once bold enough to write that, as regards pure and beautiful sound, the *Mass of Life* is to me a more musical and endearing work than the ninth of Beethoven. But I certainly wasn't suggesting that Delius is a greater composer than Beethoven, because music can soar far above and beyond sound. Listening is not just a matter of sitting back passively, letting the music pass through your mind. You must collaborate. You must listen with the inner ear as well as with the outer ear. And as I have always said, and shall go on saying till my last breath: "If you have to study scores, study them at home. Don't take them to concerts."

RD: What is the difference in your response to recorded music compared to a live performance?

NC: These days, when I listen to the gramophone, I prefer to hear piano music or chamber music. My living-room is too small to contain the vast orchestral canvas of a symphony.

The gramophone is a marvellous invention. I think it was Compton Mackenzie who once said that the gramophone had done for music what Caxton had done for literature. The gramophone enables you to get to *know* music. But we must guard against imagining that recorded music is anything more than a substitute for the real thing. It is only a photograph, as it were, or a reproduction; just as you might have in your home a reproduction of a Lowry.

Although I've said that, as I've got older, I listen so intently that I don't open my eyes, the fact remains that in the concert hall I am in the presence of a creative artist. Take as an example the adorable Kathleen Ferrier who, as I talk to you now, has been dead some twenty years. I would implore everybody who listens to Kathleen Ferrier on record—no matter how much they are charmed by her voice—to remember that they are experiencing only 50 per cent of her. The presence of Kathleen on the platform . . . you felt a *spiritual* communication.

If you listen to a recording of John Gielgud in Shakespeare, you are only hearing Gielgud's voice. You must go and see him on the stage and experience the living presence of him. On the other hand, there are some artists who perhaps *gain* by the gramophone, or at least don't lose very much. I'm thinking of the technicians who have little to give in terms of presence, spiritual communication. Without wishing to make any disparagement of von Karajan, who is a technically accomplished conductor, I don't think you lose much by experiencing his conducting via the gramophone—except in tonal balance, which is the responsibility of the engineers.

In the concert hall, Karajan doesn't communicate to me as a personality, a spirit, in the way that Klemperer did. When Klemperer was on the rostrum, you felt you were in the presence of a Jehovah-like conductor. The greatest artists must be seen and felt. By listening to a gramophone record, you can't get any real idea of the concert-hall atmosphere created by Schnabel. You had to be in his presence.

It all depends on the personality of the artist. Some can communicate almost all of their personality via a gramophone record, but the really beautiful and rare spirits only communicate 50 per cent of themselves on a record. The gramophone should be enjoyed, just as all the other good things of life should be enjoyed—in moderation.

RD: One of the biggest dangers in recording music is the striving for absolute accuracy.

NC: Arrau has told me how exhausted he gets when he is asked to play the same few bars over and over again: he once spent nearly a whole morning over fifteen or twenty bars. A mechanical perfection is destructive of the composer's intention. For instance, in the Twenties there was a superb quartet from Budapest—the Léner Quartet. In Schubert and Mozart and even in early Beethoven, their style—their sheer beauty of tone and naturalness of phrasing—was apt. But in the last quartets of Beethoven, their playing was *too* beautiful, *too* fluent. They brought these quartets into the ethos of sensuous enjoyment. I don't of course mean to suggest that the last quartets of Beethoven are ungracious to the ear, but they are not to be played in an unremittingly extrovert way.

I owe such a lot to the gramophone, but it has to be used with discretion. I remember a conversation I heard, on a staircase in the Festival Hall, during the interval of an Artur Rubinstein recital. One young man said to his friend, "I prefer him on the gramophone, because in his recordings you don't hear any wrong notes."

I think it is most important for a pianist to play the right notes, but if he does play wrong notes he must do so in such a way as to convince the audience that he could play the right ones if he wanted to!

RD: Another big danger of recorded music is that we have too much of it. We hear the G minor symphony in restaurants, on aeroplanes, and in railway stations. And we don't always hear *Mozart*'s G minor symphony. My musical sensibility is nauseated by these hotted-up versions, but I can't help smiling when disc jockeys try to give them a veneer of respectability by calling them "contemporary arrangements".

NC: Oh, I agree. This, like the motor car, is one of the *curses* of modern life. We hear so much about traffic blocks, over-crowded streets, pollution. What about the music-pollution which is causing traffic blocks in the air? Mozart has collided with Mantovani. There's a traffic block of pop singers cheek by jowl with Wagner. I can picture a sort of musical Oxford Street, with Beethoven jammed against César Franck, and César Franck jammed against George Gershwin; and all the music is polluted.

In America, so I understand, they don't do anything without music. They listen to music while they're in the bath, while they shave, while they eat their breakfast, and while they drive to work. I'm very naïve about these things called cars—I've never driven a car in my life—and I was amazed some years ago when I got into a car to be driven to a friend's house. We set off at about 50 miles an hour. He turned on the radio and, amid a lot of static and interference, we heard the G flat impromptu of Schubert. That heavenly music—in a *car*.

All this musical traffic is cheapening music. All of the arts except music are more or less made out of the materials of everyday life. Literature, from Shakespeare to P. G. Wode-house, is made out of words. Even a surrealist painting uses symbols from the external universe. But music is a thing in itself. Music, in the words of Schubert's "An die Musik", is "Du holde Kunst"—"Thou noble Art". Music is the art presided over by St Cecilia.

I remember the time when music was looked upon as miraculous. When I was young, it was almost like a miracle to go to a concert and hear beautiful sounds coming out of instruments made of wood and brass. When I heard the begin-ning of the prelude to *Tristan*, it was like a visitation. It was like an alchemy, a transformation of printed notes into golden sound.

Music is now becoming too familiar. We've had to pay a great price for the advantages of recorded music.

RD: Why is great art great?

NC: The public amuse me when they say that a critic should always be consistent. As you grow older, you do change your mind. I have never turned a double somersault about music within a few months, but in the course of 20 or 25 years I have found that a given composer is not quite as great as I used to think. And then I get letters reminding me of what I said 25 years ago.

A critic's mind should, if at all possible, remain pliable. A critic, as he goes from stage to stage in his personal development, should continue to let works of genius pass through the sieve of his mind and imagination; and if he finds he is no longer responding, he doesn't label a composition as "no good"—he says that his reactions have changed. To my dismay, I now find that I don't want to hear a lot of music which I *know* to be wonderful music; but I would be very much annoyed if a young man said that.

Some music has yielded all its mysteries to me, whereas other music never becomes stale. I remember an evening in the Opera House in Vienna during Act I of *Rosenkavalier*, with Lotte Lehmann as the Marschallin. I thought to myself, "This is the perfection of delight in an opera house. For entertainment and charm no opera can match *Rosenkavalier*." I wouldn't say that now, but I would be annoyed if you or any other young man in his twenties or early thirties didn't respond wholeheartedly to *Rosenkavalier*.

I still think there are moments of great enchantment in *Rosenkavalier*, but there are other parts that make me want to slip out to the bar. On the other hand there is no moment in *Così fan tutte*, or in any Mozart opera, when I would want to slip out. And there is not a single bar of music in the "Unfinished" symphony that causes my attention to wander.

Some music is *perenially* fresh; other music—which in the past has given you much pleasure and which your intellect continues to tell you is the work of genius—no longer makes the same impact. Why is this? It is a mystery and I can't solve it. I don't want to talk in religious terms, but the answer to this question has something to do with the spirit behind the music. To discover the source and nature of that spirit would be to discover one of the most deeply-hidden secrets of our universe.

Great music is more than just music. When I'm listening to the *adagio* of the ninth symphony, I'm not just listening to Beethoven. This *adagio* is much more than an arrangement of notes. It is much more than a statement of two themes and an account of the contrasts between them. This *adagio* is Beethoven's essence, his spiritual essence, transformed into music as a kind of tonal ectoplasm. It *is* Beethoven.

What we know of the mortal Beethoven is that he was deaf, that he died and was buried. But the *essence* of Beethoven—his creative mind and the substance of his being—lives on in his music. As a man who would describe himself as an agnostic, I am always bewildered when I come to examine my lack of religious faith—for I cannot believe that Beethoven and Mozart and all the beauty and creativity in the world are a mere accident. To me, listening to great music is like the Catholic doctrine of transubstantiation: it means tasting the blood, and eating of the body, of the composer. It is a sacrament.

Schopenhauer said that it is through music, more than through words, that you can get to "the thing in itself", because music transcends the ordinary symbols of life. Let's take as an example *Così fan tutte*. *Così* is more than a farce; it is a comedy. It depicts a cloud-cuckoo-land, and there is a scene in which the two officers test their lovers, to see if they can be trusted. The officers pretend that they have to go away; later they will come back in disguise. We hear the great farewell quintet. It is so sad: it could be an *Abschied*, a farewell, to life. It is so poignantly beautiful, coming as it does in the middle of a comedy. Here is Mozart, writing a comic opera, and, without knowing it himself, something eternal speaks through him—it is something that *I* cannot define. I can't accept the atheist belief that all beauty, all life, is a chemical accident. On the other hand, I can't accept the theological explanations.

I've been speaking about the great spiritual experiences in music, but equally enduring is music that doesn't express emotion requiring metaphysical explanation. A nocturne or a mazurka of Chopin is not on the same plane as Mozart or Beethoven but it is music I never tire of. Chopin's music is the music the piano itself would have composed if it had been a composer. Chopin's music evokes the *essence* of the piano.

We find manifestations of genius in every walk of life, even in the supposedly mundane world of sport. What was there

about Denis Compton that so enchanted us? It was something
Denis Compton didn't *really* know about. When you watch a
rationalistic cricketer, you admire him, you are amazed. In
astonishment, you watch a Hutton or a Boycott or a Bradman.
But you know *how* he achieves his effects, his strokes, his
successes. You know *how* he was made: he has evolved from the
science and the technique of cricket; he's like a marvellous
machine. But we will never know how Denis Compton could
take a ball near the off-stump and stroke it round to the leg
side, and do it perfectly correctly. That was inexplicable. This
for me is what keeps things eternally fresh—when I cannot
explain them.

No one can explain the joy in a Johann Strauss waltz. A
thing of wonder doesn't need to be heaven-storming. You
don't have to gaze at Mount Etna. You don't have to study the
ninth symphony of Beethoven. The smallest object can be a
revelation. Have you ever seen a bird's nest? The perfection,
the texture . . . No mortal hand could make a nest so
exquisitely.

I'm not a highbrow. I'm just as happy listening to *The
Merry Widow* or a Strauss waltz as to a great symphony or choral
work; but there are different levels of happiness. Listening to
Johann Strauss is like drinking a glass of wine or making love
to a beautiful girl: it is part of the sensual enjoyment of life.
But if I go to hear Beethoven's *Missa Solemnis*, I'm seeking
something more than entertainment.

Although there is a great deal to be said for today's wide-
spread propagation of music—you can hear it all day and
everywhere—I fear it is tending to make many people think
of music as just another form of entertainment. In certain forms,
it is. *Show Boat*, *The Merry Widow*—this is marvellous entertainment. But when you are listening to a work such as the
"Unfinished" symphony, you are in the presence of something
more: you are listening to uniquely beautiful music, a product
of the mind and metabolism of rare genius. I don't want the
arts to become just another part of the media.

RD: You've been a music critic for over half-a-century. How
do you retain your joy in writing about the same works over
and over again?

NC: A truly great piece of music will have different meanings to you in different periods of your life. There used to be in Manchester a famous philosopher of the name of Samuel Alexander. He belonged to a school of metaphysics that is now out of date; along with Bertrand Russell, he was one of the last metaphysicians to be awarded the Order of Merit. In a book on aesthetics, Alexander made a statement that was very revealing to me when I was young: "A great work of art can accommodate many imputations." In other words, there are many ways of getting onto the wavelength of a great work of art.

You're on a very different wavelength when listening to the fifth symphony of Beethoven at 20 or 25 than at 60 or 70. While hearing the fifth symphony at 20, I used to think about "Fate knocking at the door". To a young man, this was a dramatic idea. So dramatic that it was once mis-spelt in a concert notice —"Kate knocking at the door".

As you get older, you tend to do away with such elementary extra-musical ideas. By then you've had experience of life and you know more about the language of music. That language has become second-nature to you: certain keys, certain tone colours, now have special associations.

Today when I listen to the fifth symphony I no longer have an image of "Fate knocking at the door", but I do have the feeling of a man, a great mind, trying to solve profound spiritual problems, and in the end succeeding. This music resembles the experiences of life—by contrasts of tone colour, by struggles to move from one key to another, by persistent rhythmic figures, by tensions and resolutions, by humour and heroic striving. The last-movement transformation of the *scherzo* theme, with new orchestration, is like the transition from one major experience to another, and even more life-shaking, experience.

I have often said that the Sibelius symphonies are unpopulated: they are neuter; there is no eroticism in them. At one time, I used to see them as descriptions of Finnish landscape. Once I had learned to listen to Sibelius in this imaginative way *then* I could begin to find out how he achieves his effects. Similarly, when I first look at a portrait by a great painter, I say, "My God, what a wonderful likeness. This is a living portraiture of So-and-so." What do I look for next? I look to see how he has done it, and I now notice individual curves, shadings, touches of colour. He has re-created a human being onto canvas; in addition to my initial imaginative response, I want to share in the artist's technical processes. I try to see the painting from the inside of the artist's mind, as it was *while* he was painting.

I object to the critic—of any of the fine arts—who splits off description of technique from discussion of the artist's conceptual process. Equally, I object to critics who try to turn history upside-down, for example by saying that Wagner wrote *Tristan* just because he was in love with Mathilde Wesendonk. My own theory is that he had already been formulating *Tristan*: his mind and his imagination were ripe soil for *Tristan*. And it was *because* he was in the process of composing *Tristan* that he fell in love with Mathilde. He had to find a human channel, as a complement to his creativity. Once he had completed *Tristan*, and had got the opera more or less out of his system, Mathilde ceased to be important to him. She was, according to Newman, the conductor—not the generator—of Wagner's lightning: ". . . when the *Tristan* lava-tide in him ebbed, he no longer saw her as a haloed vision in an artist's dream of paradise." Wagner then switched his affections from one married woman (Mathilde) to another—Cosima von Bülow, wife of the first great conductor of Wagner's own works! I don't of course suggest that every composer should behave like that.

RD: What prompted Ernest Newman to say, "The trouble with you, Cardus, is that you love music"?

NC: It was in the Thirties. I had been to a performance of *The Valkyrie* at Covent Garden, Bruno Walter conducting. Lotte Lehmann sang the part of Sieglinde with vocal and visual appeal and mastery not equalled, in my hearing, before or since. I forget who the Wotan was; probably Rudolf Bockelmann. I came out before the end because I had to write my notice that night. I missed my turning and went completely the wrong way. The contrast between the wonder of Wagner's world and the reality of the dark street was too much for me, and when at last I returned to sanity I found I was a mile from where I should have been. It was getting late and so I took a cab to Fleet Street.

The next day I described to Newman how I had lost my way after being so overcome by the music. He looked at me intently —it was the look of a stern father—and said, "Having read your notice earlier this morning and having now heard your story about getting lost, I'm in some *doubt* about your future as a music critic. You labour under a serious disadvantage." I was very much in awe of Newman at that time: I was only in my forties whereas he was in his ripest period. I thought, "My God, what limitations has Newman discovered? Perhaps I don't know enough about the technique of music? Perhaps I made an awful blunder about the diminished seventh?" "W-W-What is it?" I asked. He said, "You *love* music, my dear man, you actually love it. This will be the ruin of you."

I can now see more clearly what he meant. He probably thought that, by falling too much in love with music, I might lose my critical sense. When a young man beams "I've just found the most beautiful girl . . .", and you see her the next day, you wonder what on earth he saw in her.

By contrast, one of the sad things about my time of life is the number of composers whose music I no longer want to hear. I don't want to go to *The Ring* again, but I should be very much annoyed if a young man were to come to me and say, "I can't sit through the whole of *The Ring*." I'd reply, "Don't be a damn fool. You can't expect to know what it is all about until you're at least 40."

I've been thinking lately of the sad ravages in the garden of my musical culture: it seems that the harvest of the years has taken so many things away. There are only a few blooms left. It is alarming to realize that there are great masterpieces I don't want to hear any more. And I can't quite account for it.

These present feelings of mine have nothing to do with highbrow standards. For example, I don't want to hear the ninth symphony of Beethoven ever again; whereas tonight I would gladly go to *Carmen*. And if I could go to a Viennese production—especially if it came near to the quality of Viennese productions of 30 or 40 years ago—I would like to see and hear *The Merry Widow*.

A rather curious thing has happened to me during the last twelve months. I now prefer my music as far divorced as possible from human participation: I'm even getting tired of listening to singing. I like to hear music that is more abstract—a string quartet. And I never tire of hearing the piano well played.

I remember once discussing the subject of piano-playing with Artur Schnabel. He could play the great classical concertos

with the bigness of mind and fullness of stature that they
deserve. As a soloist in the concertos of Beethoven and Brahms,
he has only been approached, in my lifetime, by Claudio
Arrau and perhaps one or two others. I had heard Schnabel
in Manchester playing the D minor concerto of Brahms. At
supper afterwards, I said, "Artur, it must be marvellous to be
soloist in a concerto, with a whole orchestra round you." "No,"
he said. "Good God, why not?" I replied, astonished. "It is
an adaptation every time. In only two or three rehearsals, I
have to adapt myself to the conductor. I also have to adapt
myself to the orchestra: 60 or 70 players, each with a different
wavelength. Sometimes they don't play well: perhaps one of
the horn players will get out of tune, and that will upset me.
Sometimes they play good, but even then I am being conditioned. However, when I am giving a recital I am *alone*. And
I can forget everything. I can even forget my technique!"

If, in another incarnation, I could be granted one gift by
whatever gods there be, I would ask to be a pianist combining
the qualities of Schnabel, Horowitz, and Rubinstein. You might
say that's a tall order to ask of the Almighty. Well, if he is
omnipotent, he could easily grant me my wish.

I wouldn't want to flaunt my new-found gifts in the concert
hall. I'd rather play at home, alone. The literature of the piano
takes you from the exquisite lyricism of Schubert to the profound thinking of Beethoven, and you can play all this music
alone.

This may sound like a monkish idea, but I'm talking as an
octogenarian. I don't expect everybody to take an austere view
of music; I didn't feel like this when I was 30 or 40. I loved to
go into an opera house. I loved to feel the stir of life all round
me. But as you get older you want to encounter what the
Germans call "the thing in itself"; you want to get to the
essence.

RD: In a concert notice you once wrote of "the ache for far-off
receding loveliness"; and in *Full Score* you said you have tried
to be "an artist in the reception of visitations of delight". Is
there anything of the mystic in you?

NC: I wouldn't say I'm a mystic in the generally-understood
sense of the word. I don't believe in universal love, in the
theological sense. I don't believe in mysticism as a cult. And

I certainly don't go through certain rituals or say prayers or wait for God to manifest Himself. But things happen to me that challenge all my beliefs. Simple things—not the awe-inspiring things you read about in books of philosophy. I've spent a lot of time reading books by philosophers and I don't get many visitations from *them*.

Philosophers can give me clues to the meaning of the world, but the things that give me a mystical vision of life, helping me to see that life is more than bricks and mortar, more than governments, more than the welfare state—these things come accidentally, such as when I hear a bird singing on a stormy day. Thomas Hardy in "The Darkling Thrush" wrote about "An aged thrush, frail, gaunt, and small" singing in the twilight, in such a way

> That I could think there trembled through
> His happy good-night air
> Some blessed Hope, whereof he knew
> And I was unaware.

I can get a visitation from the beauty of a great painting; I can get a visitation from something quite simple. I was walking the other day in Queen Mary's Rose Garden in Regent's Park. Out of a bush came a squirrel and it scampered up my leg; I happened to have a few nuts with me. To see that beautiful little creature grasping a nut and then running away to hide it —that touched me just as much as beautiful music touches me. I have lived for more than 80 years and I feel I am in the middle of a great symphony. I'm still in the slow movement; I can't imagine what the *finale* is going to be like.

The whole complex of life is like an enormous and often tragic symphony, and I have been listening to it ever since I was born. There was a period between 1870 and 1900 when no wars really touched Europe. During the years leading up to the First World War, there were plenty of industrial and social troubles—there were very rich people and very, very poor people—but, as young men, we believed that there would never be any more major wars; and our belief wasn't only based on the grounds of ethics and humanity. Norman Angell wrote a book called *The Great Illusion*, published in 1910, in which he suggested that the great powers had become so interdependent, through the increasing flow of trade, that it would be economically ridiculous for them to go to war. In 1913, and even in early 1914, when the first war-clouds were darkening the sky, I never believed—and I couldn't find any young man in Manchester who believed—that there was ever going to be another war. We were convinced that weapons were going to be turned into ploughshares.

When the Boer War broke out, people thought it was terrible, the end of the world: when 3, to 4,000 of our troops were killed, it was considered a black week. Then came the First War, and half a million men were slaughtered in the battle of the Somme, all for the gain of a few hundred yards of territory. This shows how *relative* disaster is.

In the First War we had the frightening new experience of aerial bombardment, and an aerial bombardment in those days was a German in a kite-like biplane dropping bombs by hand. After four years of conflict, we all believed, along with President Wilson and his Fourteen Points, that this would be the *end* of all war. Then we had the 1939–45 War, which was the first war with massive civilian losses. And now, only 50 or 60 years after the German with his hand-bomb, some people seem to be accepting nuclear war, with its vast potential for destruction, as inevitable. Are the young people of today—in whom I have a great deal of faith—going to prevent it? This is a question which *you* will see answered.

RD: You've been talking about suffering and world wars. How do you explain the presence of beauty in the world?

NC: That question has baffled me all my life. If we knew what it is that gives us a sense of beauty, then we would have solved one of the great mysteries of life. If you have religious beliefs, then it may not be so difficult to find the source of beauty; but you also have to explain the source of ugliness and evil.

As far as I know, man's sense of beauty is a gift not shared by the rest of the animal kingdom. Perhaps a bird does perceive the beauty of nature? But I shouldn't think so, because beauty is a conception, an abstract idea. When I use the word "beauty" I don't just mean a beautiful woman or a beautiful cat or a beautiful piece of music; I mean also an aspiring conception of life itself, with an ultimate purpose that transcends ordinary everyday human activity. You may call it beauty; you may call it religion. There's a famous passage in the first part of Goethe's *Faust*: a great outburst of passion because Faust can't find the right words to express his love for Margaret:

> Then call it what thou wilt—
> Call it Bliss! Heart! Love! God!
> I have no name for it!
> 'Tis feeling all;
> Name is but sound and smoke
> Shrouding the glow of heaven.

Margaret tells Faust she has heard a priest talk like that:

> Almost the same the parson says,
> Only in slightly different phrase.

Do the words matter? "Call it Bliss! Heart! Love! God!" Faust had no name for it; the *feeling* is all. Beauty is, ultimately, indescribable. It is one of the great mysteries. I, who have lived my life more or less as an agnostic, not because I've been determined not to believe, in the way that a lot of atheists seem determined not to believe—I seek and seek but I can't fit my awareness of beauty into any theological formula.

I once had a long discussion about aesthetics with a very famous rationalist philosopher whose name I won't mention— his surname began with the letter "R". He was a dogmatic atheist. I said to him, "Do you really believe that the universe is the result of an accidental chemical explosion, and then gradual evolution and adaptation, Darwinian theory, and all the rest of it?" Yes, he did. At that stage I didn't feel the need to refer to Mozart and Beethoven, and other human miracles. Instead, I spoke about a bird's nest.

Anyone who has seen a bird's nest must be astounded at the weaving. The subtlety and delicacy of the inside of a bird's nest is a work of art which no human hand could improve upon. No weaver, no human craftsman, could make a nest so beautifully. Not even the Bayeux Tapestry has such beauty of texture. A bird has to make a nest in order to survive, and yet it also makes a work of art—out of twigs and bits of straw. That to me is a miracle.

So I said to this atheist philosopher, "Do you really believe that a bird's nest is an accident of adaptation and survival of the fittest?" "Yes." "And a Mozart opera?" "Yes." It was presumptuous of me to argue with him, because, compared to him, I was an infant in philosophy, but I knew him well and he was a charming man with a nice sense of humour. "So you believe that a bird's nest, and Mozart, Beethoven, and Goethe, and the face of a beautiful woman, and the loveliness of nature, and a little baby in a cradle, and a kitten playing about the room—you believe they are just accidental by-products of a blind struggle for existence?" "Yes." I made him laugh when I said, "You remind me of the night in Willis's Club in London when a stranger walked up to the Duke of Wellington and said, 'Mr Brown, I believe?' And the Duke of Wellington replied, 'If you can believe that, sir, you can believe *anything*.' "

RD: Beauty often seems to have a fragile and fleeting quality.

NC: Yes, the essence of real beauty is that it is fugitive. But of course it is not beauty that is passing; you yourself are passing. When I was young I felt a saddening poignancy when I realized I couldn't hold on to beauty. As I got older I came to see that Mozart isn't going; love isn't going; the spring isn't going. Spring will come again next year: a little squirrel will run up the tree in just the same way. No, it is you and I who are going.

I would like to tell the Almighty that I don't want everlasting life, out there, in another dimension. I want to have life *here*, despite all the troubles we have to contend with. Troubles are relative to the age. People talk about "the comfortable Edwardian period". I lived in the Edwardian period and I can assure you that, for most people, life wasn't comfortable. I had to go slogging for my living. There were a lot of troubles in the world when I was a boy, but today there are tens of millions more people to be fed, and the weapons of war are infinitely more dangerous.

The Battle of Waterloo was fought in a few fields: you could almost have put grandstands round them. You could almost have watched the Battle of Waterloo in the way that people watched England and Poland at Wembley in 1973, fighting for a place in the World Cup. At the Battle of Waterloo only the combatants were in danger; today we've reached the stage when innocent children are likely to be blown up in the streets. It is sad to think that—after centuries of philosophy, arts, and international diplomacy—nations still want to ravage each other as a way of settling problems. Only the weapons have changed: man now has the capacity to wage war on a world-wide scale.

The ultimates in life are the creative achievements of the human spirit. No wars, no brutality, can nullify the eternally-existing masterpieces: the works of Michelangelo, Beethoven, and Chopin; the G minor symphony, the songs of Schubert, the boisterous and idiotic humour of Bertie Wooster.

We've got to learn to live with the Devil, and I would advise anybody who is perplexed about the condition of mankind, today or in any period, to read carefully and with great patience Goethe's *Faust*. The reader will be left with some problems not solved, but *Faust* will help him to see something of the ultimate meaning of life.

I am optimistic enough to hope that the battle for beauty— and for a full, enriching life—will eventually be won. I still believe that somehow the Beethovens and the Mozarts will win. I know it will take a long time.

RD: You frequently stress the importance of responding to beauty in all its manifestations; not only in the obvious and spectacular ones. I am always deeply moved when I read, in Gibran's *The Prophet*, "For in the dew of little things the heart finds its morning and is refreshed." A friend once said to me: "The true aesthete finds beauty not only in Rembrandt, Rodin, and Mozart, but also when he is walking down Camden High Street."

NC: I agree with your friend. The important thing is to use your creative imagination. You shouldn't see Camden High Street just at face value; you should see something more. Like William Blake, you've got to learn to see

... a World in a Grain of Sand,
And a Heaven in a Wild Flower.

Dickens, who was a social reformer as well as a novelist, went round London and saw "professional" nurses who were foul and unscrupulous, and had had little or no training. He then created Mrs Gamp, one of the most satirically humorous figures in all literature. He saw people, places, everyday events, with the eyes of the imagination.

Some people have a naturally sensitive retina; others haven't. Those who haven't may never become poets or artists, but they can be educated to *see*.

RD: How?

NC: Most people have aesthetic sensibility when they are young, but education often ruins it. I've seen children of three and four drawing and painting wonderful little pictures—not anatomically precise, but charming in conception. And their poems might be nonsense, but they are delightful nonsense. Then you see these youngsters at 18 or 19, when they've taken their "A" levels. Something of their freshness and originality has gone. They all use the same vogue-words, and have the same ideas. One of the drawbacks—and curses—of modern education is that it has become too technical, too standardized, too much geared towards this examination or that examination.

A young person's antennae can be made more sensitive by reading, looking, listening, by trying to be creative. By painting, drawing, singing, writing, children can get to know art by experiencing art.

I'm not a wholesale advocate of self-education. I'm not going to submit myself to an operation by a self-taught surgeon. I'm not going to be transported in a plane that has a self-taught pilot. And I admit that certain aspects of certain of the arts have to be taught. But no one can *learn* originality. Originality is a gift that, from days of youth, has to be jealously preserved.

If a youngster of 12 or 13 wants to be a writer, let him read as many good books as he can get hold of. Not just high-faluting highbrow books. I don't want him to spend all his time reading Sophocles and Shakespeare. He should read the world's best literature—from Aristophanes to Dostoevsky to P. G. Wodehouse—and the bigger the range the better.

I don't claim any virtue for anything I've written or for having worked hard in my studying of music and literature. I wasn't trying to make good; I've read and studied out of sheer lust for pleasure. When I was a young man, employed in an insurance office, I spent a lot of my spare time in the Free Library. I didn't wander about the streets looking for girls— not because I was austere, but because I couldn't see myself in Oxford Street, Manchester with any little servant girl, after I'd had an evening with Beatrix Esmond.

I had an affair with Tess and I had a long acquaintance with Becky Sharp, the most attractive rogue who ever lived: she said she could be a good woman on five thousand a year. I lived, at one time or another, with most of the famous, and infamous, women of literature. Some people say I got my pleasure second-hand. No, I got it first-hand: reading for me was and is a real *experience*.

I didn't need to get drunk. I got drunk *in my mind* every night. I didn't need to spend my money on pot. I could get my "trips" without cost, by going into the Free Library in Manchester. I shall always remember the terrible state I got into when I first read *Tess*, because I adored her. Oh, the *cruelty* of Thomas Hardy: ". . . the President of the Immortals (in Aeschylean phrase) had ended his sport with Tess." I wept.

When I got older, I knew what it was to be in love. Having been educated in the company of heroines of literature, I was equipped with a kind of personal radar: I knew what to reject and I knew what to accept. Whenever I met a woman in real life, she either did or didn't have some of the qualities I wanted.

If I say I want good *breeding* in everything, the English will accuse me of snobbishness. But they take enough trouble over the breeding of their horses! I want breeding in music. I want breeding in cricket. And I don't just mean the aristocrats. Emmott Robinson, who symbolized real Yorkshire as well as the comedy of the game, was a well-bred cricketer, just as Hammond was—in his own and different way.

My concept of breeding has nothing to do with class-distinction. You find good breeding in actresses such as Peggy Ashcroft and Sybil Thorndike. But it also takes good breeding to produce a George Robey, a Marie Lloyd. On the music-hall stage, she was the apotheosis of the Cockney, the barmaid, the common life of the pubs and pavements of those days. And why? Because she understood people, because she had imagination, because she was an artist, because she had breeding.

I see art and breeding in all aspects of life. A man may drink and savour wine like a connoisseur, and yet, as often as not, he won't savour cricket in the same way. But cricket should be treated as an art—and I don't here mean art with a capital "A". Emmott Robinson, bowling for Yorkshire and trying to prevent Lancashire from scoring, was to me as full and vivid of character as anyone in a Dickens novel. And when I saw Wally Hammond make 240 at Lord's in 1938 against Australia, after we had lost three wickets for 31, McCormick bowling with the fury of a thunderstorm, I ranked that double-century, for sheer classical elegance, along with the Elgin Marbles. And I won't retract a single word of that simile.

RD: What, in your opinion, is the purpose of the arts?

NC: I've never considered the arts as a means of moral improvement. I don't quite know what morals are. The immorality of one age, or of one section of the community, is the morality of another.

The arts give us an idea what life is capable of. Shakespeare put the Cleopatra type of woman into apotheosis; just as the humbug, the hypocrite, was made into a marvellous comic apotheosis in Mr Pecksniff. A barmaid can be boring, but Marie Lloyd was the barmaid in apotheosis. A clergyman can be boring, but George Robey, with a dog-collar round his neck, was the clergyman *sub specie aeternitatis*. The arts should illumine life. It is almost as if the artist sees life through the eyes of God. I picture God not so much as the Almighty Jehovah, but as the divine artist, struggling with His material; and he made a lot of mistakes. Now he lets human artists, the Mozarts and the Rembrandts, complete His fundamental conception of the world.

Artists are God's messengers. They are doing the work which the Almighty didn't have time to do; just as, in Browning's poem, Andrea del Sarto wanted to go to heaven—with Leonardo da Vinci, Raphael, and Michelangelo—to paint the four great walls of Paradise, because he realized that the Almighty wouldn't have time to paint them Himself.

The artist helps to make life fit to be lived. The forces against him are formidable, but, without the tribulations and the sufferings, there would be no art. Without the challenges to man's spirit, there would be no Beethovens. A land of plenty, with manna from heaven, would be a dull, a stultifying, place.

One of the most difficult of all metaphysical problems is to reconcile the struggle between beauty and ugliness, good and evil, God and Satan (as the old theologians used to put it). A philosopher once said, "There can be no God without the

Devil." There can be no affirmation without a negation. Only by acknowledging, and by working with and within, this clash of opposites can man win through to a resolution, a synthesis.

If, in the hereafter, God said to me, "I'm going to give you your life over again. Would you like me to change anything?" I would reply, "Oh Lord, *don't* take away any of my trials. Let me have my struggles and my heartbreaks. You might care to give me one or two more luxuries, but I can attend to my own pleasures."

16

FINALE

RD: Which of your writings would you like to be remembered by?

NC: The people who like my cricket books—good luck to them. And the people who like my books about music—well and good. But if I were asked which three books *I* would choose to be remembered by, I would reply *Second Innings*, *Ten Composers*, with my autobiography third.

Of my non-cricket books, the one I like best is *Second Innings*, which I wrote after completing my autobiography. In *Second Innings* I felt I could cast my net wider; I was freer from the ego; I was freed from the urge to document my own life-story. I wasn't happy about the title *Second Innings*: it sounded too much like a cricket book, which it wasn't. I wanted to call it *Remembered Pleasures*.

And my cricket books—well, you can take your choice. I can't read the early ones any more. They are too adjectival; and yet they are the books that the public continue to read.

I can still read my music books and I wish to God I could still write as I did then.

RD: You have always displayed—especially in your cricket writings—a strong sense of characterization and a natural gift for dialogue. But you've never written a novel. Why not?

NC: I've often been asked that question. I've often asked it myself. I think the main reason is that I've got no long-term power of invention. I can see a character, can get inside a character, but I could never picture myself inventing a plot— although nowadays novels don't have plots!

The nearest I got to starting a novel was when I was working on my autobiography, in my flat in Sydney. I can see it now. It was a beautiful afternoon. But I was too engrossed in my writing to go out for a walk. I had come to the description of my wonderful Aunt Beatrice and she almost took over the book.

I had written 1,500 words about her when all of a sudden I exclaimed, "This is my autobiography, Beatrice; not your biography. I'm sorry but I'm now going to have to kill you."

A year or so later, around 1949, when I was at the National Liberal Club, I tried to make my Aunt Beatrice the central character in a novel. She was on the way to a Hallé concert. A man picked her up in a tram; eventually he was to discover that she had a good voice.

I think it was Somerset Maugham who said, "You just create the characters; then they write the novel for you. They gain free will and go on and on." This didn't happen with me. The characters in my novel dropped down dead at the end of the second chapter, so I gave up. I'm sorry I didn't persist with my novel. I might write it even yet.

RD: One of the ironies of being a critic is that you yourself receive a lot of criticism: from members of the public, from touchy musicians, and even from your fellow-critics, the book reviewers. But you have also received, all through your career, much praise. Have you learned how to accept both praise and criticism?

NC: Naturally, one likes to get praise; but the irony of it is that you usually get praised for the wrong things. The pieces you've had to put all your labour and heart into—they seldom get noticed; the reviewer tends to pick out and comment on the most obvious passages which anyone could spot.

I've often come away from a concert not knowing what to say about it. If I've been to a mediocre performance, my technique, my experience, carries me through, enables me to say *something*.

Nowadays I'm not sure who my readers are: I've lost contact with my audience. It's a new audience, with different values; and literary values are not as strict or as high as they were in the heyday of the *Manchester Guardian* or in the heyday of arts criticism in London. You had James Agate, one of the greatest of all drama critics, writing for the *Sunday Times*; you had Desmond MacCarthy writing literary criticism; you had Ernest Newman on music. These were men of the highest culture, writers whose style was recognizable in a single sentence.

I don't remember receiving any praise from Ernest Newman

until the end of his life. One or two friends organized a birthday
book for me when I was 70, and Newman was one of the
contributors. He said he had always appreciated me and my
companionship and he even went so far as to say that he had
learned something from me. He certainly never told me that to
my face!

Nowadays when I am writing I sometimes feel—in addition
to not knowing my audience, because values have changed so
much—that I don't even know the instrument I'm playing on:
the *Guardian* is still a great newspaper but it too has changed.
I feel the way Yehudi Menuhin would feel if he were asked to
play an unfamiliar violin at an important concert.

During the editorship of C. P. Scott, Crozier, and Wadsworth, there was a *Guardian* public: it was unique, a set of
readers entirely different from those who bought *The Times* or
the *Telegraph*. I was aware of a strong rapport with my readers.
I got inspiration from the fact that I knew my audience and
my audience knew me. Occasionally I would overhear a conversation on a tram top in Manchester—"Montague was in
good form this morning"—or I might pass a table in a café and
hear somebody say, "Cardus wasn't at his best today." That
made me feel I was in touch.

But for a long time now I have felt out of touch. I feel I am
writing into a void. I still get letters—and curiously enough
the letters I get these days are mostly from young people. They
say they don't want to read so much about Stockhausen and
about electronic music. In their letters they keep saying to me:
"Why don't you write more about Beethoven and Mozart?"

These young people remind me of when I was a young boy.
I went to my first-ever performance of *Don Giovanni* in the
Theatre Royal, Manchester, and it was given by the Carl Rosa
Company, one of the touring companies of those days. I sat in
the gallery, for which I paid sixpence, and I was *enchanted* by
the music. At that time there were no gramophone records
and no radio. I was trying hard to memorize the music because
it might be a long while until I heard it again—perhaps not
for years. I felt as though I had entered into another and
enchanted world.

The next morning I went into the Free Library to read the
notice of this performance. It was written by Ernest Newman
who was then music critic of the *Manchester Guardian*. He said

the performance was not a good one and he added, "Rather than perform *Don Giovanni* in this way, it would be better not to perform *Don Giovanni* at all." And yet I had been thrilled by the music. Ever since, whenever I have been writing a music notice or an opera notice, I have always reminded myself, "Quite a lot of people in the audience were listening to this music for the very first time." If a performance is not very good, I am duty-bound, as a critic, to say so; but I always try to say something about the merits of the work itself. I often hear fellow-critics moan, "How many more times do we have to hear the C minor symphony of Beethoven? That *hackneyed* old warhorse." But the concert-goers want to hear it and readers of newspapers want to learn more about it.

My criticism of criticism in the newspapers today—and it is not the fault of editors—is lack of space. After a performance in the Festival Hall of, say, the fourth symphony of Brahms, conducted by Boulez, a critic only has space to comment on the tempi and the control of texture. *Nothing* is ever written about the music. The critic says to himself, "Everybody knows Beethoven. There is nothing new to say about the C minor symphony." I don't agree. There is something new to experience in a great masterpiece every time you hear it.

Only second-rate works give you few new aspects to write about. For instance, if Artur Rubinstein was going to play one of the Saint-Saëns piano concertos, I could write a notice now, without going to the concert. But if I went tonight to hear the ninth symphony of Beethoven, conducted by someone of the stature of Klemperer, something new would be *revealed*. A great masterpiece can always inspire newness of interpretation: it is always capable of touching the artistic imagination in a new way.

A critic should always write about the music, no matter how short his concert notice. He cannot give the public any idea what the performance was like unless he relates the performance to the work itself. It is no good my saying that Boulez's basic tempo in the *adagietto* of the fifth symphony of Mahler was too quick. I must show why it was too quick. I must try to explain what Mahler is trying to say in this movement. Then the readers can judge for themselves whether or not the conductor's tempo was appropriate.

In the same way, if I was trying to describe John Gielgud's

Hamlet, and wanted to show how and why he was so moving in "To be, or not to be", I would relate Gielgud's performance to a discussion about the character of Hamlet. Of course, I would need space for this. Many editors don't give enough space to the arts. It seems that the larger the newspapers become, the smaller is the space given to the arts.

RD: You are—so far as I know—the only music critic to receive a knighthood. Indeed, very few writers of this century —who did not also achieve fame in some other field, such as politics—have been knighted. And you have received many other honours, from this country and from abroad. But I would imagine that the two honours which have touched you most deeply were the Presidency of Lancashire County Cricket Club and your 50th-anniversary-with-the-*Guardian* concerts in 1966 —in the Free Trade Hall and the Festival Hall—given by Barbirolli and the Hallé Orchestra.

NC: One doesn't know where these honours come from. You never expect them. They just come, like Christmas presents. But you are right: the two that moved me the most were from Lancashire Cricket Club and the Hallé, because in both cases I was reminded of my childhood in Manchester. I first went to Old Trafford at the turn of the century when I was 11 or 12, and I went to my first Hallé concert around 1907 when I was 18.

I used to stand in a queue for hours, waiting to get into the Free Trade Hall. In those days a Hallé concert was by no means a democratic event. On the contrary, it was a very fashionable occasion. There was space for about 300 people right at the back of the Hall, miles away from the orchestra. We would huddle together. There were no seats, just a bench or two.

I think of that boy. He is so far from me now that I can talk of him as though he were my grandson, a little waif wandering about the streets of Manchester, walking all the way from Rusholme to Old Trafford—I couldn't afford to go by tram— and on cold winter evenings waiting in the rain to enter the Free Trade Hall in Peter Street. Then in the course of the revolving irony of time I find myself at a Hallé concert given in my honour, a marvellous gesture by Sir John Barbirolli, and a few years later I find myself President of Lancashire Cricket

Club. A wise man goes down on his knees and says *Nunc Dimittis*; he is thankful.

I can claim—without false modesty—that never in my life have I written anything or done anything with any *ambition*. I only wanted to enjoy myself. I didn't want to work for my living. I define work as an occupation you would give up tomorrow if you inherited £50,000. I sometimes wonder what would happen to this country if everybody suddenly inherited £50,000. Not 5 per cent—not even 1 per cent—would stay in their jobs.

I didn't want to be in an office. I wouldn't have worked in a bank even if, when I was 15, I had been assured, "One day you'll be general manager and earn £20,000 a year." No, if I possibly could—even if I starved, even if it wrecked me—I was determined to do the things I loved doing. I wanted to play cricket and I wanted to be a writer. And I never stopped wishing and working.

After working all day in an insurance office, 9.30 till 5, I went home and had a quick tea. Then off to Dickenson Road Library: boys only; girls weren't allowed in. I'd go into the reading room and stay there for hours. I enjoyed reading. I wasn't making any sacrifice. I wasn't a boy making good. The reading room was to me what the cinema, pub, or disco, is to a young person of today.

At one stage I got into a *cul-de-sac* of casual labour. I had to push a handcart up Brook Street—up the hill near Moseley Street—a handcart loaded with planks. Nowadays they wouldn't allow a young boy to do this, but I didn't think it was such a bad job. I remember the great joy I used to feel when I was going back down the hill: then my handcart used to go of its own volition.

I remember once taking that handcart down the hill. As I was going down Upper Brook Street I saw a poster and I can still see it now: it gave a wrench to my young heart. I was about 15 at the time. On the poster in big block letters were the words: DEATH OF DAN LENO. And this was in Manchester where Dan Leno seldom if ever appeared because he always had so many London engagements. His death was national news.

And I shall always remember the day—it was a Saturday—when I came out of my insurance office in Bridge Street and

saw a poster which said: DEATH OF HENRY IRVING. The next
day all the newspapers had a black border round their front
pages. Henry Irving and Dan Leno were just as famous as the
prime minister and probably much more in touch with the
public. I told you I never saw Dan Leno, and there were no
gramophone records and no television in those days, so how
did I know what he was like? I got to know him by hearsay.
Superb writers such as Shaw and Max Beerbohm used to
describe his antics; the picture story of his life, drawn by a
great artist such as Phil May, used to appear in the newspapers;
and every Christmas McGlennon's Song Book was published.
It included all of the songs of Dan Leno, together with some of
his patter: only the platitudinous parts of his patter; not the
cream of his jokes. Every music-hall comedian jealously guarded
his own jokes and wouldn't even allow a fellow-comedian to
come to a rehearsal, for fear that his jokes would be plagiarized.

I never saw Dan Leno and yet he was more real to me than
all the comedians I see nowadays.

RD: In *Second Innings* you wrote: "to grow old wisely and well
is to understand the perspective of years". Perhaps you'd like
to talk about your own evolutions.

NC: Evolutions can only be seen with hindsight, because, when
things happen to you, you don't really know how or why they
are happening: perhaps the way things happen is *always* a
mystery.

My own life makes me believe in some sort of fate, some sort
of destiny. It was quite natural for a working-class boy of nine
or ten to play cricket, but at that age it must have been ten
million to one that I would ever know anything about music,
let alone become a critic. To this day I don't know how I was
able to learn music, and I have never understood how I came
to be a writer—except that when I was young I *wanted* to be a
writer. But if you ask me why, from the age of ten, I wanted to
be a writer—coming, as I did, from a more or less illiterate
family—I don't know.

I had the great luck of having a wonderful aunt, my Aunt
Beatrice, whom I've written about in my autobiography. She
was not what the world would call "a good woman"; but she
did encourage me to read reasonably good books. She used to
insist that I should read W. T. Stead's "Penny Readings".

W. T. Stead was a famous publisher of that period, of popular classics for children, and he used to bring out books costing a penny: potted Shakespeare, potted Homer, potted novels.

Then when I was about 13 I started to go into the Free Library in Dickenson Road. Reading was my *passion*. I didn't read in order to be seen as a good boy or to "get on" or to become a famous person. I just could not exist without reading. I read almost to the point of blindness.

I don't know why I wanted to write. It was probably because I was so much in love with reading; and I must have thought it would be marvellous to be able to write. I used to bring out a paper of my own which I called *As you like it*. I used to fill my paper with stories and reviews. Sometimes I used to imitate the austere style and tone of the old *Athenaeum*, the literary weekly that was later to be incorporated in the *Nation*. When you begin, you've got to have models and ideals. Your intuition can lead you in the right direction. Many times in my life I've wanted to get the right quotation to round off an article, and something has led me to the right page of the right book.

As I've said, you can't see evolutions at the time they are happening. At the age of 16, 17, 18, I didn't know where I was going. I had an ambition to be a cricketer: this was an understandable ambition because it is natural for an English boy to play cricket, whether he is poor or rich. But for me to want to be a music critic, never having had any musical education except at school, where we were taught tonic sol-fa—that was an extravagant, a crazy, ambition.

When I started going to concerts and to the opera I had an immense amount to learn. I find it incredible to recall the evening when I heard my first performance of *Tannhäuser*. I was then about 19 and had been listening to music for quite a long time—or so I thought. I found the pilgrims' chorus straightforward enough but when the overture suddenly plunged into the Venusberg music it had a bewildering effect on me, the same effect that the music of Messiaen and Stockhausen has on me today.

The evolution—or it might be more correct to say the devolution!—of music in the last 30 or 40 years has been fantastic. I was lucky to be born in a late-summer period of the arts; but even at that time transitions were evident. In the 1890s the post-Impressionist painters were giving way to the new movements of Symbolism and Realism, and composers such as Mahler were pointing the way to the future. By contrast, the young people of today are living in a tilling-of-the-soil period for the arts: the harvest will probably come 50 years from now.

RD: Your most important evolution began during the First War when you joined the *Manchester Guardian*.

NC: In 1916 I wrote to C. P. Scott asking for work as a clerk in the counting-house. A few weeks later he invited me to fill a vacancy that had occurred on the reporting staff. I went to Cross Street and Haslam Mills said, with the obvious pride of a *Guardian* man, "We'll put you on the *decorative* side of the paper." To start with, I wrote about the theatre and music-hall, and then of course on cricket. If I had been a wealthy man, I would gladly have *paid* £2,000 a year to write for the *Manchester Guardian*.

In 1927 I was appointed music critic. To follow Langford was like going in to bat after Bradman. I was following in the tradition of a great master and so I had to concentrate totally on writing music criticism. With music in the winter and cricket in the summer, I had no time even to think about writing a book.

By 1940, when I went out to Australia, I'd written one or two cricket books, and a further one or two containing essays on cricket that had been selected from my writings in the *Manchester Guardian*, but I hadn't written the kind of book I really *wanted* to write. And I particularly wanted to write a book on music. Then, all of a sudden, and providentially, I found I was the one-sighted man in a country of the blind. Australian music has developed enormously since I was there, but in the Forties it was rather provincial. It was relatively easy for me to write music criticism in Australia: I didn't feel I had to match up to the great *Manchester Guardian* traditions of Johnstone, Newman, and Langford. Now *I* was setting a tradition: this gave me more time to relax and get down to writing books. Every day I used to sit at my desk and write, ignoring the temptation to go outside and enjoy the sunshine: I never used to get out of my pyjamas until 5 o'clock in the afternoon. In Australia I wrote my autobiography and *Second Innings* and *Ten Composers*.

I

RD: You had to go to the other side of the world in order to find your deeper self and express it in your writings.

NC: Yes, this is an example of what I was saying about the questions of destiny and personal evolution. If it had not been for Hitler, I would never have lived for seven years in Australia; I would have continued as music critic on the *Manchester Guardian* and I certainly wouldn't have had much time to write books.

When war broke out in 1939 we had the blackouts of the "phoney war" period: we expected an air-raid every night but there were no raids for some months. Newspapers were reduced in size, cricket was stopped, and in Manchester and elsewhere there was little of the musical life I craved for. One bleak December afternoon, when I was feeling terribly depressed, with no work to do, and, at my time of life, of no great military use to the nation—out of the blue came a cable from Sir Keith Murdoch of the *Melbourne Herald* inviting me to go out to Australia to cover the Beecham tour. I went with the idea of being there for three months; I stayed for seven years.

When you look back on your life, you wonder how these things happened. People with a religious turn of mind would call it "the work of God". I have another description for it— destiny. The longer I live, the more I've come to believe in destiny. As I look back on my life, I ask: "Why did that happen? What made me go this way instead of that way?" The answers to these questions remain an absolute mystery to me. Life *should* always remain a mystery. Perhaps that is why I have a philosophical disinclination to believe in a definite theology. If I were to believe in God and the hereafter as firmly as the Archbishop of Canterbury does, then for me the mystery, the enigma, of life would be gone.

I feel like quoting George Meredith, from *Modern Love*, which few people read nowadays and yet it contains some of the most marvellous sonnets since Shakespeare. One of them has this couplet:

> Ah, what a dusty answer gets the soul
> When hot for certainties in this our life!

I don't want certainties; I want mystery.

I have never attained the belief-in-God that I would like to have. I *envy* the man who believes he has an immortal soul. I envy the man who believes in a just providence. I envy the people who believe they're going to meet their loved ones again, in heaven. I can't fit any of this into my own personal perspectives and understandings—and *nobody* has tried harder than I have. My present position is that I'm just as impatient with a positive atheist as I am with a positive believer.

I've often imagined myself face to face with God at the Last Judgement. "Have you always believed?" He would ask me. I would probably try to escape his wrath by saying "Yes". "Have you never had any doubts about my existence?" "No." "Have you never been afflicted by doubt?" "No." "Was it so easy to understand me that you accepted me wholeheartedly, without question?" "I did." "Well then, Cardus, go into Purgatory for a thousand years and learn that disbelief is the beginning of belief."

RD: You once told me that, if you could have your life over again, you would like to be a pianist. Is there a part of you that would have liked you to have been an artist?

NC: When I was 17 or 18 I wanted to be an artist. In those days photography was in its infancy. Papers such as the *Daily Sketch*, the *Graphic*, and the *Illustrated London News*, had artists: "Black-and-white artists", we used to call them. There would be Parliamentary sketches by men such as Reginald Cleaver, and drawings of major events at home and abroad.

Later on I wanted to be a humorous artist in the style of Phil May: he used to draw for *Punch*. Among his greatest character drawings were those of old Cockney women. He used to draw their faces with the care, the sympathy, and the insight, of a Rembrandt; the rest of the body he would dismiss in four or five large elliptical sweeps.

I found I wasn't quite good enough to be an artist and I developed an itch, a great desire, to write about music. Every day I used to read Ernest Newman in the *Birmingham Post*—this was just after he had left Manchester—and of course I also read Langford in the *Manchester Guardian*. I wanted to write about music long before I ever dreamt of writing about cricket; and these days my love of cricket has declined very much compared with my love of music.

If whatever Gods there be asked me, "Would you like to be a writer as great as Bernard Shaw and T. S. Eliot, or would you rather be a pianist in the class of Arrau, Rubinstein, and Schnabel?", I would be in a great dilemma.

I certainly wouldn't want to be a conductor. I once thought it must be marvellous to stand in front of an orchestra and take charge of 80 or 90 players, but now I'm not so sure I'd like to cope with so many people.

At the piano you are alone; and the piano is one of the most wonderful instruments ever devised by man. If I had the technique of a Schnabel, I would sit down in my spare time and play transcriptions of operas—*Tristan and Isolde*, *Mikado*, *The Merry Widow*, *The Ring*, *Fidelio*—as well as working through the whole range of my favourite music written specifically for the piano.

Before going on to the platform for a public performance I would call to mind what Schnabel used to say to his students when they were nervous about playing in front of an audience: "You will only be nervous, when you go to the piano, if you are thinking about yourself. Think of Beethoven and then *he* will play." Schnabel wanted the pianist to be a medium—so far as a human being can be. Whenever I heard Schnabel play, I felt he *was* a medium through whom the music was speaking. There are very few pianists today whom I would put in that category.

RD: Neville, why has your love of music outlived your love of cricket?

NC: Whatever I may have said about cricket, and the human characteristics it can reveal, it is only a game. And I hope to goodness it will remain a game and not be made into a Saturday-afternoon entertainment.

But the world of music is like the world of literature—you couldn't master it, or exhaust its potential, even if you lived to be 800. I have been listening to music ever since I was about 16 and yet there is a *vast* amount of music I know nothing about. Given the period in which I was brought up, and wanting to be a music critic, I had to concentrate on the music of the eighteenth and nineteenth centuries. In my younger days we never heard a note of Monteverdi or Palestrina or the other early Italian composers. In fact when I first started going to concerts the music of Bach was very seldom played in this country. It was all Handel and Mendelssohn, the great choral works.

In my early days in Manchester we heard hardly a note of Bach from one year to the next, apart from the occasional performance of the B minor Mass. I can't remember Richter ever conducting Bach. Bach was looked upon as cold, remote, baroque. Only since the Twenties and Thirties has his music become widely known in England. One of the first artists to introduce Bach to the general public was a most beauteous woman, not a technically great player, but a warm and sympathetic player—Harriet Cohen.

In the period leading up to the First War, even Mozart was not a popular composer in this country. The overtures to *Figaro* and *Don Giovanni* were known, but not much else. Beecham was the first conductor to bring Mozart to life in England. *Così fan tutte*, for example, was virtually unknown to us when Beecham conducted it at His Majesty's Theatre in 1910. People often talk about what Beecham did for Delius, but he did as much for Mozart—and for Haydn.

RD: Are there any authors or composers, or any subjects in the whole range of human knowledge and learning, that you wish you had had time to study?

NC: I would certainly like to correct certain blind-spots. You can have a blind-spot and not know why. For some reason your personal radio-set won't tune-in to certain wavelengths.

If some young man were to come to me and say that Bach is a boring, second-rate composer, I'd reply, "Don't talk absolute nonsense." But if this young man retaliated and asked me: "Do *you* want to listen to Bach?", I would have to admit "Very seldom".

I *know* Bach is a great composer. Virtually all critics and composers—from Chopin to Strauss—have acknowledged the greatness of Bach, but on the whole his music doesn't absorb me. I don't want to listen to endless polyphony. I want to hear those marvellous Schubertian shifts of mood, which even in a simple song, when he goes into the minor, take your breath away. I want the Wagnerian chromaticisms, his harmonic inspiration.

I find much of Bach's music—especially his instrumental

music—predictable. Even when I hear one of his works for the first time, I feel sure, after I've heard the first 50 or 60 bars, that I could write the rest of the score. I don't say that of the Passions: they contain some incredibly moving passages. But even Strauss, who was an admirer of Bach, said: "When it comes to the Passions, they may be Bach's, but they're not mine."

I suppose I'm the last of the romantics. A romantic, in my definition of the word, is never sentimental. To me, a romantic is someone who puts beauty and feeling—what the Germans call *Gefühl*—before intellect and reason; though I *insist* that the expression of romantic feeling must be controlled by the intellect. In a score such as *Tristan*, heart and depth of feeling are controlled by an active and powerful brain. Wagner himself said that when he was composing *Tristan*, he was *aflame*, except for one part of him, which was standing back, cool as an ice chamber: controlling, watching the effects, stopping exaggerations, preventing excess.

As for literature, there is no writer I particularly want to read now whom I haven't already read. I feel like Charles Lamb who said, "The older I get, the more I go to an old book and read it again." And if a book isn't worth reading 50 times, it isn't worth reading once. I can go on re-reading Dickens and Thackeray; I can go on re-reading George Eliot. But I can't remember when I last read a modern novel. I've hardly read anything since Priestley.

I get annoyed at the present-day author who shows off the fact that he knows something about psychology. By contrast, the psychological insight of great novelists such as Balzac and Chekhov comes naturally through their presentation of character: *they* don't say to the reader, "Now look, see how I am relating this personality to Freud's work on . . ."

Talking about modernity, I read somewhere the other week a critic who was discussing Thackeray in a very patronizing way. He said that Thackeray was inhibited in the writing of *Vanity Fair*: we are never given any descriptions of Becky Sharp's exploits in bed. Well, anybody with a pennyworth of imagination will infer that Becky was seldom *out* of bed: Thackeray doesn't have to *tell* you that. When somebody chided Becky for not being as good as she ought to be, she made the classic statement: "I think I could be a good woman if I had five thousand a year." The whole of her way of life is revealed in that sentence.

Why do so many of today's writers think they have to tell the reader about the stages of personality development and also interpret every last word and gesture? Description of character should be allowed to evolve naturally out of the plot. You pick up a novel by Thomas Hardy and in the first chapter you read of a grey afternoon in Wessex. A man comes to a crossroads and he can't decide which way to go. Eventually he goes to the left; and the whole of his life is altered because he went one way instead of the other. That's what I want in a novel: *implicit* irony. Hardy doesn't tell us right away, "By taking the left turn, the whole of his life is changed." Hardy doesn't underline events as they happen; he leaves you to realize when you come to the end of the book: "My God, just because he went down that road. . . ."

The whole tragedy of *Tess of the D'Urbervilles* stems from a letter that was pushed under a door. If Tess had seen this letter things might have turned out differently, but the letter was pushed under a mat. Hardy doesn't say, "Because a letter was accidentally pushed under a mat, the whole direction of this novel has changed, and we must now explore the subconscious intentions of the principal characters." Hardy lets things happen; he makes them real. He then lets the reader use his own imagination and make his own interpretations, in his own time.

RD: You were talking recently about the so-called permissive society. How do you see contemporary attitudes to sex in the perspective of your own lifetime?

NC: The present-day attitude to sex amuses me very much: it strikes me as being a kind of inverted Puritanism. I've always held the opinion that the English are congenitally incapable of seeing or enjoying anything absolutely aesthetically. In Victorian times virtually every novel and every popular play had a happy or a moral ending: the bad man hit rock-bottom and the good man went to the top. We even used to play cricket ethically. If someone said to you, "That's not cricket", you felt hauled up in moral judgement.

The permissiveness of today has become so self-conscious. Almost everybody *claims* to be permissive: "We're living free.

. . . We can all go to bed with one another. . . . Shall we go to a wife-swopping party or to a full-scale orgy?" It has become almost a moral *obligation* to be permissive.

I was brought up in the hypocritical period in England when the squire went to church on Sunday and then paid a visit to his mistress. The men who lived in the great houses of London nearly all had a mistress. I can remember the time when, if you were a member of high society, you were considered very *bourgeois* if you were seen with your wife; you wanted to be seen with a beautiful mistress.

And in the working classes—among whom I was brought up—bastards were being spawned in the night like mushrooms. Talk about nudity—everybody in my house walked about in the nude. There was only one towel for the whole family, and my Aunt Beatrice used to come out of the bathroom, beautiful in her nakedness, and scream out, "Where the *hell* have you put the towel?" So I have never thought there is anything wrong about nudity.

As for jumping into bed, it is not a modern idea. There's a wonderful scene in Henry Fielding's *Tom Jones*. Tom Jones and Mrs Waters arrive at the inn in Upton. An Irishman, Mr Fitzpatrick, pretending he is looking for his wife, bribes the chambermaid and is shown to Mrs Waters's room. He bursts in and who should he find in her bed but Tom Jones, who has only just met her and scarcely knows her name. Meanwhile, Tom's girl-friend, Sophia Western, is on her way to the inn with her father. At this stage, Sophia doesn't know that Tom is at the inn and she certainly doesn't know of his affair with Mrs Waters. There's one night at the Upton inn when I don't think anybody is in the right bed. Before long, Tom falls in love with Lady Bellaston who, as you might guess, is, or was, one of Sophia's friends. In the eighteenth century they had permissiveness with *style*.

In the Victorian age we had a top layer, a superstructure, of religion and morality, but you can take it from me that in the working classes and in the upper classes there was plenty of permissiveness. But there was no television and no big advertising campaigns to ram sex down our throats. In my *Manchester Guardian* days, we reporters didn't talk about sex any more than we talked about breathing. You wouldn't dream of saying to me: "I'm breathing well today." We took sex for granted, as a natural part of life. Nowadays there's even a debate in Parliament: the Cinematograph and Indecent Displays Bill. Parliament should have known for the last two or three hundred years what permissiveness is.

RD: What, in your opinion, are the three greatest curses of modern life?

NC: The motor car, TV, and plastic!

I have little doubt that if TV cameras had been present at the Crucifixion the camera crew would have used more film on the two thieves than on Jesus Christ, because theft has more news-value than goodness.

RD: What are the characteristics of the happiest and most fulfilled people you have met and known?

NC: That's a difficult one. I should say that the most important thing in life is to be doing the kind of work you want to do. And if you have the *will*, you can make your work—even though it may not be too pleasant to begin with—a part of yourself.

No occupation is as hard to master as the *apparently* simple business of writing. Very few people achieve a good prose style which is immediately identifiable—so that you could pick up a newspaper which had no by-lines and say with certainty, "That is So-and-so."

Writing can be a terrible grind. Sometimes I think I would rather go out and dig in a quarry than sit down and write. Unlike a painter, a composer, or a playwright, a writer doesn't see the effects of his work on the public. He seldom sees anybody reading one of his books; and the critics usually say they don't like your work. Being a writer is a lonely way of life, but you can make it more enjoyable by really devoting yourself to your writing.

If you have to do some work which is not pleasant—which may even be dangerous—you can make it much more tolerable if you start it thinking, "I'm going to do this job better than anybody who has ever lived." There's a lot of discussion today about the need for—as the current jargon puts it—job satisfaction. Heaven knows, we have plenty of social problems in England today. I think these problems would have a better chance of being solved if, instead of having "talks", trade unionists and Cabinet Ministers sat round a dinner table at a nice inn and related to one another as human beings.

People don't enjoy a job more just by getting more money for doing it. I've discovered that from experience. In fact, many people I know have become more and more miserable, the more money they've acquired: they come to you, complaining miserably about surtax and capital-gains tax—things which previously they never used to have to worry about.

We're going through a period when the devil seems to be winning. People should show more self-denial—in *all* things. All of the most miserable people I've met in my life have been very rich. So far as we know, Jesus Christ managed to live on less than £10,000 a year. He offered the world a complete code for civilized living, but the majority of people reject Him. The fact that He went to the Cross as an ordinary man— divesting Himself of all power—moves me much more deeply than the description and theology of the Resurrection.

RD: During the course of our conversations you have talked of Beethoven and the music-hall with equal relish. You seem to find natural links between Stanley Matthews and Hammond and Yehudi Menuhin.

NC: This is no more than the unity inherent in life itself. I have my receiving-set: if I meet someone who is interesting and individual, I don't care if he comes from the New Forest or the Old Kent Road or Buckingham Palace.

If an artist has charm, if an artist has humour, if an artist has character, I can respond equally to Marie Lloyd, or Mrs Patrick Campbell or Sarah Bernhardt. And yet each has a unique identity.

What I strongly object to about television is that the millions of people who watch it will one day all look alike and talk alike—and they are already beginning to. I hardly hear a sentence on the radio or television that doesn't begin with "I mean" or "You know" or "Basically". People in Northampton, Northumberland, Glasgow, Bolton, and Kensington, will soon be using the same vocabulary.

At one time there were regional differences. For example, when I lived in the north of England, people seldom said "Darling". My Aunt Beatrice, one of the most wonderful creatures in my life, who took a great deal of care of me when

I was a little boy—if she said "Darling", it was like a Christmas present. We had a different vocabulary from people in the south.

When I first used to go from Manchester to London, just after the First War, I sometimes felt embarrassed, trying to adapt myself. I felt I had come from a lower stratum of social life. I felt I was probably not fully accepted by southerners. I don't mean Cockneys in the East End; I mean the people I met in Piccadilly and Bond Street. They looked different from northerners; they *were* different.

People tell me that nowadays, if you are walking down a main street in Tokyo, you might think you were in Tottenham Court Road. I think this levelling-down of character is due very much to television, that enormous sprawling octopus, which is standardizing life in such a corrosive way.

RD: Do you fear for the future of the individual? How is individuality going to reassert itself?

NC: I'm not sure. It's going to be a battle. My hopes rest with the young people of today. In the flux of history there is always action and reaction. I have a firm belief that people will adjust themselves—in the face of pressures to conform.

The young people I meet today—and I meet quite a lot—are extraordinarily well developed, in maturity of mind, compared with the period when I was 16 or 17, just after the turn of the century. My only worry is that they might be achieving their maturity too academically and perhaps too much by imitation. This sudden avalanche of the media seems to me to be interfering with people's own personal development of character.

Television is miraculous: by turning a knob you can see what is happening in Africa—or on the moon. But I find it depressing to think that tonight at 8 o'clock *millions* of people will be sitting at home *passively* receiving.

When I was young I used to go to the library—not passively receiving, but actively taking part in a book. If you reach out to a book and its characters, you are collaborating, experiencing. You can be creative when you're reading. In fact, a child reading a fairy-tale is often as creative as the author. A child will use his imagination when reading and, by making up new stories, new material, will take part in a creative act.

The communication you receive from the hands of a great genius such as Dickens or Shakespeare is much more penetrating than a fleeting television show, which is only an image on the retina—and I don't think it goes very much farther than that!

The trouble with television is that it is not a live experience; and I always favour personal experience. You can't experience the personal presence and full genius of an artist by proxy. Surely we're not going to believe that a machine is a more powerful influence than live contact with a human heart and mind? And I do believe in the heart as well as the mind. I don't subscribe to the modern rationalist idea that we are conditioned and governed by our intelligence. I think that intelligence, intellect, and knowledge, are probably the least important aspects of an artist. I'm sure that if you analysed a great genius such as Mozart or Shakespeare—in the way that a clinical psychologist analyses people—he would score highest in imagination, human sympathy, the capacity to laugh, and the ability to see and feel beauty.

RD: Your writing gives you an outlet for creativity. How can the man in the street be creative?

NC: Life itself is an art. The whole business, the whole secret, of life is to be creative—to be creative every day. If I were a shoe-repairer, I would repair shoes so that they could *last*. If I were a waiter, I'd set out to become the best waiter in the world.

RD: During our conversations we have talked about war as well as about beauty. Life *is* a mixture of brutality and beauty, failure and achievement, cloud and clarity. On which side of the scales has your own life mostly tipped?

NC: Despite the philosophy of men such as Aristotle, despite the wisdom of the great religions and of metaphysics, despite the inspiration we've had from poets, some people in some countries still think they can settle disputes by dropping bombs. That is the biggest disillusion of my life.

Personally, I don't remember any real brutality in my life. I was brought up in a very strict home in a semi-slum, and if I was naughty I had my bottom slapped—I took this for granted. In fact, I would rather have had my bottom slapped by my wonderful Aunt Beatrice than have her say something to me which would make me feel ashamed of myself: words can hurt much more than the cane. At that dreadful board school I didn't mind getting caned, but I didn't like the headmaster to come in front of the class and tell me that I had disgraced the class or that I had been lazy or that I ought to be ashamed of myself.

You spoke about the sunshine and cloud in life. I did have a struggle, between the ages of 18 and 22, when I had to do all kinds of *menial* work. There was no welfare state then; you were thankful to get whatever job you could. I sold burial-insurance policies, collecting a shilling a week from homes in the slums of Manchester: poor people had to pay to be buried and yet they had scarcely enough money to keep themselves alive.

In another job I had to push a handcart up and down the streets of Manchester. I can't call this a "cloud" period of my life because I lived in a dream world. During the day I could look forward to half-past five when I could finish work. By seven o'clock I would be in the Free Library and I would enter the world of *Tess of the D'Urbervilles*, the world of Becky Sharp, the world of Dickens. This was a marvellous period in my boyhood.

At various points of our life we have heartbreaks—a love that disappoints; illusions and ideals that are not realized— but it is the cloud that gives worth and meaning to the sunshine. Schubert said that all of his most cheerful songs derived from his sorrows. I'm sure he didn't mean what I call abstract or universal sorrows. The war in Vietnam is a horror, a tragedy, but it is not a sorrow that I have experienced personally. I feel sorry for the men, women, and children, who have been killed thousands of miles from here, but the sorrows that kindle an artist's creativity are the sorrows he himself feels or the sorrows communicated to him by other artists.

Few tragedies in the material world—because they are happening every day—are more moving than the tragedy of *Tess of the D'Urbervilles*: in writing the story of a girl who went wrong, Hardy made her the subject of great and enduring prose.

To me, the fact that 10,000 people might get blown up or maimed in Vietnam tomorrow is no more tragic than if I saw a little boy get run over by a car in Baker Street. I could not, even if I were a Beethoven, write a symphony about Vietnam; but I could write a symphony deriving from the personal tragedies I have seen in my life, such as the beautiful girl I knew and loved who, though seemingly in the bloom of health, died suddenly—for no reason I could then or even now understand.

Or a beautiful artist dies. Seeing Kathleen Ferrier in the bloom of loveliness, when she was about 30, you would have thought she was going to live like a beautiful flower till the autumn of her life. Then she is snapped. That to me is a more poignant tragedy than Napoleon's Retreat from Moscow or the Russian and Austrian casualties at the Battle of Austerlitz.

Somebody once asked me: "How can religious people believe in a just God when a lovely and sensitive artist such as the violinist Ginette Neveu is killed in an aeroplane accident when only about 30?" I have been an agnostic all my life but I replied, "Curiously and paradoxically enough, it is the tragedies such as this, when an artist is suddenly taken away, that make me *believe* in some mysterious power." I can't reconcile this with my logic, but it is the tragedies that have happened to me—not the successes—that have made me believe.

Supposing, by a great stretch of imagination, I picture myself as the Creator. I would not make the world a completely happy place. I would allow disasters and tragedies to happen; otherwise people wouldn't acquire a sense of the mystery of life, and we would have none of the great masterpieces of art. We would feel only half alive if we had no trials, no tests.

As Creator, I'd make it very difficult for mortal beings to believe in me. I wouldn't want anyone to say, "Thank you, God: I believe in you because I am happy." I would want people to say: "I believe in you because you've been cruel as well as kind to me. You've tested me. Why have you done this? There must be a reason. You must value me or you wouldn't take the trouble to send occasional tragedy into my life."

To my mind, the real religion is to accept the whole orchestration of life. Curiously enough, out of all the discords and unhappinesses there comes a harmony. For instance, the whole musical world loved Kathleen Ferrier when she was alive. Then she died and everyone who knew anything about beauty mourned for her; but she is still loved and she is more alive than ever. And that is the belief of an agnostic!

RD: Are there any compensations for personal suffering?

NC: Not always, but there *can* be. For example, Beethoven couldn't have written the last quartets if he had *not* been deaf. His deafness forced him to cultivate his inner life and he achieved one of the fullest and richest inner cultivations of any artist in history. A lot of present-day "composers" might write better music if they too were deaf!

RD: Have you a vision of what life-after-death—if, indeed, there is such a state of being—might be like?

NC: I *regret*, I painfully regret, that I cannot conceive of a personal immortality, much as I have tried. This is one of the biggest regrets of my life.

I can't believe in total annihilation, but nor can I go along with the idea of personal salvation, and I'm suspicious of the motives for wanting to go to heaven. A lot of people seem to treat religion as a sort of divine insurance-policy. I want to find heaven on earth. I believe in life *before* death.

I don't agree with the militant atheists who attempt to rationalize and materialize every good thing in life, but nor do I feel in sympathy with the bishops who act as if they speak to God on the telephone every morning, before breakfast. I believe that genuine religious awareness has an aura of mystery. On the other hand, I once told William Temple that I was going to have a tooth taken out, and he said: "Have them all out. The good Lord, for all his omnipotence, cannot create a perfect set of teeth. The Lord God Almighty is a good amateur. He makes a lot of mistakes. We've got to help Him along."

RD: Where did you meet William Temple?

NC: At the Old Rectory Club in Manchester: they allowed laymen to become members. I joined this Manchester Diocese club because I knew that, wherever the clergy were, there would be a good wine cellar! I met Temple several times. He was then Bishop of Manchester, and he was one of the great Christians, warm and sympathetic. However, he didn't talk to to me about Christianity; he let me learn and feel Christianity *implicitly*. There was something about him, an aura, not of contentment—I am suspicious of people who are content, complacent—but of a real, rich, all-embracing way of experiencing life.

I used to have arguments with Temple, and one night, when I was arguing from a Freethinker's point of view and he of course from the Christian point of view, he astonished me by saying, "Cardus, I wish I had a single curate in my diocese with your religious belief." "Oh," I said, "come, come." "Yes," he went on, "you call it Mozart or beauty or grace; we call it God. It's only a difference in words." I had no answer to that.

RD: Has any clergyman tried to persuade you to go to church?

NC: Yes, when I was in Sydney, I met a Jesuit, a very brilliant man, who used to do everything he could to get me into the Catholic Church. He didn't succeed of course; but they always win, these theologians. He said to me one night, "I don't seem to be able to persuade you to become a member of the Catholic Church, but in a way you're already in it." I was puzzled: "What do you mean, 'I'm in it'? I can't recite a word of your liturgies, not a word." He said, "I saw you in the garden feeding the birds and I thought of St Francis of Assisi."

I wonder why it is that some people have the gift of belief, while others can't ever achieve it? I've tried, but I can't believe in a wise, far-seeing God because I can't reconcile God with the problem of evil. On the other hand, there is, I believe, some fundamental force. *What* it is, I don't know; but I do believe it makes the world what it is, and who are we to say what is evil and what is good?

I want the real democracy. I don't mean a democracy based on money—with everybody getting equal pay—I want a democracy of heart and mind, as we used to have in the music-hall. Before we talk about the Industrial Relations Act and Phase Three of the Price Code, let's talk about one another and see where we each are in the human scheme.

RD: What are the world's three finest creations?

NC: A rose (including Kathleen Ferrier), Mozart, and an oyster. Why are these my choices? Because each is beyond improvement. I confess to having hesitated between an oyster and a strawberry.

RD: One of the recurring themes in your personal philosophy is the sense of beauty vanishing.

NC: I don't know where I got it from. It's something I

inherited, I suppose. It has been an enrichment to me as I've got older but I had this same awareness even when I was quite young. I remember being taken to one of my first pantomimes: a beautiful girl was dancing, and I was delighting also in the loveliness of the stage and of the theatre, and yet, even at the age of 14, I felt, "This is going, vanishing, even as I am seeing it." And I have had that same feeling ever since: as soon as I experience a perfect moment I know that it is vanishing.

Somebody once suggested that I owe this feeling to my reading of Goethe: no, I had this feeling before I'd ever heard of Goethe. When I used to play cricket I had some divine moments. I remember an afternoon at Shrewsbury when I did the hat-trick. I took two wickets and I thought to myself, "Well, I won't often in my life have the chance of a hat-trick." By sheer accident I bowled the right ball and took my third wicket. This was one of the moments of my life when I felt like chanting the *Nunc Dimittis*. I can see myself then, on that lovely afternoon, a young man of about 24 in white flannels. All the fielders were coming towards me to congratulate me and I was pleased—and I suddenly realized that this moment was going. It came and it went.

At the time, these moments are poignant, but as you get older the memory of them becomes an enrichment. I have always had a sense of time quickly passing. I remember once sitting in the *Stadtpark* in Vienna on a beautiful September afternoon, with gaiety and alluring women all around me, and, moving amongst the tables or sitting drinking tea, were Moriz Rosenthal and Weingartner and Arnold Rosé and Kreisler: men resembling the great heroes of the Vienna Opera nights. I thought, "This is one of those moments of perfection in life", and yet it was vanishing, passing—which increases your awareness of beauty. You want to make the most of that moment because you know it is going. To be an artist, you've got to have a concept of beauty vanishing; otherwise, instead of being a rare and precious thing, the material you are working with becomes fixed, mechanical, routine.

All art, I have always thought, is ideally a collaboration between the mind of the public and the mind of the artist. I am saddened that the public seems to be losing its intense imaginative love of the arts. There is plenty of culture, more now than ever before. Anybody can turn on the radio at any time of the day and hear a Beethoven symphony; anybody can go to a concert on any night of the week, but music is no longer treated as if it were a miracle. Music has become as noisy as street traffic and as commonplace as rain in Manchester. Music has become part of the pattern of everyday life: you hear Beethoven while you eat your Corn Flakes and you listen to Chopin at the end of the day while you read your evening paper.

I remember the time when we went to a Hallé concert to hear the ninth symphony of Beethoven expecting it to be an *experience*. When I was in my twenties, we used to distinguish between music as learning and music as entertainment. If you went to the music-hall or if you went to a musical comedy such as *The Merry Widow*, featuring Lily Elsie—that was entertainment. If you went to a play by Oscar Wilde—that was entertainment. But if you went to see *Hamlet* or if you went to hear the ninth symphony, that was *not* entertainment. That was something much more serious; you were going in order to *learn* something and intending to be spiritually involved. You were going, so to speak, to a cathedral of life.

We had our different degrees of artistic experience. Nowadays, it seems to me, people go to *Tristan* in the same frame of mind as they go, the next night, to *The Barber of Seville*. They come out of the opera house saying, "The orchestra was quite good . . . the sets were beautiful . . . I've heard Birgit Nilsson sing better," but nobody comes out saying, "My God, what a revelation! What music! To think that one day the beginning of that second act didn't exist and Wagner came downstairs and wrote down some notes in black ink on white paper: he had composed the haunting beginning of the second act. The 'Day' motif was born." If people could only approach art and life in this frame of mind, individual experiences and memories would remain with them for the rest of their lives.

A great pianist, even if he has played the "Appassionata" six hundred times, treats his next performance as if it were his first. A routine way of doing *anything* marks the death of the soul of man; and this applies not only to the creative artist, the pianist, the composer. When I was quite young I used to go and watch a bootmaker in a little shop in Rusholme: it was as though I were going to a studio to watch an artist paint a picture. His knife was his brush, and leather was his canvas. To him, making boots was a work of art. One of the tragedies of modern life is that the craftsman is dying out; his work is being done by machines.

Here we are, in the throes of industrial disputes and massive wage claims, and only the other day I had a vision of this man in Grove Street, Manchester, in his little shop, sitting cross-legged, shaping a boot as though it were a beautiful diamond. He was proud of his craft.

I remember the way my old grandmother used to make a potato pie. She would put all the ingredients into a dish—using nothing out of a tin!—then roll the pastry with a rolling pin, put the pastry over the top of the dish, and trim the edges. Before putting the pie into the oven, my grandmother with a fork used to make a little pattern on the pastry. Why did she make that little pattern? It was a touch of love, of art, a creative thing. She made a potato pie with the same care with which Chopin composed a nocturne. Until we return to the individual's love of whatever job he is doing then I don't see a flourishing future for the human race.

The greatest religion (in the worldly sense—I don't refer to God's love because that is a mystery beyond all mysteries) is to have a passionate love for whatever you are doing.

RD: You are now fifteen years past the biblical three score years and ten. What have you learned about yourself in these last fifteen years?

NC: The tragedy of what is called "old age" is that the body gets older and the mind gets younger. I was much older in the head at the age of 35 than I am now. I was very intellectual when I was 35: I used to sniff at P. G. Wodehouse. I read him now, because I have worked through the Goethes, the Dantes, the Chekhovs and Ibsens, and I have become younger. I now find myself reading books which I would never have dreamed of reading when I was 35. I will no longer read anything that isn't witty or written with charm. I will not read anything that doesn't entertain me. I *must* have wit. I am now returning to writers who are not read often enough these days: Max Beerbohm, Shaw at his best, and writers who can offer me not only thought and experience but also wit, which is a form of youth.

The irony of so-called old age is that the more my mind is quickened and made sensitive by experience, the more my body fails to be able to respond. This is what annoys me. I *want* to go for an eight-mile walk. My mind goes for an eight-mile walk, but my damn legs won't go.

RD: On the last page of your autobiography you wrote, "I have stored my mind and heart with good things." Does that say anything about the way you face death?

NC: I know people who have faced death with great courage, but the prospect of coming face to face with death is something that has never occurred to me. I keep saying to myself: "No man can live for ever, and you have gone well beyond the life span. You have fifteen years to your credit and the odds are against your being alive five years from now." But my mind won't accept this at all.

I've always been of the opinion that a man should live his life from day to day. I never think of next week or next month. I never make a plan. Never in my life have I made plans. To me, life is a matter of gathering rosebuds while you may. If I can make a good thing of today—well, that is another rosebud I've gathered. Whether or not I will gather one tomorrow, I don't know.

I remember a remark of Max Beerbohm. When he was still only about 60—he lived into his eighties—he said he felt sorry for young people. Somebody asked him why. He replied: "They're so young and they might be run over in the street. They might die. They might miss the glory and richness of life."

For me, one of the most moving experiences in life is to meet a very gifted young boy or girl; and I don't remember a time when young people had so much promise. I hope to heaven that they inherit a congenial social and political environment. By that, I don't mean "Make it easy for them"; but give them peace and opportunity. I've got faith that these young people will change things for the better. I only hope they don't try to bring about change in the way people have tried to in the past—by violence. Sustained growth comes not by violence but by human companionship.

RD: Lastly, Neville, what are your most precious possessions?

NC: The gifts I would most thank the gods for are a sense of humour and the capacity to love.

EPILOGUE

London
Sunday, 2.iii.75

NEVILLE DIED TWO days ago. I am shocked and numbed by his death: by the suddenness of it, by the loss of a good friend, by the fact that he did not live to see the results of our work in book form.

I had so much been looking forward to planning, with the *Guardian* and my publishers, the celebrations that were to have taken place in 1976 to mark Neville's 60th anniversary with the *Guardian*. Until last week, apart from some of the lesser ailments that beset old age, he had enjoyed reasonably good health. I went to the hospital on Thursday. Following his stroke, he was too confused to see visitors but it seemed likely that I would be allowed to see him at the week-end. Ten hours later he died peacefully in his sleep.

By the grace of providence, we finished our work six weeks ago. He reminisced about Alfred Cortot and we discussed aspects of our conversation on pianists: he was most anxious to do justice to Solomon. This was our usual practice: once we had worked on new material, we revised the old. I would verify factual details with him and discuss the wording of specific sentences or passages. Thus the whole of our book of conversations—the overall structure and balance, and the text itself—had Neville's *imprimatur*.

For more than two years we had been working on this book. We allowed it to grow and evolve in its own time. And, all the while, our mutual understanding and rapport were developing. I would leave the noise and rush of Baker Street, descend the slender staircase that led to his flat, and within minutes we would be deeply immersed in the aesthetics of cricket or the metaphysics of music or the seductiveness of Marie Lloyd. Although we were separated in age by more than half a century, there was no generation gap. Our conversations, here recorded, were entirely spontaneous. There was no preparation, no use of notes, no advance questions.

Neville was fascinated by the new material our conversations were yielding. He said to me recently: "When questions are put to you, your subconscious is invaded. Certain strands in your personality are touched during conversation that are not touched in the process of writing, a process which is much more detached and self-conscious." The very last time we met he expressed a wish to work with me on another volume of autobiography: "A lot has happened to me since the 1940s."

His mind remained active and lucid to the end. He had a sense of his own destiny, and a realization that he had fulfilled it, and he did not fear death. His generosity towards others was the generosity of self-harmony and of a full, varied, and well-composed life. Neville may not have been religious—in the usual, narrow, confining way in which we tend to use that word—but, in the wider sense, he was the most religious of men. He was modest about his own gifts: he believed in, and experienced, artistic inspiration. He was as responsive to people as to art; and in his loves, of both people and art, he was a man of enormous range. He had reverence for the miniature as well as for the epic, for the simple as well as the sophisticated: in one and the same evening I have seen him charm a duchess and a waitress.

Nicholas de Jongh spoke for me also when he said sadly, "I feel I have lost my best supporter."

ROBIN DANIELS

INDEX